Advance praise for *Design by Deficit*

"The thrill of reading this book is like finding secret passages in a house you've long blithely lived in. It's essential reading for anyone who wants to understand the world around them--full of insights, sharp analysis, memorable aphorisms, and vivid images. Policymakers and academics will understand their fields in new ways, and casual readers will find joy exploring with Dieterlen hidden worlds of decay, ruin, neglect, and forgetting. She shows that the blank spaces in our built environment and our social world, the places nobody brags about or plans for, are key to our future. The book powerfully communicates not only important ideas, but strong and inspiring new reasons for hope."

-Ava Ayers, Director of the Government Law Center and Assistant Professor of Law, Albany Law School

"*Design by Deficit* is an important and impressive contribution to conversations regarding the urgent issues facing built environment academics and professionals. Dieterlen has coalesced relevant topics that provide strategies for rethinking our cities and enabling cross-disciplinary conversation. This is a passionate volume that does not shy away from the complex political challenges for academics and professionals dealing with cities and the people who live in them."

- Jesus J. Lara, Ph.D., Professor of City and Regional Planning, The Ohio State University, Author of Latino Placemaking and Planning: Cultural Resiliency and Strategies for Re-urbanization

"*Design by Deficit* meticulously breaks down the long overlooked comprehensive influence of neglect on cities and their occupants. With unique and insightful consideration of both the negative and positive impacts of neglect, along with questions in need of further exploration, it's a must-read for anyone with an interest in urban design and development."

"*Design by Deficit* shines a much-needed light on the forces of neglect that shape our cities, arguing both for a designer's attention to why and how the spaces and systems we live in came to be, as well as the need to maybe keep a little bit of our cities wild to reconnect us with nature, entrepreneurship, and creative expression."

"Those of us in the forestry field look for every tree under our purview to thrive. However, Dieterlen's book shows us how too often forces of neglect thwart our efforts – neglected communities lacking adequate tree cover, neglected budgets forcing fewer tree resources, and neglected acknowledgement of the benefits of nature. Dieterlen's book opens your eyes to where this neglect lies, forces an assessment of the reality, and through that, a real opportunity to help people and nature flourish."

"As the making of resilient cities gains attention nationwide, Susan Dieterlen has given us an motivating blueprint. A more equitable blueprint for shaping our city environments and neighborhoods."

"*Design by Deficit* takes a novel approach to the social, political and ecological issues that many American cities are facing, especially those that have lost a large portion of their population and are struggling financially. Susan Dieterlen argues that the neglected maintenance that characterize such cities are the physical manifestation of a resource that, if properly managed, presents a unique opportunity to redesign urban infrastructure and how it can be repurposed to make cities more culturally and ecologically resilient in the face of climate change and social justice. In short, the book demonstrates how a holistic approach to urban land use practices can help solve some stubborn problems challenging American cities today."

DESIGN BY DEFICIT

Neglect and the Accidental City

Susan Dieterlen

DEFTSPACE LAB

WWW.DEFTSPACELAB.COM

DeftSpace Lab
1948 Litchfield Turnpike
Woodbridge, Connecticut 06525
U.S.A.
www.deftspacelab.com

This book should not be used as a substitute for the advice of a professionally licensed landscape architect, architect, planner, or engineer familiar with the locale of your site, project, or city.

Book Layout © 2014 *BookDesignTemplates.com*

Design by Deficit: Neglect and the Accidental City/ Susan Dieterlen. -- 1st ed.
ISBN 978-1-7376280-0-2 (paperback) | ISBN 978-1-7376280-1-9 (ebook)

Publisher's Cataloging-in-Publication data

Names: Dieterlen, Susan, author.

Title: Design by deficit : neglect and the accidental city / Susan Dieterlen.

Description: Includes bibliographical references and index. | Woodbridge, CT: DeftSpace Lab, 2021.

Identifiers: LCCN: 2021918432 | ISBN 978-1-7376280-0-2 (paperback) | 978-1-7376280-1-9 (ebook)

Subjects: LCSH Urban ecology (Sociology) | Urban ecology (Biology) | Cities and towns--Growth--Environmental aspects. | Sustainable development. | Nature. | BISAC ARCHITECTURE / Sustainability & Green Design | NATURE / Essays

Classification: LCC HD75.6 .D 2021 | DDC 307.1/216--dc23

Contents

Failure Forces Your Hand
Buildings and GHG emissions
Heroic Weatherstripping

Inequality Is a Massive Problem
Not Someone Else's Problem
Historical Roots
Redlining
Impact on Residents, and Which Residents
Neglect by Neighborhood
A Subjective Interpretation of the Table
Neglect Affects Some Neighborhoods More...
...but Neglect's Effects Are Both Bad and Good
Trees and Inequality
Wild Vegetation and Wildlife
Segregation, Still
Who Benefits Most from Neglect?
Downtown/Central Business District
Inner City
Gentrified Urban Areas
Inner Suburbs
Suburbs
The Imaginary Suburb
Infrastructure Isn't Free
City Parks, Suburban Playing Fields
Suburban Neglect Is Less Visible
Mostly Somewhere Else
Exurbs
Rural Blight and Inequality
A Universal Cost
Neglect by Region
Midwest: Neglect's Darling
The Southwest Is Different

The Hidden Bottom Line
Public Health and Urban Environments
Walkability
Street Trees
Neglect's Impact on Health
Infrastructure Failure and Health

Acknowledgments

This book grew from years of study and teaching. In those years, I was very fortunate to have the help of several student assistants. Each of them contributed to this book through their work. Thanks, Ella Braco and Ingrid Brofman, research assistants on the "Criminal mischief—tree canopy" studies. Thanks, Meghan Holtan, whose long-lost "Zone of Vision" project paved the way for later studies and thoughts. Some of our abandoned "Under Western Skies" study is in here, too. Thank you, Ely Margolis and Cathy Ponte, for your work, especially photos, but also for entertaining many oddball discussions with open minds.

Special thanks to my beta readers. Your contributions made this a better book!

Cathy Ponte

Amy Warren

Jess Koscher

Mieka Clark

Chris Gottbrath

Stephanie Nick

Organizing and teaching a class is the best way to refine your thoughts and critique your arguments. There's no better place to take an idea for a walk. Thank you, students in each of these classes, for your work, your insights, and your tolerance for serving as impromptu focus groups:

Studio|Next: Building the Post-Carbon City (versions 1.0 and 2.0)

People in the Environment

City Wild Seminar: Abandonment, Invasives, and Losing Control

Design Studio V: Research + Design, aka The Unnecessary Studio

Enduring thanks to my partner in life, Tim LaBreche. I couldn't have done this without you.

Illustration Credits

Much appreciation to the following individuals for permission to use these illustrations. All other illustrations were photographed or otherwise created by Susan Dieterlen.

Erica Grohol, figures 1, 13-18, 21
Meghan Holtan, figures 10 and 19
Ely Margolis, figures 3 and 24
Cathy Ponte, figure 9

THINGS FALL APART: AN INTRODUCTION

BEHIND YOUR BACK

Every city has a shadow. It's the things we don't see, that we choose
not to see or teach ourselves not to see. What we don't see still exists,
though. It works out of sight, behind our backs, and it's all the more
powerful because it's unobserved. We underestimate what we don't
notice. We mount no defense against what we never see.

No matter where you live, I guarantee that something near you un-
raveled while you slept last night. Things do that: they fall apart. They
do it constantly, without cease. Steel doesn't get your permission to
rust. Wood doesn't require legislation to rot. Last night, wherever you
are, pavement cracked a bit more. And another weed seed germinated,
someplace dark and out of sight.

That falling apart, whether you call it decay or entropy or disorder,
is a force with power, and it never stops. There's even a thermody-
namic law about it. For a lot of us, the cities in which we live are
great examples of this, either as a whole or in part. Those parts may
be places we try not to go, but they exist all the same, even when they
are out of sight. If you're someone who studies cities or governs them
or shapes them in any way, this unraveling is not something you talk
about much, or perhaps not something you want to look at. Cities are
supposed to grow. For a lot of us concerned with cities, our particular
take on them is predicated on growth, particularly continual building

and land development. It's an article of faith that our city will continue to build. To look at the opposing force, at decay and disorder, feels a lot like failure. It feels like that fear that keeps you up at night.

In fact, a lot of our top fears fall into the category of "things falling apart," whether you worry about climate change or crime or whether your car will get you home from work tonight. Things can come apart in terms of how we get along with each other, how systems work, or how structures endure.

Neglect is this falling apart that affects cities like yours and mine. "Neglect" means that it's something someone has looked away from. Neglect is what happens behind your back. *Neglect* is also a verb, and you can neglect something by ignoring it or not seeing its distress, but also by not paying for what it needs. These are fundamental statements, but you get the idea: neglect is all the ways, big and small, that cities unravel. No matter what city you think of, neglect is shaping it right now. Neglect is a constant, because there's always something we should be paying attention to but can't afford. The bottom of someone's to-do list is tomorrow's neglect. Neglect doesn't need our permission. It doesn't need us to notice it to be at work. In fact, our inattention can turbocharge neglect. It's a shaping by unintentional consequence. It's powerful because we **don't** pay attention to it. It thrives on passivity and apathy.

If neglect shapes the environment of your city, it's influencing you, too, through that environment. You probably don't notice how it affects you, and once again, that makes neglect a little more powerful. That's sinister, and it should be, because neglect hurts us, and it hurts some of us a lot more than others. Except when it doesn't. Neglect, in some ways, shapes urban environments in ways that benefit us. **Some of us, some of the time, are better off because of neglect.**

This is ambiguous, which is what makes it worth learning about. It's also worth learning about because it's an unstoppable force that's shaping our cities, as you read this, in ways that affect our health, our climate, and our opportunities in life. It's working right now, outside your window or behind your back. It's just out of sight.

Never Enough Money

Our cities are falling apart. This isn't news—pick several recent headlines and connect the dots.[1] Our government is characterized by dysfunction and inaction: gridlock, shutdowns, and most especially, the inability to pass legislation that majorities of the country's people support. We've grown used to this, so we don't think of it this way, but that doesn't make it less true. Dysfunction and inaction are the essential characteristics of governance in this country, particularly at the federal level, but not only there. Failing water mains and the over-burdened electrical grid are not partisan issues. We all use water and electricity, and no one supports dirty water or power outages. Yet, inaction persists. Dysfunction at its most basic and undeniable.

In too many cities, it's been a long time now since there was enough to go around. Enough money, enough labor, enough staffing, enough political will, but really, it all comes down to enough money. Rust-Belt decline and shrinking cities are often portrayed as a new or newly urgent problem, but really, they aren't. There's nothing at all new about this decline, or about the disinvestment in cities that has accompanied it. In a strange twist, the lack of newness is exactly **why** it matters—these are long-term trends and thus, their effects are much bigger. Because they are long-term, they are more difficult to stop or to reverse. It's not a bad year or a bad decade or someone's poor governance during his term in office. It's forty years, or more: 1950 is usually cited as the peak year of urban population, or the year in which the most people lived actually within the city itself, not its many suburbs or in neighboring bedroom communities. And friends, 1950 was a long time ago, over sixty years at this writing. This at-mosphere of scarcity in our cities is not a blip, and the next election won't change it.

So here's a bit of logic. It's pretty basic, but it escaped my notice for many years, even as I learned about, shaped, and studied cities, because it happens out of sight. That persistent atmosphere of scarcity, the budget that's never big enough, the coffers that are always overdrawn? What that means is choices. Just as in your own home or your own life, when there's not enough money to go around, you choose where to spend what you do have. In city governance there are all kinds of possible shenanigans involving deficit spending and various ways to rob Peter and pay Paul, but really, are those so different from credit cards in our own homes? Not really.

When times are tight at home, you might opt to pay the electric bill and avoid eating out, if you are able to cook at home and shop for groceries. If you do this enough—say, if times are tight for sixty years—you will always have the lights on and never eat out. The electric company wins and the restaurant down the street loses. Although your intent was to keep the lights on, you may find you weigh less and thus escape the host of obesity-related diseases with which we are plagued because you have eaten home cooking for sixty years instead of more caloric restaurant food. You may also enjoy better health due to dodging the related host of diet- and nutrition-related diseases with which we are plagued, because, again, you've not eaten at a restaurant in sixty years, so you likely consume less salt, for example. You've undoubtedly become a great cook with all that practice. Your pots and pans have gotten a lot of wear. You've been at home for sixty years of dinner-time telemarketer calls. Your kitchen has needed to be cleaned frequently, with all that use. You may be very tired of mac and cheese and spaghetti. All of these are consequences of your choice repeated consistently over decades to pay for electricity and not for eating out. They are unintended, yet consequences all the same; some are positive and some are negative. You could say that you've neglected to fund eating out for sixty years, and thus caused all these consequences, good and bad.

THE BIG HYPOTHESIS

Couldn't the same thing happen with city budgets and competing priorities for municipal resources? If, for example, police protection and trash collection always get funded—and they are important—what doesn't get funded to provide for them? What's the dining out in this comparison? And is it always the same priorities or tasks or programs that don't get funded? And what does that mean?

This book is about a question—a hypothesis—and what's already known about it, what new connections can be drawn between those bits of existing knowledge, and what new insights can be produced from examining all this material together.

This central hypothesis is this: all these bits and pieces are observed effects and outcomes from a larger trend or dynamic: neglect. Decades of scarcity have resulted in the same priorities going unfunded repeatedly, and those unfunded priorities express themselves in the physical environment of our cities, in consistent and predictable ways. In short:

Neglect is a major yet unnoticed shaper of our cities.

An intriguing sub-hypothesis: Some impacts of this neglect may be positive—we urban residents may actually be better off in some ways because of the environment created by neglect.

IS IT TRUE?

That's a hypothesis of sorts, which means that it's not a proven statement, but rather a statement of one possible reality. It begs to be tested. This book explores that idea, not with the scientific method, because this isn't about rigorous testing of narrowly defined questions about established phenomena. Rather, this is an initial exploration—the first voyage, not the definitive survey. Science comes later, but we'll use it as we examine conditions in cities we know, explore what's known about their issues, and define what's left to find out. This is an exercise in defining questions that matter. Asking the right questions is essential. Ask them, and you're on your way. These questions are identified throughout the text through formatting as

▶ *Questions that Matter.*

WHAT DO WE KNOW?

Who knows about neglect in cities? By its nature, neglect is not something anyone is really comprehensively on top of (because it's out of sight). Plenty of people are alarmed about failing infrastructure, as we'll see. This alarm gained new urgency since the Flint drinking water crisis began in 2014.

A handful of scholars discuss urban wilds, or uncontrolled, often spontaneous, natural areas in cities. Much more about this later (especially in Chapter 7: Accidental Nature), too, but there's more about this in qualitative or speculative terms than in writing or projects using hard data. Urban foresters can tell you all about vegetation in cities, and there are wildlife biologists who specialize in urban wildlife, usually one species at a time. From these scientists, it can be difficult to grasp the big picture, because science does what science is best at: investigating narrow questions in as much depth as possible. Neglect is not in the foreground of these studies, either—it's a background condition, the phenomenon that allows the shrubbery to grow, the groundhog to thrive, and the coyote to eat the groundhog.

Lots more people are happy to tell you about failing systems in cities, but they tend to be systems that aren't spatial, things like schools and law enforcement. Disinvestment in cities is an old story. Its sad fruits are well documented.

But each of these experts only looks at part of the overall picture. It's not just the wildlife, or the trees, or the cracking pipes. It's all these things, all together, all the time, all in the same places. Outside the lab, in the real world, everything affects everything else, often in surprising ways. If we want to look at neglect's impact on urban environments and their inhabitants, we want to know:

▶ *What kind of impact does neglect and the environment it shapes have on urban residents?*

▶ *Do these impacts help or hurt urban residents, and are those hurt or helped all part of one demographic or social group?*

▶ *How does this help/hurt break down geographically, meaning whether suburban residents are helped by some of the same impacts that hurt urban residents, or vice versa?*

And one of the most interesting aspects of this idea:

▶ *Is neglect good or bad on balance?*

Could there be benefits from letting everything run to ruin? If we fixed everything, what would be lost? What's the benefit of neglect and what's the cost? Who gets the benefits and who pays the costs?

ORIGINS OF THIS BOOK

It's hard to see the absence of something – in this case, the absence of intention or attention. How do you learn to see it? You start paying attention, and once you focus your attention on it, it becomes visible to you.* In my case, learning to see neglect has happened over

---

* Some Native Americans have a traditional belief concerning the ability of elements in the environment to decide which humans can see them and when. That is, a given person may not see the pictographs or the bison not because s/he is inattentive or short-sighted, but because the pictographs or bison do not choose to reveal themselves at that moment to that that person. The agency is with what's (un)seen, not with the one who sees. This is another way to think about how the way the world

seven years of study. More accurately, seven years of thought, then reading, then more thought, then teaching classes exploring aspects of neglect and the city, then some genuine studies, then writing and more thought.

This is how research interests evolve when you start studying them from scratch. You notice something, you start to wonder about it, you ask questions and find no one has answered them to your satisfaction, and then you go down the rabbit hole.

This particular rabbit hole appeared in the fall of 2011, when I first taught what was then a rather standard Environment and Behavior survey class in the weedy, rusty environs of Syracuse, New York. I developed a collection of work on the topic of neglect as urban shaper, completed from 2012 to 2018. This collection encompasses studies, papers, presentations, and proposals. It also includes several college classes that I developed and taught, including City Wild Seminar (2013–2015), Studio | Next (2014 and 2016), People in the Environment (2011–2014), and Studio | Research + Design (2014), as well as a few independent student projects I advised during that time. These courses featured projects and papers, and student work from those assignments forms a valuable and substantial part of this collection. These classes provided an invaluable forum for discussing and developing the ideas within this book, and I hope every former student reading this book will recognize parts of it from our early days exploring this topic. As a topic formed by connecting dots from different disciplines and professions, my ideas about neglect sometimes looked like classes, and sometimes like studies, before they took shape as this book. A number of study proposals and plans for proposals helped clarify the central logic of this idea.* My blog[2] City

---

looks changes to us as we learn to focus on different things or pay attention to different things. Is neglect revealing itself to you?

* Or, as my graduate adviser put it, even unfunded proposals are worth doing, because they make you get your shit together.

Wild became a playground for neglect ideas, after its beginnings as a way to share neglect-oriented news items that students sent me. In many ways, this collection of work forms the backbone of this book. It's the chords beneath the riff.

OUTLINE OF THE BOOK

We open with how neglect shapes the built environment of cities. Part I starts with "The Other Cities," on places where chronic disinvestment has become the norm. The following chapter, "Invisible Infrastructure," discusses failing infrastructure, a major sign of neglect in the built environment, and a crisis in its own right. "Vacant Buildings, Vacant Land," the final chapter in this section, deals with two additional well-known effects of neglect.

This book isn't just about the physical environment of cities, but also the people who live in them. Part II focuses on this: on how neglect interacts with the way we behave toward each other and toward places within the city. We start with the good news: "Wild and Healthy" about the documented benefits we receive from exposure to nature—including accidental nature within the city. The next chapter, "Places No One Cares About," is about how we act toward these places, and how we act within them. It's a mixed bag of good and bad. "The Scary City, Crime, and Fear," the final chapter in this section, looks at the darker side of human behavior and neglect.

People aren't the only occupants of the neglected city, and Part III looks at some of those other residents: urban nature. The initial chapter, "Accidental Nature," discusses places within the city where nature appears to have taken over, and invasive species, both flora and fauna. "The Price of Nature," focused on benefits we humans derive from functioning natural systems, closes this part of the book.

The built environment, people, and nature, taken together make up "Portrait of the Neglected City," the topic of the next chapter. Two important ideas occupy center stage here: the tendency of neglect to "pile up," or occur in multiple ways in the same physical location, and the critical question of whether neglect unintentionally designs certain parts of the city more than other parts.

These questions point toward larger societal issues, and Part IV takes on those connections between neglect and some of the most important public conversations happening today. "Climate Change," "Inequality," and "Public Health" look at each one of these crucial issues and their interactions with neglect in the city.

The value of a book like this is largely in how readers can put what they've learned into action. "Sail with the Current" focuses on this. It includes a kit of parts that readers can use to apply what they've learned to situations in their own cities. It also includes a very important idea: that neglect is a trend that can be harnessed to do what we need to do in our cities—not just a problem, but a problem that can create solutions.

Without further ado, let's wander into the Neglected City.

PART I

NEGLECT AND THE BUILT ENVIRONMENT

YOUR REAL ENVIRONMENT IS HAPHAZARD

Wherever you are as you read this, you arrived there via a specific path of travel, over road or sidewalk or shortcut. As you remember the path you took, think of it as a series of places, or spaces, through which you moved. It's almost like scenes in a movie, strung together into spots along the highway. Or it's vignettes along the sidewalk, as you walk to school, across campus, up the stairs, down the hall, through the door and to the seat where you sit right now. Your life (my life, our lives) takes place in a variety of settings. Everything that occurs happens in a place, even the unremarkable everyday happenings. Some of those places are unremarkable and everyday, too, but they always have an influence, because they set the scene. They are omnipresent, more powerful because you don't notice them. They are unexamined, unquestioned, covert.

Shut your eyes and think of a few of those places you moved through today. Pick one in particular, and focus on it. See it in your mind. Now ask yourself this:

▶ *Who shaped it to be like it is today?*

▶ *Whose decisions dictated its physical characteristics?*

▶ *What tools made their vision manifest?*

▶ *Whose design are you seeing when you picture that place you walked or drove or biked through today?*

For most of you, this is a trick question. Whose design? No one's. Sure, maybe someone designed and built that parking lot you picture, and someone else certainly designed that road you drove on, and if you pictured a campus, someone laid out the original concept for it (more or less), and over the years, little bits have been redesigned, piecemeal, but in terms of the whole scene you see? For most of us, most of the time, the landscapes in which we live our lives are not intentional spaces created deliberately by a single design mind.*

Usually, when we are outdoors, we're in environments that are haphazard accretions of unintentional consequences and, yes, some decisions made along the way. I say neglect is a covert sculptor of urban environments, and by that, I mean that the "designer," as such, of the scene you're picturing may well be inaction: putting things off, letting things go while you pay attention to somewhere else. Most places in which we live our lives happened by accident.

THE BUILT ENVIRONMENT CHAPTERS

This part of the book begins with shrinking cities, those places where neglect is the most influential and prevalent. Shrinking cities know a lot about disinvestment, both public and private, but they aren't the only places you find neglect. The overriding imperative to spend less and cut costs creates some strange stories.

One of these stories is the recent big story about Flint, Michigan, and its drinking water system. This is especially germane to our investigation here because it hinges on failing infrastructure as well, another hallmark of neglect. Infrastructure gets its own chapter in this

---

* This is a dirty little secret of landscape architecture—so don't tell anyone.

section, too, so the saga of Flint's pipes serves as an apt introduction to both:

FLINT, WATER, PIPES, CRISIS

Prompted by the need to cut costs, Flint officials switched sources for the city's municipal drinking water system in 2014. The new water supply was the Flint River, which provided the city's drinking water until the 1960s. Although Flint, like many older cities, has a number of lead-containing pipes in its water system, the decision was made not to treat the water to protect against corrosion within the pipes, a customary procedure to avoid lead contamination in drinking water. Residents began to complain almost immediately about the appearance and smell of the tap water, and the water was soon found to contain *E. coli* bacteria, prompting officials to increase the amount of chlorine added during water treatment. However, a few months later, Flint's drinking water also was found to contain disinfection byproducts called total trihalomethanes, suspected carcinogens created by a reaction between chlorine and organic matter in the water. In 2015, outside researchers found very high levels of lead in Flint's water— many times more than the level regarded as acceptable by the EPA[3].

In October 2015, Flint switched back to its previous water supply, that used by nearby Detroit. However, problems continued to mount, with blame falling on officials at several levels of government. Lead seriously affects children, but its impacts take a long time to become fully visible, so this aspect of the crisis will continue to unfold for years. New tests run in 2016 found Flint's water remained unsafe, partly because residents—understandably— had switched to using bottled water, which so decreased the volume of water flowing through the system that it hampered the effectiveness of additives to re-isolate the lead in the pipes.[4]

In spring 2018, the state of Michigan stopped providing Flint residents with bottled water, saying that the municipal drinking water was now safe to consume. However, many lead pipes remain in the city's water system at this writing, and of course, residents' trust in public officials has been nearly obliterated.[5] Many homes in Flint also have lead-containing pipes within the homes themselves or between the house and the main water line. These remaining lead sources are an ongoing concern, with opinions divided about whether the water is now safe to drink, years after the initial switch in water supply.[6] City government continues to advise residents to filter their water and reports that the EPA seconds this recommendation for the foreseeable future[7].

One of the most alarming things about the Flint crisis is this: Flint is not unique, and neither is the state of its water system. The unscrupulous behavior of the public officials charged with the protection of the public health and welfare of those drinking Flint's water is without question a smoking gun here. Nonetheless, that gun smokes because of the state of the water system to begin with, which took decades of neglect to achieve. One aspect of this neglect is the lack of good reliable records about the condition and materials of water pipes in a given location. In some cases, the location itself is in doubt. Water pipes and other underground utilities suffer from being literally out of sight. It's easy to lose track of structures underground. We tend to forget about them until they break, and even then, it can be a substantial task to find the break. Water pipes and other older systems by their nature are composed of piecemeal additions added over decades, if not centuries. The original system tends to be in the oldest part of town, built to serve that oldest part when it was the only part of town (or at least the only part of town deemed worthy of public water service). The planners and builders of that original system had no way to know how much the town would expand in the future and in what areas those expansions would take place. **No one uses a crystal ball to design utility systems.**

As new neighborhoods were developed, water service was extended to them, adding to the original system, and as more neighborhoods developed beyond those, new additions to the water system were added to the additions. This continues, creating a patchwork of sorts, all underground. As time passes, records go missing, employees move on or pass on, and information about the system is lost. Eventually a city reaches the current condition, at which point it's a massive, expensive task even to map where the pipes are and what their condition is. Guess what? If your city doesn't have the financial wherewithal to maintain a water system, chances are your city also cannot afford to do this expensive mapping of the water system. So neglect accumulates.

VACANT BUILDINGS, LAND, AND OTHER SYSTEMS

Naturally, it's not just the infrastructure that ages, needs maintenance and repair, and falls into disrepair without it. Buildings do, too. **Disused or abandoned buildings are a major symptom of neglect.** Anyone who has ever owned an older building will tell you that maintenance and repair is a never-ending effort. Shockingly, the effort needed actually increases when a building sits empty, since empty buildings fall apart more rapidly.[8] They fall apart quickly, but they don't vanish all by themselves, not for a long time, anyway. Once a building is too far gone to repair and re-occupy, demolition is the only answer, and demolition is far more expensive than you'd think. **The kind of city that tends to have a lot of abandoned buildings can't afford demolition, and so, neglect keeps piling up.**

Even when the buildings are gone, land without purpose creates its own set of problems. Vacant land is another classic calling card of neglect, but one that's difficult to cast as all bad or all good. "Too much land" is a phenomenon explored along with abandoned buildings in the final chapter of this section.

OTHER STRESSED SYSTEMS

Before we move on, let's note that neglect doesn't just impact the built environment of the city, through buildings, land, and infrastructure. Neglect wreaks havoc with other urban systems, too. These other systems include those without obvious implications for the physical environment—school systems, policing and police relations with the community, community itself. Disinvestment in cities is an old story, and a lot has been said about its impact. This story, the story of neglect as city shaper, is less well documented, but it's important to remember, as we explore it, that nothing happens in a vacuum. **A neglected city is the way it is because all these stressed systems and symptoms happen together,** interacting with each other. That can mean the first line of defense against a specific problem is unavailable or on the verge of failure itself. In this way, neglect doesn't just pile up, but spreads, as the collapse of one system overtaxes interconnected systems, pushing them closer to collapse, too.

CHAPTER 1

THE OTHER CITIES

A SHRINKING WHAT?

Urban wilds are characteristic of the shrinking city.

That's a sentence with not one, but two catchy jargon phrases. A shrinking city is one whose population isn't growing and is instead either declining or holding steady. That may sound simple, but the catch is that pretty much everything we, as professionals and as a society, think or study or know about cities is based on the idea that they grow. Even the way we conceptualize cities is based on growth—the hustle and bustle, economic expansion, opportunity, population density, bright lights, etc. A city that is shrinking is therefore not really a city.

Much of our collected expertise about managing or studying or succeeding in cities becomes irrelevant when faced with a declining population. In particular, fields that have to do with physical space or land—architecture, landscape architecture, planning, real estate development, construction, civil engineering—are all based on the notion that we can control or shape or profit from **new** growth. The primary mechanism for zoning enforcement is approval of proposed plans. New architectural styles become part of new buildings. Yes, there's renovation of older buildings, and there's adaptive reuse, but that's not the bread and butter of these fields. The economics of these fields don't work without new development. Thus, shrinking cities are difficult for us to grapple with, and we handle them poorly or not at all. But if we experts in shaping and managing space don't deal with shrinking cities, who does?

A shrinking city is disturbing, conjuring up apocalyptic visions and echoing the end of empires and civilizations. For some of us, there's a certain romance to that. I'm as vulnerable as anyone to post-apocalyptic chic. Some of us love that grunge/punk design ethic, and some of us are eco-fanatics excited about crafting livelihoods based on reuse. But for most people, shrinking cities are an emblem of failure and decay, maybe even of mortality itself. Particularly in the United States, the melting pot of Manifest Destiny and habitual superpower, we want cities to grow. A shrinking city is un-American, right?

Or it could be un-American, except that the United States contains plenty of shrinking cities, or more accurately, shrunken cities. Sixteen out of twenty—that's 80%—of the most-populous American cities in

Figure 1: Shrinking cities in the midwestern states of Indiana, Ohio, and Michigan, showing population change from 1950 to 2010.

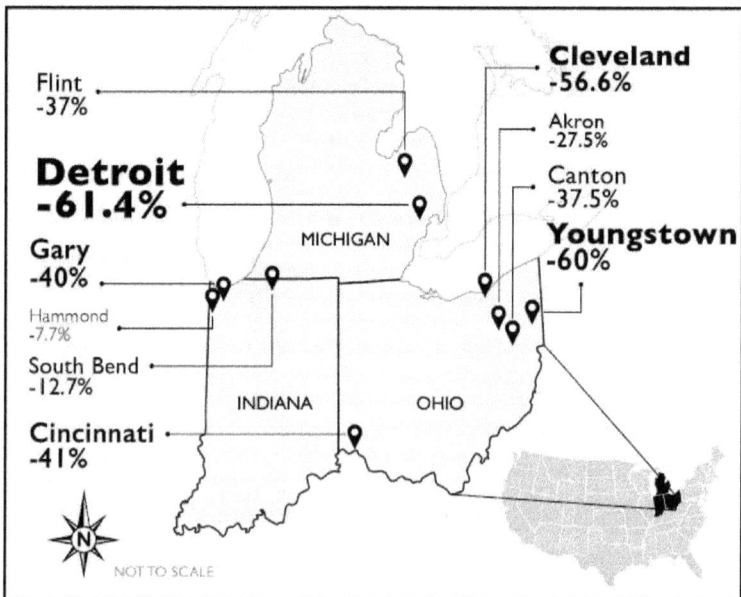

the 1950s had fewer people by 2009.[9] A 2008 analysis added 151 additional smaller shrinking cities to this tally, with 2000 populations of less than 150,000 residents.[10] Some cities have declined in population across their entire metro areas. Far more have declined within the city itself but grown in the suburbs, a hollowing out of the metropolis.

Some cities have a contradictory trend of "sprawl without growth." This means expanding in geographic area while declining in population so that the density of the metro area is falling as people leave more urban areas for more sprawling suburban and exurban areas. Let's look at Syracuse as an example, because Upstate New York is a great place to observe this phenomenon, as others have noted.[11]

In Table 1, "Syracuse city" is just what it sounds like: within the city limits, not including suburbs surrounding the city. "Syracuse urbanized area" includes the city and all its suburbs, or in the language of the Census, the adjacent densely settled area. In 1950, that was confined within Onondaga County, but by 2017, the urbanized area sprawled beyond Onondaga County and into adjacent Oswego and Madison counties.

Table 1: Syracuse, New York, urbanized area growth by population and area, 1950 and 2017

	1950	*2017*	*Percent change*
Population, Syracuse city	220,583[12]	144,405[13]	-35%
Population, Syracuse urbanized area	341,719[14]	409,915[15]	20%
Size (square miles), Syracuse urbanized area	44[16]	194.9[17]	343%

A careful look at this table reveals that "without growth" is not technically true here: The population of Onondaga County as a whole, including Syracuse, did indeed grow between 1950 and 2017. However, that modest population growth was far outstripped by the amount of land it consumed. "Sprawl without growth" refers to the consumption of land by urbanization outstripping population growth, indicating that the population is spreading out more than simply increasing. These figures for Syracuse and its county show 20% population growth simultaneous with a whopping 343% increase of urbanized area. What makes that contrast even more astonishing is the dramatic decrease in population within the city limits during that same time period: a decrease of 35%.

REASONS

Why do cities shrink? Cities in the United States have shrunk because of economic transformation. The big one is deindustrialization, or the movement of manufacturing to other places from the center of cities, particularly in the Northeast and Midwest, aka the Rust Belt. It's important to note here that contrary to popular belief, manufacturing does not have to move to another country to leave the Rust Belt high and dry. Instead, production can move to other states or even just to the suburbs or more rural areas nearby. Cities in the United States have also shrunk because of demographic trends, some intertwined with deindustrialization. In the new century, the established trend has continued: more population growth in the West and the South; less population growth (or even decline) in the Midwest and Northeast.[18] Some of this growth is due to immigration, but much of it is people moving around within the United States, including from rural areas to cities.

US cities that have decreased in population due to deindustrialization and suburbanization typically had a peak population in 1950, with decline since then. They may have stabilized in population or they may continue to decline or even grow a bit. Nonetheless, a city has the label "shrinking" if its current population is less than at any point in the past, even if it's not **currently** getting smaller from year to year. Some examples of cities that have shrunk due to these forces are Youngstown (and nearly every other major city in Ohio), Buffalo, and of course, Detroit—the iconic city in decline. More about Detroit later.

Table 2: Populations of selected "shrinking" cities, 1950 and 2016

City (Census Designated Place)	Population in 1950	Population in 2016	Change, 1950–2016	Percent change, 1950–2016
Youngstown, Ohio	168,330[19]	64,312[20]	-104,018	-62%
Buffalo, New York	580,132[21]	256,902[22]	-323,230	-56%
Detroit, Michigan	1,849,568[23]	672,795[24]	-1,176,773	-64%

Why else do cities shrink? Much more recently, the housing boom and crisis of the 2000s resulted in concerns about shrinkage in the normally booming cities of Phoenix and Las Vegas. The housing crisis also added even more population loss in some cities that were already declining for other reasons, such as Detroit (again).

Cities may shrink because of disasters like Hurricane Katrina, which walloped New Orleans in 2005. The most recent estimate of New Orleans' population is 391,495[25] residents, over 93,000 less than its pre-disaster 2000 population of 484,674 residents.[26] At this point, it's widely recognized that the disaster in New Orleans was a combination of human-created and natural factors, with contributions from some pre-existing characteristics of the city, such as severe social inequality and the low-lying topography and inadequate transportation systems of the city. These characteristics made New Orleans a fragile city—the opposite of a resilient city. We see the result of that now, in part in the smaller population.

A major factor in that population decline was the pre-storm poverty of the city. For people of limited means, especially those without access to a car, relocating or evacuating is a substantial expense. Even going to a hotel in another town for a few days can be financially out of reach. This played a tragic role in who suffered and died in New Orleans, but it also plays a role in who returns once they leave, if they leave. We can all relate to how expensive moving is—it always costs more than you'd think. If you were barely making ends meet to begin with, it may simply be too expensive to move again back home, even if you want to. And of course, some people don't want to go home or have made new lives they prefer somewhere else.

OUTSIDE THE UNITED STATES

These causes of urban population decline aren't unique to the United States. In fact, during the 1990s, more than 25% of cities with more than 100,000 residents were shrinking worldwide.[27] Most of these are in the United States and Europe. In some respects, Europe and North America have shrinking cities for the same reasons, but Europe also has a number of shrinking cities due to the continuing historical legacies of World War II and the Cold War. The division of Europe into East and West during the Soviet era and, prior to that, into Axis and Allied during World War II, had profound economic consequences. As in the United States, Germany cranked up its industrial production during the war, including manufacture of bombers, tanks, and so on, as well as the raw materials for them, such as iron and steel. Due to the war, materials couldn't move freely from country to country, so parallel industries grew up within Germany. Of course, the war also seriously limited the ability of people to move from place to place, and its impact (that is, people killed) was also far heavier in some places than in others. Some cities literally shrank in habitable space due to bombing.

After the war, people and goods still weren't free to move due to the rise of the Iron Curtain, Soviet domination, and the Cold War. Again, parallel industries grew up on both sides of the Iron Curtain. The Soviets also removed resources from Eastern Europe, in colonial-like fashion, creating lots of mines and other extractive industries. These industries required labor, which affected where people lived and what cities grew. Again, people weren't free to move or to live where they wished.

With the fall of the Iron Curtain, all this changed, and even today the process of readjustment continues. People were free to leave and pursue opportunity elsewhere or be reunited with relatives elsewhere, as we saw with the former East Germany. People were free to simply pursue better housing and infrastructure and services, as we saw with the former East Berlin. Those parallel industries were no longer needed, since goods like iron and steel could now be purchased for less from the rest of the world. This led to Rust Belt–like population decline in many formerly industrial cities in Eastern Europe, and to some extent within the former Soviet Union/today's Russia itself. Western Europe has also experienced deindustrialization similar to that of the US Rust Belt, as industry moved to areas of cheaper labor and less regulation, as we see in western Germany, such as the Ruhr area, and in Britain, particularly northern England and lowland Scotland. Some of the most prominent cities in Shrinking Cities literature fall within these categories, like Berlin and Sheffield (UK).[28]

China is also home to a number of shrinking cities. A 2016 study reported 180 cities in China whose population had fallen between 2000 and 2010[29]. This appears to be a newer set of shrinking cities than the well-studied ones of the American Rust Belt, Western Europe, and Britain. China's cities are feeling the effects of population shifts, possibly connected with the growth of the middle class and greater mobility. Observers also note that many of China's shrinking cities are those that boomed with economies based on a single local resource, such as mining or timber, and then experienced a corresponding bust when that resource became exhausted. Obviously, this raises substantial environmental questions as well as economic ones.

WILDS AND THE SHRINKING CITY

If you recall, that second buzzword at the beginning of this chapter was "urban wilds." Urban wilds enter this discussion about shrinking cities because a city with less people is a city with too much land, too much space, and too many structures to maintain. Shrinking cities are usually cities with financial commitments they can no longer meet. Fewer people and fewer businesses mean a smaller tax base and less private investment, so in essence, there's less money coming in. People who do stay are disproportionately people with fewer options to leave—more poor folks, more old folks, more disabled folks, more people within marginalized groups—so the burden of social services also goes up per capita. In this way, services in cities are a bit like insurance: the fundamental way they work is that richer people (or other entities) offset the poorer people (or entities). A city with no affluent taxpayers is like an insurance company with only sick policy holders. Neither one works as well as you'd like.

Yet much of the city's expenses are fixed due to the existing structures and infrastructure of the city. The number of schools and firehouses and parks is the same. The number of miles of streets and sidewalks and water lines is the same. Garbage must be collected, and snow needs to be plowed. All of that now has to be done with less money, so there are shortfalls. **The shrinking city is a city of financial scarcity.** Hard decisions about financial priorities have to be made, and maintenance and upkeep of public spaces, buildings, and especially landscapes is almost always considered expendable. In addition, private property slides into vacancy and abandonment, and standards of upkeep may fall among occupied properties, especially with absentee landlords (slumlords) and land held in speculation. All of this provides more space and opportunity for nature to encroach and take back urban areas. **A shrinking city is a wilder city.**

CHAPTER 2

INVISIBLE INFRASTRUCTURE

Infrastructure Fail

Changes and dynamics that created shrinking cities aren't limited to urban population trends. They've also been working on urban infrastructure. However, neglect of infrastructure is far from being restricted to shrinking cities, or even urban areas of any kind. Rather, the United States is in the midst of a full-blown, nationwide infrastructure crisis.

Books[30] and articles appear regularly about this, but no one is on top of it like the American Society of Civil Engineers, aka ASCE. Their assessment: our infrastructure is, in a word, crumbling. Press about this peaks whenever there's a particularly egregious crisis. When those water pipes or dams[31] or bridges[32] or subways[33] break, we pay attention. This is the unspoken truth about infrastructure: we rely on it to make our daily lives possible, but pay no attention to it until it doesn't work.

When it doesn't work, it makes our daily lives spectacularly impossible—if you want to experience living in a previous century, make all your infrastructure fail at once.

Natural disasters showcase this with devastating thoroughness. But once the shocking headlines are replaced by new ones, we stop paying attention, even as the crises continue. Case in point: can you tell me whether the city of Flint ever got reliably clean drinking water?

Second case in point: the eleven months Puerto Rico was without electricity after Hurricane Maria, a massive, nearly category 5 storm, hit the island on September 20, 2017. The size and severity of the storm resulted in tremendous damage, compounded by a slow and inadequate response from the US federal government. Many assumed this inadequacy to be due to Puerto Rico's physical separation from the mainland United States, its second-class status as a territory rather than a state, and the lack of political power of its primarily Latina/o residents. Maria decimated the island's already fragile power grid, knocking out power completely, including power to water treatment facilities. Virtually all structures—up to 90%—in some towns were destroyed. Unimaginable amounts of rain—up to 30" in one day— caused severe flooding and damage in its own right.[34] The power is back on in Puerto Rico, more or less, but full recovery from the devastation wrought by the storm continues, hampered by repeated political posturing in Washington, DC, over federal funds.

Yet these crises quickly fade from public view, supplanted by newer news. Were you thinking about Flint and Puerto Rico and their infrastructural woes when you started reading this paragraph? Probably not, unless you are in Flint or Puerto Rico.

INVISIBLE (WORKING) INFRASTRUCTURE

Most of us have the luxury of ignoring the infrastructure that serves us. That's because it's working. Infrastructure that's working is made more invisible to the general public by our tendency to view the entire built environment as naturally occurring and therefore neutral. We don't see it as changeable or changing, so we assume it's always been what it is, arising at some primordial time and remaining inert throughout human history. It's just the background, so how could it favor anyone or any place over anyone else?

This is, of course, nonsense. Anyone who's worked in any job related to design, planning, or construction can tell you that an enormous amount of effort goes into shaping the built environment. Anyone responsible for the facilities or physical plant of an organization can tell you that an enormous amount of effort goes into merely keeping their portion of the built environment the same—that holding off decay and deterioration is a full-time job for lots of people. Any property owner can tell you that about their little piece of the physical world, too.

Historical "then and now" photos of streets or points of interest are entertaining precisely because they show how the built environment we know **has** changed, often dramatically, more quickly than we imagine. Perhaps the appeal of these photo pairs is that they contradict an unconscious yet near-universal fallacy: that nothing ever changes with the built environment, and things have always been just as they are today.

The comforting belief that "nothing ever changes" leads us to the even-more-comforting assumption that no maintenance is needed and that if we ignore maintenance, nothing will actually fall apart. The bill won't come due. The piper will never need paying. This is an appealing assumption—who doesn't want that free lunch?—which makes it all the harder to resist. And it's false, in infrastructure as in so many things. You know what they say about a free lunch.

FRAGILE BY DESIGN

If infrastructure is only visible to the public when it fails, let's look at what failed in Puerto Rico to help us see infrastructure. When Maria blew through, she took the power grid with her. For anything to happen when you plug your toaster into the outlet at home, you must have power generation happening, at power plants or alternatives like solar arrays or wind farms. You must also have the system of substations and transmission lines that connects your outlet to the place where power is generated. Knock out any part of this—the grid—and your outlet is just some funny looking holes in the wall.

Of the two, power generation is the less vulnerable, although it's worth mentioning that because fossil fuels are heavy and bulky, one of the best ways to transport them has historically been via ship, and that generating electricity from fossil fuels is a steamy business, meaning that the cooling available via bodies of water has always been appealing. This means a disproportionate number of power plants are located on water, whether ocean or river or lake. Where there's water, you can have flooding, and where there's flooding, climate change can make it worse. Power plants on ocean shores are intrinsically more vulnerable to damage from worsening hurricanes and to sea level rise. So power generation the way we currently do it is not exactly unassailable.

Nonetheless, the vulnerability of power plants is nothing compared to the vulnerability of the power distribution network. We overlook this, because power lines are mundane and not fun to look at. But— power lines are lengthy, often inaccessible (due to rough terrain, lack of roads, or being underground), and, well, just lines, not massive masonry structures like dams, for example. Three-quarters of new power lines in the United States are above-ground,[35] as are the vast majority of older power lines. This situates them perfectly for damage from falling trees, wind, and ice storms. The "grid" moniker might lead you to expect that the power distribution network connects every location to every other location in a level hierarchy (like, say, a grid), but that's misleading. Rather, the power distribution network looks more like the veins in your body, in a riverine or "tree" system. Each point is connected to a line, which connects to larger lines, then to larger lines, and so on to the power plant. Knock out one point in one line, and you lose the connection to every point downstream, including your outlet with your non-functioning toaster. The generation of power in a few main plants makes this a centralized system. **Centralized systems, by their nature, are vulnerable to disruption. They are, unintentionally, fragile by design.**

Figure 2: A riverine or tree system versus a grid system

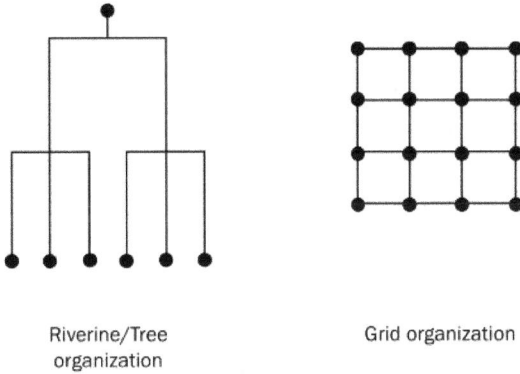

Riverine/Tree
organization

Grid organization

Let's also note that the general consensus among experts is that the main grid of the mainland United States (never mind Puerto Rico) is in terrible shape. Components are aging and frequently overtaxed, both because there are more people than there used to be and because we all use so much more electricity than we used to. The digital age has revolutionized nearly everything, and the digital age is made possible by the grid—a centralized system, fragile by its nature, as a fundamental platform for daily work, commerce, communication, and social life. And it's...crumbling.

How to Build a Failure

This gets us back to neglect and cities in the "why," as in "why is the grid crumbling?" Our power grid is crumbling, in essence, for the same reasons that the rest of our infrastructure is in such a dire state, namely, deferred maintenance and increasing demand. More minor points are physical stress from climate change, and, surprisingly, large, concentrated investments in infrastructure in a few past eras. That last point is the most esoteric, so let's start there.

CONCENTRATED INFRASTRUCTURE INVESTMENT IN PAST ERAS

Infrastructure formed a considerable part of the tsunami of public works projects constructed during the 1930s, in the federal government's New Deal programs to create jobs and stimulate the economy during the Great Depression. The Works Progress Administration (WPA) and Civilian Conservation Corps (CCC), among others, designed and built roads, dams, public buildings, parks, and countless other projects. Rural electrification, through the Rural Electrification Administration (REA) and other organizations like the Tennessee Valley Authority (TVA), brought electricity to over one million rural dwellers by 1943, up from the approximately 10% of farms with electricity before the New Deal. The continuation of these programs eventually boosted the share of farms with electricity to about 97% by 1960.[36] Not only were a huge number of projects built in a short time period during the New Deal, but they were built to last, with solid materials and techniques, partly because they were job-creation efforts, and if you're creating jobs, there's no point in doing things halfway. We benefit still from the infrastructure and buildings constructed during the New Deal, but at 80 years and counting, the age of these investments is starting to show. Quite possibly, the very solidity of WPA and CCC structures encouraged us to put off maintaining them over the years. How could one more year matter to such a robust stone building? Would that wall really notice if we didn't maintain it this year...or next year...or the year after that?

A few decades later, the United States again invested heavily in infrastructure during the economic boom that followed World War II, during the 1950s and '60s. The emphasis this time was on the interstate highway system and its cousin urban freeways and bypasses (with quite a bit of overlap between these and the interstates). The establishment of these roads encouraged and perpetuated a massive move away from urban areas into the surrounding countryside, creating suburban communities across the country. Those new suburbs in turn needed a massive amount of new infrastructure in their own right, including secondary roads, electrical lines, water and sewer lines and treatment plants, and more broadly, schools and parks. The movement of such large numbers of (non-Hispanic white, native-born) people out of the cities accelerated efforts to "renew" the cities by demolishing neighborhoods judged problematic (usually African-American neighborhoods; sometimes immigrant, Jewish, and/or Latina/o neighborhoods as well) and building large public structures and infrastructure in their place. These "urban renewal" projects included the aforementioned urban freeways, but also government buildings, civic centers (ironically), and sometimes parks or sports arenas. While not built with the same classical solidity as the New Deal structures, these postwar projects are also twenty to thirty years newer, and so, we continue to benefit from them as well.

SOCKS

However, the benefit is starting to wear thin, because all of this, the New Deal projects and the postwar projects, is aging. Since it was all built at the same time, it's all reaching its dotage at the same time. It's a similar situation to having bought all your socks at one time, then wondering why all your socks seem to be wearing out at the same time. You got used to having lots of socks and never needing to buy more—never needing to think about socks at all, actually. After a while, you fell into assuming that socks would always just be there, without you having to do anything—to invest—in your sock supply at all.

DEFERRED MAINTENANCE (AND SOCKS)

It's exactly the same with infrastructure. The investments of the two big pushes of the 20th century are wearing out, and we've gotten very used to never investing in these kinds of projects, expecting they would somehow just always be there to use. Deferred maintenance which is exactly what you'd think— putting off repairs and upkeep— is a major contributor to our infrastructure crisis. We can stick with the sock analogy to understand the cost of deferred maintenance as well. Probably many of you have never darned a sock (and are now wondering what "darned" means). To darn is to mend a sock, with a needle and thread—to sew closed a hole. When your sock first sprouts a hole, you can readily fix it (darn it) with a needle and thread, and you can continue wearing the sock, hole-free, for a while longer. If you don't darn the first hole, it becomes a bigger hole, and soon your whole heel or multiple toes are hanging out, and you toss that sock.* Trying to patch a hole that lets your entire heel through is much tougher, and unlikely to be satisfactory. You need more skill and materials and time to do it than just needle and thread, and so, out goes the sock. You then purchase a new sock to replace it, the cost of which far exceeds the small amount of thread and the needle with which you could have darned the first hole.

Again, it's the same with infrastructure and buildings. Maintenance tasks left undone become bigger problems, which then require more maintenance. It's generally easier to fix problems sooner, when they are smaller, and it is without question less expensive. At some point, just like our hypothetical holey sock, the problems have become so large and the cost of fixing them so prohibitive that it is more feasible to simply replace the structure. **This is how deferred maintenance causes infrastructure failure.**

Obviously, we should fix problems when they are new and small, and keep up with the maintenance. This is simple, right? But—small problems are easy to overlook and easy to ignore. Like that first hole in the sock, they really aren't that bad a problem and don't compromise the use of the structure or whatever too much. In the case of

---

* Full disclosure: I don't fix holes in socks.

infrastructure, it can also be difficult to get whatever authority is relevant to provide funds to fix small problems, because they are only small problems, after all, and there is always something more pressing. Remember that point about how we only see infrastructure when it fails? Sometimes it has to fail before anyone will pay to fix it. Your whole foot has to stick through the hole before the sock gets replaced.

INCREASING DEMAND

The sock analogy gets weird when extended to increasing demand ("imagine you grow two more feet..."), so we leave it behind here. Increasing demand is easy to understand, anyway, because it is exactly what it sounds like. We now need more from various bits of infrastructure because there are more people using them or because each person using them now needs more from them. These dynamics can operate at the same time, too, so to have demand really skyrocket, you have population growth, and each person in that population using more of whatever service the given piece of infrastructure provides.

Increasing population is simple. For example: in 1950, the total population of the United States was somewhat more than 151 million people.[37] By 2010, that had risen to over 309 million people.[38] That's a lot of growth at the national level, but of course, it wasn't evenly distributed. Some cities and towns grew even more, proportionally speaking. Increasing individual demand includes shifts like car ownership increasing from one car per household (among households that could afford cars) to one car per person within the household (among households that can afford multiple cars). Where each house only had one car a generation ago, now each house has two or three cars. Note how the total number of cars goes up even if a generation ago each house had, say, five or six people (more children) and now has only two or three people. The number of houses is the same, the total number of people in those houses is actually fewer, but the roads serving those houses need to carry more cars.

Technological developments like televisions and computers have created tremendous increases in electrical demand, first with their widespread adoption and then with their change from a single device typically shared within a household to devices typically belonging to each individual member of the same household (again, among households that can afford such luxuries). Air conditioning is another technological innovation that greatly increased demand on the electrical grid.

PHYSICAL STRESSES FROM CLIMATE CHANGE

Air conditioning is the perfect segue into the final factor tightening the screws on our infrastructure: physical stresses from climate change. It will not be news to anyone that we use more air conditioning when temperatures go up. Some of you may participate in a demand management program run by your power company with just this relationship in mind: on the very hottest days, power demand peaks in large part because of all those air conditioners whirring away on "max," and for a little discount on your electric rate, you let the power company send you a little less power on those days. Public institutions frequently participate in these programs, so sometimes you notice that when it's really steamy, the air conditioning is off in the library or similar places.

Hotter summers mean more demand for air conditioning, in terms of more electricity needed to run air conditioners we already have as well as more places deciding that air conditioning is now a necessity and adding new air conditioning units and systems. Less obviously, warmer temperatures and other climate change impacts stress infrastructure in additional ways. Heat stresses asphalt, making it softer and more prone to developing ruts. This can actually shorten the life of pavement, making it fail and require replacement sooner. Somewhat paradoxically, severe cold, like that from the polar vortex we've become familiar with in the eastern United States the last few winters, also increases stress on pavement of all kinds through freeze/thaw cycles, especially during more volatile winters with sudden large drops and rises in temperature. The opposite poles of flood and drought both stress roads, as the soil beneath them absorbs water, then dries out.

Heat and drought may also stress dams built in a cooler, wetter age. Take the case of Oroville Dam—north of Sacramento, California—an earthen structure built in the 1960s. The dam on the Feather River created Lake Oroville, a 15,500-acre reservoir providing water to multiple counties as well as flood control on the river and hydropower generation. The dam made headlines in February 2017 when the partial failure of its spillways prompted the evacuation of over 180,000 people living below the dam.[39] A comprehensive investigation by the state of California concluded that Oroville's original flaws were made worse by years of inadequate repairs—deferred maintenance, again.

Many others connected Oroville's crisis to climate change, particularly the increase in frequency and severity of storms. More rain means more strain on flood control infrastructure, like dams. In this case, lots of wet weather followed an exceptional multi-year drought, swinging from one extreme to the other.[40] It's easy to see how floods stress dams, but drought brings its own stressors, too. Earthen levees and reservoir banks can be weakened in a number of ways by extreme drought, including cracking and subsidence. In essence, soil normally contains a certain amount of water, and when that water is removed through drought conditions or extra pumping of groundwater or other means, the structure of the soil can be affected.

The type of changes and their severity can vary with the type of soil as well, so the situation becomes more complex where there are multiple soil types (such as loam, sand, peat, etc.) adjacent to each other or layered on top of one another. In the case of a levee, the soil below the levee may be different from that forming the levee structure itself, especially with structures built long ago without benefit of engineering expertise.

All this means that drought can weaken levees, reservoir banks, and the slopes around dams and spillways. When that drought ends with an extremely wet year and flooding, as it did in Oroville in 2017, the new stress of flooding bears on areas previously weakened by drought. Since climate change means more extreme weather, expect more droughts and floods—and more Orovilles. When this increased weather stress from climate change meets the band-aid repairs of deferred maintenance, well, bad things happen.

Circling back to Hurricane Maria, extreme weather events notable for their severity and frequency are a clear strain on all kinds of infrastructure, for reasons we're all familiar with. The destructive impact of any kind of storm is familiar enough, but a little less visible to the layperson is the cumulative impact of increasing precipitation totals and more frequent severe precipitation events on infrastructure that manages stormwater. This includes underground dedicated storm sewers as well as above-ground portions of the system such as detention ponds and ditches. More broadly, this includes flood management infrastructure along watercourses, such as levees and floodwalls. In the many US cities where stormwater is carried along with sewage in a single combined sewer system, increasing precipitation and storms overburden these systems, leading to more combined sewer overflow (CSO) events or demand for wastewater treatment or both.

The individual stresses of climate change on infrastructure components are many and varied, but the underlying dynamic is easy to understand. **Simply put, change in the climate means that our infrastructure increasingly inhabits a different world than the one for which it was designed.** Roughly, the older the infrastructure, the greater the mismatch with the climate conditions for which it was designed, since climate change is increasing over time. Older infrastructure, in general, is also more prone to problems and eventual failure because things wear out over time. Increased demand is naturally also a more severe stress on older infrastructure, generally, for the same reason: conditions have changed more since the infrastructure was designed and built.

Once again, the hotter it is, the hotter it gets. **Failure loves company, and neglect piles up.**

ALL THE FAILURES HAPPEN HERE

Neglect piles up.

Let's unpack that recurring statement before we go any further. In terms of infrastructure, "neglect piles up" means that stressed infrastructure tends to occur in different systems **in the same physical location**. Spatially speaking, it can pile up literally, as different systems weaken in the same spot where other systems are weakened. So in your city, a certain neighborhood or street corridor or even intersection can suffer from multiple problems in different infrastructure systems, simultaneously. At this point a few spots within your own city may occur to you—the places where everything seems to go wrong.

Is this coincidence, or just bad luck? Possibly, but there are also a few logical reasons why urban infrastructure failures should cluster geographically. Let's return to that list of factors contributing to the infrastructure crisis in US cities: deferred maintenance, increasing demand, physical stress from climate change, and large concentrated investments in infrastructure in a few past eras. Think about the spatial implications of these causes in your city, the **where**. What kinds of neighborhoods or places are most affected by these factors?

Generally, older neighborhoods have older infrastructure. An exception to this is where systems within an older neighborhood have deteriorated to the point where they have been replaced, or where they've been replaced for some other reason, such as combined sewer systems replaced to avoid the construction and expense of additional wastewater treatment plants. In the context of the cash-strapped city, system replacement is rare because it's expensive, and because

infrastructure is notoriously unsexy—citizens or voters or taxpayers (whomever you need to please) do not get excited over spending money on improvements they neither see nor pay attention to
until these systems fail. Another exception is where infrastructure
improvement follows money, beginning in the most affluent neighborhoods, regardless of when they were established, and continuing
down the socioeconomic scale of political power to the poorest and
least-connected neighborhoods in the city. As discussed in my previous book, these least-connected urban neighborhoods can include
former workers' camps, such as those adjacent to railroads or vintage
factories, and as such may be right in the heart of the city, especially
along watercourses or in floodplains.[41]

So exceptions exist, but in enough places, neighborhoods of older
houses and other buildings are neighborhoods of older roads, water
systems, sewer systems, electrical lines, and bridges. Things wear out
over time, so, generally, older systems become progressively more
prone to failure. Where maintenance is being deferred, it likely has
been deferred longer on older systems, and those older systems also
need more maintenance than newer ones, so more is currently being deferred as well. Increasing demand and climate change are both
harder on older infrastructure—in general—because more change in
conditions has occurred since that infrastructure was designed and
built. In a sense, it's been longer since that infrastructure was adequate to current conditions.

All of these factors are intrinsically associated with older infrastructure, and more strongly associated as that infrastructure ages. If
your neighborhood has older infrastructure, it's likely more affected
by all three of these factors than is similar neighborhoods with newer
infrastructure. Remember, urban areas likely to have multiple older
systems are logically those with older housing and building stock.
Again, neglect piles up, this time in overlapping infrastructural failures: Potholes and water main breaks. Wobbly electric lines and street
flooding. Combined sewer overflow events and crumbling sidewalks.

If all this is true, it means citywide statistics about infrastructure failures are misleading, because those failures aren't evenly distributed across every neighborhood. Some newer neighborhoods with newer systems have virtually no infrastructure failures—it's all somewhere else. **The burden of living with infrastructure failure and its repairs is borne primarily by people living in the oldest areas of the city.**

Before we leave this topic for now, ask yourself two questions about the cities with which you are most familiar:

▶ *Where are the neighborhoods with the oldest average housing and building stock?*

▶ *Who lives there?*

PAYING THE PIPER, PRIVATELY

What happens when infrastructure fails, or becomes too unreliable to count on? Ideally, systems would be fixed in a comprehensive, effective, and timely manner, and we'd all go on with life knowing the lights would work and the water coming out of the tap would be clean and safe. But in the best possible scenario, infrastructural systems are expensive and large, which means fixing them is neither cheap nor simple nor fast. This means, best case, it takes a while to get the system fixed once problems develop. And it's so rarely the best case.

How does daily life go on, as repairs are delayed and replacement is deferred endlessly?

Short answer: you pay for it.

Longer answer: When infrastructure fails, the need it was intended to fill does not disappear. The pavement disintegrates, yet transportation and traffic still need to move from here to there. The water main breaks, yet we still need to drink, wash, cook, and clean. The power line breaks, and all hell breaks loose with it, because we need electricity for everything in contemporary American life. So infra-structure failure means need goes unmet. Perhaps there is some allow-able amount of failure, a portion of infrastructure that can go offline without anyone really noticing, because no one was really using that bit anyway—like a sidewalk crumbling along a street with no pedes-trians, or a streetlight going dark on a street where no one drives. Logically, there are cases of this: spots where existing infrastructure is overbuilt for current usage and therefore has extra capacity that no one misses when it stops working. But eventually, failure cuts into what you need, and it's far more common for infrastructure to be just big enough or a little undersized.

When needs aren't met by the infrastructure we rely on, people find ways to work around failing systems and meet their needs on their own. If your water isn't drinkable, buy bottled water. If your power is unreliable, get a generator. On the face of it, this sounds very independent and self-reliant—adjectives Americans tend to like. This is privatization of public services, in a way, with everyone paying his or her own way, and plenty of Americans like the idea of privatization an awful lot.

What's Wrong with Privatization?

▶ *What's wrong with taking care of our own needs and privatizing everything infrastructure does?*

1) It can be far more expensive.   Bottled water is the perfect example, and that takes us back to Flint. A truly inconceivable num-ber of bottles of water have been consumed by the citizens of Flint since the drinking water crisis began in 2014. As of 2013, bottled water cost, on average and in quantity, $1.22 per gallon, a staggering 300 times the average cost of tap water.[42] You get an even worse deal if you buy that one bottle at a time: the average price shoots up to approximately $7.50 per gallon, a jaw-dropping 2,000 times the aver-

age cost of tap water.[43] For Flint, though, the state of Michigan got a pretty good deal, relatively speaking: $2.35 to $2.90 per case of water, part of a year-long contract.[44] A typical American uses around 32,000 gallons of water per year in his or her home,[45] although in Flint, some of that could be supplied with filtered tap water. There are around 96,000 people living in Flint, Michigan, as of 2018.* You can do the math, but as a hint, in March 2018, the state of Michigan estimated it was spending $22,000+ per day on bottled water for Flint.[46]

Not everything is as stark as the comparison between bottled water and tap water, but there are economies of scale involved, as well as the difference between for-profit companies selling you the privatized substitute and public utilities providing services to everyone.

2) **It can be far more expensive in ways other than money.**
Again, the bottled water and Flint: Where have those all those empty bottles gone? How about fuel and labor to transport those myriad bottles to Flint from far and wide? How about the time spent by citizens—again, these are American citizens—going out to pick up water again and again, and getting rid of those bottles by whatever means? What could they have done with all that time spent acquiring all that water that they used to get just by turning the tap, like the rest of us do?

3) **Not everyone can afford the extra expense.** Privatization of failing infrastructure, in cases like these, means you pay twice for the service, because you pay taxes to support the infrastructure and the public services it provides, and then you pay again to make up

---

* And falling, because lack of safe drinking water is a pretty powerful argument to leave, but it's also nearly impossible to sell a house in a city that's famously without clean drinking water. Just sit with that predicament for a moment. Flint's population has fallen about 6% since 2010, before the water crisis began (population figures from U.S. Census Bureau, U.S. Census Bureau QuickFacts: Flint city, Michigan, 2019, available at: *https://www.census.gov/quickfacts/fact/table/flintcitymichigan/PST045217.*

for what the failing systems don't provide to you. Take roads. Roads can fail in a multitude of ways, from the lowly pothole to congestion from inadequate capacity to outright disintegration of pavement. The civil engineers of ASCE are all over this, since roads are kind of what they do, and they make this case for the cost of privatization very well: almost $147 billion for US households and businesses in 2015. Incredible, isn't it? That includes costs related to your vehicle, but also travel time lost, safety costs, and environmental ills.[47]

If you're driving over crumbling or congested roads every day, this number may astound you. The cost hides itself pretty well because it's hidden in a number of places: Car repair is one, and increased maintenance from the wear and tear your vehicle receives bumping over all those potholes. You need extra gasoline because you're sitting in traffic instead of moving smoothly toward your destination. Once failures advance to the point where roads have to be closed, you pay in extra gas, lost time, and wear on your vehicle when you have to take longer alternate routes around the closure. You pay every time you arrive late at your destination, tense and fuming with road rage. As I said above, you pay for it.

What if you can't pay? You do without, or you do without something else to be able to pay this additional cost of privatization, this hidden tax on top of taxes. In most places in the United States, to be without a car is to be without the means to reliably get to and from employment, as well as grocery shopping and medical care. To be without water is life-threatening. To be without electricity is not life-threatening for most of us, most of the time,* but it is certainly costly: $20–55 billion in annual costs to the US economy, varying mostly according to severe weather in any given year, according to a 2012 source.[48] Cruelly, this cost is more of a hardship for those of us with less money to begin with. For those of us with ample financial

---

* Unless it's running the dialysis you need to survive or running the heat that's keeping you from freezing to death.

resources, a refrigerator or freezer full of spoiled food is an irritation, but for those without the means to replace that food, it's far more hazardous.

4) It damages our idea of ourselves as a community and our reputation with others. This damage is not as concrete or immediate as the other problems listed here, but perhaps ultimately worse. Infrastructure failure and resulting privatization of services changes how we see our cities and our country, and the ways others see them, too. Americans assume clean drinking water to be our birthright, but should we, after Flint? We assume electrical service to be a birthright, too, unless we deliberately take ourselves away from it. Should we, when the lights went out in Puerto Rico for 328 days?*

To be a part of the developed world is to take these kinds of modern conveniences for granted, and to be free to build lives that depend on the constant availability of these kinds of services. If we can't count on these services, are we still a developed country?

---

* Yes, ABSOLUTELY Puerto Rico is America. Puerto Ricans are American citizens. They have been since 1917. The island has been US territory since 1898. This shouldn't be news.

CHAPTER 3

VACANT BUILDINGS, VACANT LAND

DEFINING THE PROBLEM

Neglect provides the city with a wealth of urban ruins. Abandoned buildings are a substantial problem for shrinking cities and for areas of growing cities plagued with disinvestment. **Along with vacant land, abandoned buildings are perhaps the most readily recognizable sign of neglect in our cities.**

The term *abandoned building* is straightforward enough, but what is vacant land? Vacant land is a parcel of land or lot not currently seen as in productive use. This usually means that it doesn't have any buildings on it, but land can be in "productive use" and not have buildings: parks, utility easements, transportation uses, agriculture. "Productive use" is slippery—"productive" according to whom, and what must it be producing? Generally lots within cities are categorized according to their land use, which includes categories such as commercial, industrial, and residential.

In practical terms, "vacant" really means "none of the above"—it's a parcel that does not fit into any of the other categories. For our purposes here, it's reasonable to think of vacant land as vacant lots of various sizes and conditions, from small strips leftover between other uses to large brownfields.

Abandoned buildings can be a real problem – when they aren't posing for glamour shots by urban ruins photographers. Almost immediately upon becoming vacant, a building starts to decay. Your chief enemy depends on your climate, but water, mold, wind, and freeze/thaw are a few of the big culprits. Even sunshine can be a problem, because some materials photodegrade, meaning they break down over time when exposed to UV light. Things fall apart much quicker when no one is there to keep tabs on them (in buildings as in life). Decay is accelerated by the lack of heating or air conditioning, both of which dehumidify the interior air. That fights moisture, the nemesis of buildings.[49]

As a building becomes more dilapidated, it also becomes more dangerous to you and me. Rotten floors are easy to fall through; missing windows won't keep you from falling out. Less dramatic dangers are the mold and particulates you can inhale, killers like lead paint, asbestos, and fiberglass. The abandoned building is rife with opportunities to impale your foot or get a filthy cut on your arm. These environmental contaminants aren't limited to the interior of the building, either. As buildings collapse, all the substances they contain are released and able to spread through the surrounding area. Environmental lead contamination is endemic in the soil of inner-city neighborhoods, and it certainly didn't get there because someone was painting the yard.*

Consider: these are all dangers inherent in the abandoned building ,those that result from the building itself as it makes its long journey toward oblivion. A whole other category of danger comes from animals and people who move into the abandoned building (see Chapter 7: Accidental Nature).

---

* Leaded gasoline, a bad idea that finally ended (in the United States) back in 1996, is the other big historical cause of lead in urban soils. More information, including links to even more information, at "Lead," Soil Science Society, 2021, available at: *https://www.soils.org/discover-soils/soils-in-the-city/soil-contaminants/lead*.

SQUATTING

And we want to move in. Abandoned buildings are great sites for all kinds of mischief—anything you don't want someone else observing, or can't do elsewhere. Abandoned buildings are good places for seeking shelter when you have no shelter. Not everyone who takes up residence in a vacant building is up to something nefarious. People may be motivated to become squatters by simple shortage of decent, affordable housing, as happened in Britain after the bombing campaigns of World War II.[50] Squatting may also be a means of protesting against housing policies or specific development of the squatting site, such as the notable example of Grow Heathrow, also in Britain.[51] Squatting can also be a component of a larger protest-driven opting out of capitalism or consumerism itself, as with the Freegan movement.[52]

Protests and edgy alternative lifestyles aside, if you do happen to be looking to do something bad, an abandoned building is an ideal place to do it. There's also something about abandoned buildings that calls to the vandal in us. This ranges from the fairly innocent—throwing a rock at the remaining panes of a broken window—to the truly nihilistic. Detroit, again, is the metric here. The annual orgy of destruction by arson known as Devil's Night originated before World War I with a variety of Halloween pranks like soaping windows and false fire alarms. That tradition darkened into setting bonfires in the streets, and then deliberate arson, claiming over 100 abandoned buildings each year in the 1980s and 1990s, up to 800 buildings in 1984. The number of fires on the night before Halloween has steadily declined over the last twenty years. As Detroit rebounded, Devil's Night faded into the past. Halloween 2018 saw a quiet milestone: Devil's Night in Detroit had no more fires—less than twelve—than any other night.[53]

NON-HUMAN SQUATTERS

We're not the only ones who want to move into a vacant building. Neither are we the only ones driven to accelerate its decline. Wildlife of all kinds, mammals to insects to birds, show up in abandoned buildings. Sometimes that wildlife is not so very wild, but rather feral, in a kind of poetic suitability, as dogs or cats cast off by society find a home in buildings also cast off by society.[54] Also invited is the retinue of creatures that accompany us wherever we settle: rats, mice, cockroaches, and the like. They're never far away. Genuinely wild wildlife has also been known to take up residence in abandoned buildings, and these raccoons, skunks, and friends can be the last straw for increasingly exasperated neighbors.

All the problems of abandoned buildings are magnified by the sheer abundance of them in shrinking cities. Looking solely at housing, studies have found a vacancy rate of around 15% in larger shrinking cities like Cleveland, and an even higher rate—17%—in smaller shrinking cities like Gary, Indiana. Of course, these numbers soared during the housing crisis of the early 2000s, but even now, there remain more vacant and abandoned buildings than there were in 2005.[55]

What's a cash-strapped city to do? The essential solutions here are pretty clear: you can get someone to move in and fix the place up, or you can demolish it. Land banks have taken charge of the "move in and fix it up" strategy. A land bank is a governmental or not-for-profit organization that acquires vacant and abandoned properties and transfers them to new owners. A specialty of land banks is property that owes more than its market value in back taxes, not an uncommon situation in distressed neighborhoods, and a very effective deterrent to buyers. Land banks may also hold properties for public use. Properties are leased or sold to new owners for uses aligned with local planning goals, so land banks can also be a tool to further community-strengthening goals such as increasing local businesses or alleviating urban food deserts.[56] (We'll revisit land banks later, in Chapter 13—Sail with the Current.)

Demolition seems like the easy route, but bulldozing buildings is surprisingly expensive. For example, the city of Detroit budgeted $500 million for demolition of abandoned buildings over five years, with the hard-to-grasp goal of demolishing 200 buildings each week.[57] Obviously, that's an enormous amount of demolition, so it will reasonably cost an enormous amount, but demolition is expensive for cities with smaller problems, too.

There's a feedback loop here: people stop paying mortgage payments or taxes on their property and/or don't keep it up. This private disinvestment becomes a public cost because the city has to pay to demolish the building once it lands in city hands through foreclosure. The increasing number of abandoned buildings, along with other signs of neglect, further discourages investment in the city, so more buildings become abandoned, and the potential demolition bill grows.

Let's pause for a moment here to recognize that we have a very large and intransigent problem, if not a crisis, of abandoned buildings in this country. You might not be aware of that, because a lot of us lead lives where we do not frequent areas or cities that have all those buildings. You also might not be aware of that because we are good at not seeing the occasional abandoned building, our eyes gliding away from it like a taboo topic in conversation.

We also must recognize that we have a problem with homelessness in the United States (over a half million people in 2018),[58] and a related problem of the lack of decent, safe, affordable housing (on average, you must make at least $10 per hour more than minimum wage to afford an apartment in the United States),[59] and these exist at the same time as this inventory of excess crumbling buildings. What makes this possible, this heartbreaking contradiction? Several villains could be mentioned here, but one you might not see immediately is space, and the mismatching of it. **We have places with too many buildings, and places with too many people without a place to live,**

but they are often not the same places. That's irony. That's tragedy. That's a problem in need of someone to fix it.

Vacant Land

Vacant land lies at the heart of this examination of the neglected city. Therefore, much of what there is to say about vacant land is said elsewhere in this volume. What remains to be said here is this: there is a lot of vacant land. In a 2016 study involving neighborhoods as candidates for revitalization efforts in Upstate New York, I found that more than eighty-two neighborhoods across ten cities contained vacant land at a rate of 10%, or one in ten parcels within these areas.[60] Vacant land is not just an Upstate problem: Nationally around 17% of land area in our large cities was vacant according to a 2016 study.[61]

What's wrong with vacant land? In many ways, the answer to that is this entire book, but an important question is that same one turned inside out:

▶ *Is vacant land all bad, or can it play a positive role?*

As we dig deeper into the neglected city and its vacant and abandoned spaces, remember this core idea: Vacant parcels, along with other signs of neglect in the built environment, encourage us to see the city as a dangerous place and ourselves as threatened within it. It encourages the depiction of people who live in the city as dangerous themselves. This dangerous city is not only threatening to life and health, but also to investment, meaning it tells you to put your money somewhere else. The very prevalence of vacant land makes it one of the most obvious signs of neglect in the urban environment. We react to what we see, so in this case what is obvious is what is most important. Vacant land matters.

PROPERTY VALUES

Property values have historically been a powerful argument about land use in the city, as both cause and effect. "Highest best use" is the mantra of property development, embodying the dogma that the use that brings the highest property value is the best one for any given piece of land. All manner of racial and ethnic discrimination in housing and mortgage lending has been justified by protecting property values, and conversely, the threat of property value decline due to increasing racial integration has been used to push white residents to sell cheaply or move.[62] Low property values are often used to justify siting disamenities in urban neighborhoods, as responsible stewardship of public tax monies or construction budgets. Where land is cheap, you get more of it for your tax dollar, and so the prison or landfill joins the host of other disamenities in the poor neighborhood on the floodplain.

Property values are also the sacred cow of home ownership and all the structures and policies we've put in place to encourage, support, and reward home ownership. You buy a house expecting that it will increase in value, a solid shockproof investment because no one's making any more land. Does this work? Sometimes. The oft-cited statistic is that over time, land always increases in value. Countless homeowners burned in the Great Recession could tell you that your mileage may vary, having watched home prices nationwide plummet over 27% from 2006 to 2012. Nonetheless, protecting and increasing property values remains a cause seen as uncontroversial and noble, an American cause. Perhaps our recent experience with what happens when property values stop increasing serves to make this cause all the more treasured, more valuable because we've felt its absence so strongly.

What does neglect do for your property values? Nothing good. The open secret of property values is that they are nothing more than quantified public opinion. Land is worth what someone will pay for it, or in common parlance, "what the market will bear." What makes someone think your acre is worth more or less? In part, his or her feeling about the neighborhood and the condition of the property. That feeling is perception, and we'll see what neglect does for that a bit further along (Chapter 5: Places No One Cares About). In terms of urban property, the big bogeyman is always crime, and neglect bears on that, too (Chapter 6: The Scary City, Crime, and Fear). The intersection of perception and crime is fear: the idea that this is a place where criminal activity is likely or common. People, especially outsiders not in a given neighborhood on a daily basis, are quite unlikely to actually witness crime near their prospective purchase. Most of us don't check crime statistics.* We rely instead on our sense of the dangerousness or safety of a place. Our sense is perception, and there you go.

PARKS ARE AMBIGUOUS NEIGHBORS

Strange things happen to property values in the wild city. Generally, property near a park is a good investment. A park is an amenity, and being near that is good. It's also almost always a long-term land use, persisting over centuries while houses and businesses change hands and conditions. The house next door may crumble, but the city park endures. That stability makes them good neighbors. That stability also ensures the park will not become, say, a big box store next year or the year after that. If you're looking out your front door at a park, chances are that someone standing at that front door will still be looking at a park in 100 years.

This is expressed through property values as an elevation in them for parcels adjacent to parks. You could ask any realtor about this, or you could look at the authoritative 2001 review of relevant studies,[63] a review going clear back to Frederick Law Olmstead and the effect of the 1857 construction of Central Park on adjacent property values.

---

* Although we could—they are publicly available and often readily available on the internet, on sites like *http://spotcrime.com/* and *http://www.trulia.com.*

This review gives a nice succinct number for this effect: 20%. That's a ballpark estimate for how much more your property is worth if it directly borders or faces a park. Crompton does note that this bump is less for parks that are heavily used for "active" (i.e., noisy) uses, but even then, there's a substantial increase for the properties nearby but not immediately adjacent to the park—add a little buffer zone, and your lot is still worth more. That's the usual relationship.

But in the shrinking city, or the neglected city as we're calling it here, this dynamic may be reversed. Here properties adjacent to city parks are worth less on average. The park that raises adjacent values anywhere else here lowers them. At least one study found that in Syracuse, most parks depressed the values of adjacent urban properties rather than increasing them.[64] The author speculated that this could be because of crime or perceived crime occurring in the parks. Surprisingly, he speculates that parks with footpaths and other provisions for pedestrian use had a more negative impact on neighboring property values, while those green spaces without provision for pedestrians (such as densely wooded parcels) had a less negative effect—in essence, no park users, no threat. The big idea here is that there is a threshold beyond which urban parks are viewed overall as a liability, not an amenity at all.

This is just one study, but it's a fascinating finding. It dovetails especially well with what we know about perception of wild spaces in the city and other signs of neglect. I suspect that it's about the perception of wild parks as unkempt, unregulated, even dangerous places. **Perhaps it's also the assumption that the park is no longer a stable long-term use, but rather an unknown—an urban wild card, if you will.** Anything could happen there, and that could include activities you don't want across from your new home. This also seems to speak to a loss of faith in the authorities charged with maintaining the neglected city's parks. It's bad today—surely it will be bad tomorrow. Maybe worse.

Without question, neglect shapes the built environment of the city, leaving calling cards of crumbling infrastructure, abandoned buildings, and vacant land. That's easy to see. Few people would quarrel with that depiction, even its sometimes-provocative notion of causation. But what about us?

▶ *Does neglect shape how we, as people in the city, act?*

A much less obvious question, and also, therefore, one well worth exploring.

PART II

PEOPLE IN THE NEGLECTED CITY

PEOPLE MATTER, SO BEHAVIOR MATTERS

A city without people would be wild, surely, but perhaps not a city at all. People are central to the neglected city's design by deficit. City residents are key, particularly people in the neighborhoods thick with signs of neglect. If those residents have few alternatives due to expense, transportation issues, housing discrimination, or societal racism, that's key, too.

People in other neighborhoods, far from obvious signs of neglect, matter to this narrative as well, because of their influence on the life of the metropolis, through their political and economic power. Genuine outsiders—residents of somewhere other than the neglected city and its suburbs—affect the dynamic of neglect because they form the potential market for every effort to spur investment within the city and reverse the tide of neglect. Their perceptions of the city as a whole and as parts, like whether certain neighborhoods are dangerous, can influence support (or lack of it) in state and national policies for the neglected city.

In this case, what people think matters, and what more people think matters more. Most shrinking cities are smaller places, not stars on the national stage. There will always be more people outside them than inside them, and those "outside" people play a powerful role in the life of the city, by investing (or not) and voting (or not) the way they do.

People matter to the city, and one way they matter is through behavior. "Behavior" sounds like raising your hand in class or throwing spitballs, but here it means what we do, especially how we interact with each other. You'd think human behavior would be universal, that people are people wherever you go. That assertion misses how we're affected by the environment, our physical surroundings. That influence can be strong, and yes, it can make a difference.

This idea is surprisingly controversial. For environmental designers like architects and landscape architects, it's a big part of the broad definition of what we do: that the physical spaces in which we live can improve the quality of our lives in a number of ways. For others, though, that same statement smacks of "environmental determinism," a damning condemnation. To say that our physical surroundings influence our behavior is not to say that we are unthinking pawns of our houses and roads and rooms, but rather that we respond to stimuli in the world around us. We respond in the same way we respond to other people, to animals, to weather—to every aspect of the world. To single out the physical environment as somehow uniquely ineffectual seems at best a myopic academic straw man. The point of this volume is not to say that signs of neglect in the urban environment force urban dwellers to behave a certain way. We all have free will. Rather, we talk about influences and encouragement, and how to shape cities in which everyone, most especially those without the resources to leave or visit elsewhere, has the best chance at life's opportunities.

CHAPTER 4

WILD AND HEALTHY

NATURE AND HEALTH

A basic notion—that humans benefit in numerous ways from exposure to nature—has been explored by many researchers. In research terms, this isn't a huge collection of studies, but it is well established, with foundations in studies over forty years old. Together, these findings demonstrate that being near or simply looking at vegetation, animals, and bodies of water has a measurably beneficial effect on our mental, physical, and emotional well-being. There's also a benefit to the health and strength of social bonds within communities, meaning in essence that we tend to treat each other better when we have some form of contact with nature.

Does this surprise you? It's not common knowledge that this benefit exists, and it's supported by multiple studies spanning decades. Or you might find the idea vaguely familiar, but be surprised it's been supported with studies. A lot of us **feel** like there should be health benefits from exposure to nature. We like trees; trees are good; let's all hug a tree. If you're my age, childhood exposure to the 1970s environmental movement left you with this: a memory of granola bars and of a frog playing a banjo in the swamp. Those somewhat older may remember the passage of the Clean Air and Clean Water acts, the outlawing of DDT, and the shocking environmental horrors that preceded them—burning rivers, dying bald eagles, Love Canal.

Admittedly this is a pretty mixed bag of associations, wandering far afield from the basic notion that we benefit from contact with nature. But that idea is in there.

However: your vague feeling that something is true is in no way indicative of scientific proof. In fact, a great way to make a splash as a scientist is to demonstrate that something "everybody knows" to be true is actually not. In this case, though, what everybody knows really is borne out by the research.*

POSSIBLE PATHWAYS

We know that benefits from exposure to nature can all be thought of in terms of health: physical health, but also mental health, emotional health, and the health of social groups or social interactions. In the simplest terms, contact with nature makes us function better and treat each other better.

A lot of people are interested in exploring this link in less simple terms. A few of them did a comprehensive review of published research relating to human benefit from exposure to nature, and they found that in the broad array of studies they examined, there were four links between nature and health.[65] In other words, the way nature impacts health went through one or more of these four routes:

- better air quality

- greater physical activity

- better social cohesion

- greater stress reduction.

Better air quality is straightforward.

---

* And also, DDT really did kill eagles and our water really is cleaner and healthier and less flammable because of the Clean Water Act.

Greater physical activity is the idea, demonstrated in various studies, that people are more likely to exercise outdoors or do more exercise outdoors if they are exposed to nature (like trees) while they do it.

Social cohesion is a measure of how connected a community is— do people know each other? do they like each other? would they help each other? Social cohesion may also include how people feel about their communities, such as whether they feel that they live in a good community, and that people there generally like each other and are helpful. A rough but relatable way to understand social cohesion (and the similar concepts of social capital and connectedness) is to think of a Facebook network, but in real life. A larger Facebook network is sort of analogous to greater social cohesion, as is a more active or involved network. The big takeaway from nature-health research about social cohesion is more exposure to nature, more social cohesion.

Greater stress reduction is easy to understand, since we can all understand (and desire) being less anxious and pressured. On this list, reduced stress indicators are seen in people when they have contact with nature.

These four routes make nature-health research make more intuitive sense to the regular person (aka anyone who doesn't study nature-health, aka virtually everyone). Maybe it's a new idea that looking at trees will improve your health, but everyone probably can think of one or two health benefits realized from less stress, better relationships with people, more exercise, or cleaner air. Some of us can probably think of hundreds of benefits attributable to these factors—more exercise and less stress alone seem to be implicated in every self-help article you read and every visit to your doctor. So for all of those benefits that come to mind, consider this:

Because exposure to nature is associated with those four routes, every benefit you've thought of may well be boosted, to some degree, by exposure to nature.

EASY AND SMALL, BUT SIGNIFICANT

This is compelling. It's compelling not only because we all want better health and everybody loves the idea of finding that one silver bullet that will fix every health woe in a single stroke, but because of this: exposure to nature is easy. In these studies, exposure to nature does not mean spending a week at Yellowstone or hiking in the Alps, although those pursuits would indeed expose you to plenty of nature. "Exposure" can be as little as looking through your office or school cafeteria window at a single tree. "Nature" can be that lone tree, a flower bed, or even a house plant. That such ordinary situations constitute exposure to nature is very good, because overall, in general, the kind of benefit demonstrated by these study findings is small but statistically significant. So it's real, according to the stats, not just random chance or attributable to some other characteristic of the people in the study, like age or income or education level. But it's a small benefit. If you are dying of cancer, looking at a tree outside your window five minutes a day is extremely unlikely to cure you, but it may ease your stress levels a bit, or make you feel more like talking with a friend. A bit less stress and a bit more positive social interaction may add a bit more time to your prognosis, but it will certainly make whatever time you have more pleasant and enjoyable, in a number of ways. This would be a small health benefit.*

---

* There's some evidence that looking at that tree may fight cancer in a more specific way, too. At least one team of researchers has reported that NK cells (a type of white blood cell that fights cancer and infections) are present in greater numbers in the blood after "forest bathing," a Japanese version of spending relaxed time in nature. The study is here: Q. Li, K. Morimoto, M. Kobayashi, H. Inagaki, M. Katsumata, Y. Hirata, K. Hirata, H. Suzuki, Y. Li, Y. Wakayama, T. Kawada, Y. Miyazaki, T. Kagawa, T. Ohira, N. Takayama, and A. M. Krensky (2007), "A Forest Bathing Trip Increases Human Natural Killer Activity and Expression of Anti-cancer Proteins:

Small but significant benefits like these are best incorporated into one's daily life, in ordinary places, during routine activities: the commute to work or school or the view in your backyard, not whatever you do on vacation once a year (assuming you take a vacation at all, which we Americans do not excel at, but that's another story). This is good news for putting this research into practice within your own life or within your recommendations in design or planning or facilities management. It's not great news for designing studies to reveal dramatic benefits, because it's difficult to craft a study that isolates this kind of environmental influence and reveals its full magnitude in a realistic scenario. **Real life is not like running rats through mazes, and people make lousy rats.** Studying people and studying real-world environments is always challenging because of complexity and the number of different things happening at once. This is another reason why the benefits demonstrated by these studies tend to be small. Small...but significant.

ATTENTION AND STRESS AND CAVEMEN

So what are these benefits? Other people have compiled comprehensive lists,[66] but I'll provide an overview here.

Perhaps because our species evolved living outdoors and has only begun living life indoors relatively recently, our brains seem to be hardwired to focus easily on elements of the natural world. This ease of focusing on nature allows our ability to focus on the rest of our lives to relax and recover, giving us renewed capacity for paying attention to the people and things around us afterward.[67] This idea is called Attention Restoration Theory.

A similar idea, Stress Reduction Theory, posits that being in nature or exposed to nature allows us respite and recovery from stress, which

A Comparison with a Trip to a Place Without Forest," *International Journal of Immunopathology and Pharmacology* 20 (2 Suppl 2): 3–8.

enables us to better deal with the demands of life afterward.[68] Both theories have adherents who feel their theory is the better of the two. I see merit in both. Perhaps the two theories are different facets of the same effect, an opinion at least a few others share.[69]

These two theories, Attention Restoration and Stress Reduction, are the foundation of much of the rest of the research mentioned here. Within them lies the inference that the inability to continually cope with the demands of the world around us stresses our bodies and minds in myriad ways, producing or exacerbating a host of ills, that "small but significant" effect, again. You could rephrase that, roughly, as "modern life is killing you."

So, is modern life killing you? Why would that be? An explanation could lie in humanity's history, particularly the length of time we've been on earth compared to the length of time we've lived in environments almost entirely of our own creation. Consider: for time out of mind, humans evolved in wholly natural environments, from the savannas of Africa to the forests and plains and jungles of everywhere else. This tends to bring to mind early humans and cavemen, but consider the more recent past. What was the world of a medieval peasant like, in terms of time spent in environments created by humans versus natural environments? Anyone throughout history who lived in one crowded room, be that cabin or cottage or hut, spent a lot of time outside that room, and nearly everything outside that room was natural. Even farm fields and pastures are natural, in terms of whether you see vegetation when you look at them.

"What about cities?" you ask. Cities certainly have been around for a long time, at least for some parts of humanity, but consider again how small nearly all cities were, and how few people actually lived in them. By modern standards, the cities of the pre-industrial world were quite small: medieval London ranged from 10,000 to 100,000 residents.[70] Mexico City (then Tenochtitlan) may have had as few as 50,000 residents before the Spanish conquest.[71] Cities built around foot travel also were typically very dense, and there was no suburban sprawl surrounding them, so it was very easy to reach the edge and see the forest or wetland outside. Also, many of the few people who did live in the cities would have spent the day outside of them—in nature—farming or plying other trades.

Consider, too, what the interiors and streets of those pre-industrial cities were like compared to your home's interior and your street. There were no screens. There was no electricity. Rooms were small, dark, and crowded, for the most part, so a lot of activities that we now do inside, everyday tasks like laundry or cooking, were done outside. In a way, the pre-industrial "built" environment was a lot less built than ours is today. Even inside, light came from sun or moon or fire. Sound came from nature or other people or domestic animals—no jets overhead, no cars zooming by, no TV. No central heating or air conditioning, either, so the temperature inside was more like outside, for better or worse.

I think the role of farming is often underestimated in this discussion. If you've raised a garden, you have some idea of what it was to be a farmer in the pre-industrial world: endless backbreaking work, but all of it outside, surrounded by greenery and animals. One hallmark of the pre-industrial world is that far more people farmed or herded animals or did other kinds of food production and procurement most of the time, because industrial processes have allowed far, far fewer people to feed far, far more of us. So, most of our ancestors spent most of their time out in the natural world somewhere bringing home the bacon. This was the case until quite recently, even here in the United States. We did not urbanize until about 1920, meaning that up until about a century ago, more Americans lived outside cities than within them. One hundred years is a very short time in the 150,000+ year history of our species—perhaps 0.07% of our time on Earth. It's not nearly enough time to rewire our minds and re-engineer our bodies to thrive in fluorescent-lit, climate-controlled rooms dominated by screens instead of fields and forests.* The speculation is that this fundamental mismatch between the world we evolved in and the world we have created is at the root of nature-health benefits.

But that's just speculation. The studies upon which Attention Restoration and Stress Reduction rest are like any studies: they very carefully, deliberately, and thoroughly define a narrow question about a possible cause and possible effect, and then test whether that question is true. If all goes well, you can look at the findings of the study and say with certainty that this potential cause and effect are related to each other in some specific way: such as one goes up when the other goes down, or they increase or decrease together. But that's not about the why. It's not about the explanation behind why they rise or fall together or are inversely related. The "why" is much harder to test and determine. We can know the facts in this explanation—that for millennia, humans lived in natural environments and only very recently have lived in almost totally constructed ones. It seems very plausible that we as humans do not really function as well in these modern, totally built environments—but that last bit, the "do not really function as well"—that's speculation.

That's not at all because the research isn't done well. It's because that's the nature of research. There are things you can prove or disprove, but the "why?" often ends up being speculation. It's still speculation if everyone agrees with it, or if lots of people disagree with it. I'm stressing this here because people use this inability to prove or disprove the "why" as a way to dismiss research they don't like, and too many people believe their arguments. But we know better.

———————

* And, of course, environments dominated by these technologies weren't around in 1920. Fluorescent lights show up in the 1930s—that's after about 99.94% of human history, to date. Air conditioning becomes popular in the United States in the 1950s, after about 99.95% of human history, also to date. Smart phones are real newcomers, only around for about ten years, absent through virtually all of humanity's history up to now. These major influences on us are all very new, in terms of our species.

Physiological Health

Some of these studies have found measurable physical health benefits either after people have contact with nature or natural views or in residents of areas with more vegetation (often tree canopy or parks). These benefits are measured through health indicators such as blood pressure and cortisol levels as well as the rates of diseases like cardiovascular disorders and clinical depression.[72] People also demonstrate lower perceived stress levels in studies after exposure to nature, so you know it and your body knows it, too. These benefits may be enhanced or related to the measurable increase in physical activity and exercise by those living in places with more vegetation, and/or by the social benefits of contact with nature. However, even a view of vegetation, particularly trees, from a window has measurable health benefits, such as faster healing times for hospital in-patients.[73] The combination of stress reduction and more exercise is a really potent one for preventing all kinds of disorders and diseases and managing ones you already have. If nature is doing that for you, it's truly a wonder drug.

Mental and Emotional Health

You're probably already familiar with that feeling, and being less stressed can have mental health benefits as well, which research also indicates. Again, this is the one-two punch of less stress and more exercise, plus perhaps the better social connections and positive feelings toward place. Outdoor activities can help alleviate symptoms of Alzheimer's, dementia, anxiety, and depression. Exposure to nature has also been shown to reduce symptoms of attention-deficit hyperactivity disorder (ADHD) in children. In recent years the promise of contact with nature as incorporated in healing gardens and other therapeutic gardens has received increased interest as a tool for managing or alleviating post-traumatic stress disorder (PTSD). This is of particular interest to the US Veterans Administration and others serving veterans, due to the large numbers of vets suffering from PTSD and other anxiety- and depression-related problems due to their experiences in our recent wars.

Nature therapy has the marked advantages of being inexpensive, readily incorporated into daily life long-term, and easy to incorporate with other healthy habits like exercise and social interaction. Compare taking a daily walk in the park with taking a daily prescription drug or two and you'll see what I mean. The meds are far more expensive, even if you're not the one paying for them. They have to be picked up from the pharmacy and refilled and taken correctly at the right time and dose. They can cause side effects and interact with other medications and foods. None of this is really a problem with that daily walk in the park. On that daily walk you are walking, not just looking at trees, so you're getting the benefits of exercise, too. Over time you may start meeting a buddy or two for that walk, or at least get to know some of the other people in the park at that time every day, and this kind of social support helps with anxiety and depression, too.

It's easy to see the appeal of nature-based therapy, especially for long-term or even lifelong conditions. Exposure to nature is something you can work into your life as a daily habit that's just part of normal life, not a medication that marks you as "sick."

MENTAL HEALTH BENEFITS OF URBAN WILDS

Mental health benefits are less intuitive and familiar than the other nature-health benefits discussed here. So here's a helpful list:

Table 3: Mental health benefits of urban wilds

Reduces mental fatigue
Improves alertness, performance, memory
Reduces stress/impact of stressful events
Reduces depression
Enhances cognitive functioning
Reduces childhood ADHD symptoms
Reduces negative symptoms in dementia patients
Increases life, place, and job satisfaction

Mental health benefits matter when we weigh the impact of urban wilds in the neglected city, as we will later. Urban wilds are nature; exposure to them is exposure to nature...probably.

SOCIAL AND PLACE BENEFITS

As I mentioned in the pathways list above—better air quality, greater physical activity, better social cohesion, greater stress reduction—one of the big documented benefits of exposure to nature is, in essence, that we get along better with each other when we have more contact with nature. This breaks down into greater social interaction, greater feelings of connectedness, and perhaps more trust in each other. The kind of question used to measure this is, "Can people in this neighborhood count on one another?" So it's trust at that basic level, sort of your assessment of the common decency level of those around you.

Intermingled with this dynamic are more positive feelings towards places with more trees or other "good" nature. This shows up as greater place attachment ("I like this place," or "I value this place") and as straightforward preference for places with more trees or nature ("I like this place more than that one"). This manifests as people spending more time doing activities in places with more trees, a key finding that points toward a number of other findings on this list. What kind of activities might people be doing in those treed places? Exercise, for one, even just casually strolling or walking a dog. Playing with children, which is pretty good exercise in its own right and great for the kids, too. Socializing with other people, which ties into those social benefits. For communities or people in any kind of social group, this manifests itself in people who live in neighborhoods with more shade trees (tree canopy) rating their connections with neighbors and their communities more highly.[74] This is a benefit that's easy to dismiss, yet it has ramifications for all kinds of quality-of-life issues determining how happy and healthy you are and how happy and healthy the people around you are.

CRIME AND FEAR

If you turn place attachment inside out, you get a lack of connection with other people, which is one way to characterize crime or fear of crime. And indeed, nature-health research includes studies examining crime and vegetation. These studies generally find that places with more vegetation, particularly well-kept vegetation such as shade trees or lawn that doesn't block views of the surroundings, have lower crime rates.[75] A related but separate benefit is perception of crime, or whether people see an area as safe or dangerous in terms of criminal activity.[76] Although it seems logical that we'll fear crime more where there are more crime incidents, that's often not the case: reputation of an area and actual crime rates are two separate phenomena. Other factors contribute to a person's opinion about the safety of an area, and these factors can outweigh the actual incidence of crimes there. The average person does not maintain familiarity with crime rates in different areas s/he frequents, anyway. Nonetheless, vegetation generally reduces the perception of crime in an area —as long as that vegetation does not block views of the surroundings, and as long as it appears well maintained. Much more on that later, in Chapter 5: Places No One Cares About.

IT'S NOT A LIST, IT'S A WEB

As you read through this list of benefits, perhaps you thought one benefit or another was mis-categorized. It's in "mental," but it should be in "health," or "social," or whatever. There's a good reason for this: these benefits overlap with each other and interact with each other, so my categories, while providing a clear organization that's easy to grasp, are rather artificial.

The way we experience these benefits is more complex. For example, on a street with more trees, we may spend more time outside. This lets us get to know our neighbors better and feel more at ease relying on them, AND it increases our chances of spotting anyone on the street who's up to something nefarious, which may discourage crime and/or make people around us feel safer. At the same time, since we're outside, we may move around more, which increases the amount of physical exercise we're getting. This AND the social interaction AND the positive feelings about where we live AND the lessening of worries about crime all may contribute to a more positive mental and emotional outlook, decreasing depression, anxiety, or post-traumatic stress. It seems likely that these effects can feed into and amplify each other. In the previous example, the lessening of our anxiety and depression might make us more likely to spend even more time outside on our green street, which lets us interact even more with the neighbors, and so on.

This network of benefits and their interplay with each other may well mean that scientific studies of individual nature-health effects underestimate the benefit we receive. Studies do the best they can to isolate individual causes and effects, in order to best reveal how or whether they affect each other and by how much. They are reductive by nature because that allows you to have the most confidence that any effect you see is really due to what you intend to study. But that same reductive process may shortchange complex effects like how we're affected by nature. In short, those small-but-significant benefits may actually be a little less small than we think.

It also seems likely that the specific ways nature exposure affects us are complex and overlapping. If you sift through the many nature-health studies, you'll find different ideas about what it is about nature that causes these effects. Maybe it's an airborne substance exuded by trees. Maybe it's the light flickering through leaves. Maybe it's the physical comfort of lower temperatures or greater relative humidity. Maybe it's the lack of all the not-natural conditions we escape while we're steeped in nature, and not anything specific from trees or plants at all. The extraordinary breadth of documented nature-health effects says to me it's likely that many or maybe all of these possibilities are correct. It's not one thing; it's everything, and it's all at once.

This makes the benefits we get more robust and harder to avoid receiving, yet could also make crafting good studies to parse causes and effects more difficult. One last complexity is this: some experts speculate that we don't all benefit equally from the same exposure to natural settings. All else being equal, more disadvantaged people benefit more from the same exposure to nature, something called the equigenic effect.[77]

On the whole, nature has a lot to offer us in terms of health benefits. It's a simple notion, backed up by plenty of established research. But "nature" can be a threat as well as a friend. This relationship gets more intriguing when we look at places where that ambiguity is on display.

CHAPTER 5

PLACES NO ONE CARES ABOUT

Look around your home and ask yourself where things pile up, everything you set down "just for a minute." Do you notice that spot, or have you stopped seeing it? In your own home, a mess is just a mess, but in places we share with other people, a mess can be more than that. It's messy because no one is cleaning it up. It's unmanaged because no one is taking care of it. Outside, messy, unmanaged places can be threatening because, well, no one is cleaning them up or taking care of them or otherwise monitoring what's happening there. A place like this is outside the rules. It's uncivilized. Wild.

"No one cares about this place" is a powerful message, more powerful than it might initially appear. What happens to places no one cares about? We fill them with litter and whatever else we discard. We let them decay or grow into thickets or forests. **We often stop noticing them, because in places we frequent, we are practiced at no longer seeing places filled with litter and cast-offs.** The message that no one cares about a place is also a message that no one will notice what you do there, or monitor it, whether that's dropping litter or burying a corpse. It's a gray area where threat lives. **Anything could happen there.**

The ambiguity of urban wilds comes into its own when we talk about human behavior. Clearly there are a host of benefits we realize from being exposed to nature, as we've seen. The impact from each benefit may be small, but it's also empirically demonstrable and objectively manifest; the benefits are real. Equally real, however, is an array of negative impacts on our behavior from exposure to a certain kind of nature—unmanaged, threatening, and wild.

CUES TO CARE

This connection, between places that we see as uncared for and the perception that no one cares for them, is the finding of a number of studies. "Cues to Care" is the phrase researcher Joan Nassauer coined in 1995 for this idea: that markers of human intention in otherwise natural landscapes convey to us that someone is looking after this place, and that it is, therefore, cared for and of value.[78] These markers can be a lot smaller than you'd think—as little as a strip of mowed grass along a roadway or a fence at the edge of the woods. Those little "wildflower plantings—do not mow" signs you sometimes see are a great example of this. A sign or two makes you see an ecologically valuable if small preserve where you would have just seen a messy former field.

We tend to see attractive landscapes as good or worthwhile, realizing that "attractive" is a rather subjective term. What's attractive to me may not be quite the same to you, particularly since I'm a landscape architect and environmentalist with a doctorate in an environmentally related field. Your expertise, particularly this kind of expertise regarding ecology, makes a measurable difference in what you deem "attractive." That means you see some landscapes as worthwhile that others see as weedy wastelands. Cues to Care, it turns out, can tip the average person's view of a particular natural landscape just across the fine line from "weedpatch" to "desirable natural area." Since a lot of ecologically valuable natural landscapes are indeed messy, this is a powerful insight. Little things can have a big impact in how people perceive landscapes, and how we perceive them dictates whether we value them and take care of them.

BROKEN WINDOWS

This takes us down a dark, unmaintained path to a related idea based on similar research: Broken Windows. Broken Windows is the hypothesis that small but persistent signs of disorder send a powerful message that people in a neighborhood will tolerate bigger signs of disorder, such as crime. Litter, graffiti, and literal broken windows are this kind of sign. If they are allowed to remain, not fixed or cleaned up, the hypothesis says other people will not bother to clean up or repair other little signs of disorder nearby, and soon the whole neighborhood falls into disrepair. These signs of disorder tell anyone looking for a place to break the rules that this is it: no one will complain or even notice if you conduct your crimes here.[79]

At first glance, this seems innocuous enough. Big neglect follows little neglect, because small signs of neglect that are allowed to persist send an undeniable message that neglect is accepted here. You can watch this happen in your office or home or anywhere you are charged to maintain. A surface, like a table or counter, that's free of all clutter will remain clutter-free much longer than one that has a single item of clutter, like a pile of mail, sitting on it. That pile of mail is permission to leave things there. One more won't hurt. No one will notice. This happens even if you live or work alone. It's how we are.

The trouble begins when we over-extrapolate. In law enforcement and local government, Broken Windows became a strategy of strict enforcement of laws against minor crimes, based on the assumption that stopping minor crimes would stop bigger crimes from ever happening. These minor crimes could be as small as jaywalking. Broken Windows eventually led to stop-and-frisk, a controversial and now discredited policing policy that encouraged harassment of African Americans and Latina/os.

Think about it: enforcing laws against minor crimes in at-risk neighborhoods means the people in those at-risk neighborhoods get arrested or fined for infractions like jaywalking that most of us get

away with, most of the time. In too many cases, Broken Windows provided an excuse for loading up non-white men with arrests and fines,
disproportionately burdening them. In essence, it makes minor crimes
only a crime for people already living in a neighborhood deemed to
be at risk for crime. That, clearly, is inequitable, and in recent years
opinion has turned against Broken Windows and its use in policing.
It's also been long enough now since this policing strategy was implemented to evaluate whether it's been effective, and many people
say that it hasn't (although there are dissenters). Critics also blame
Broken Windows for fostering an atmosphere of distrust and hostil-
ity between urban minority residents and the police, which is without
question a substantial problem.[80]

What does all this mean for a city replete with signs of neglect?
By definition, a sign of neglect is a sign that no one appears to be
maintaining a place. There is accordingly near-total overlap between
the signs of neglect in an urban environment and environmental characteristics that cultivate the impression that a space is uncared for
and owner-less. **It adds up to widespread perception that no one
is paying attention to many, perhaps most, places in the city, and
that no one will notice what goes on there.**

Loose Space Is What You Make It

That perception is a mixed bag with a surprising number of positives
in it. People see wild spaces like these in many ways—eyesore, habitat, health hazard, oasis. These contradictory views come to a head
in the way people use wild spaces. We express the ambiguity of our
views about these spaces through our actions within them. What's the
right way to behave in a vacant lot? What are the rules?

Spaces like these, without clear societal rules of behavior, are
sometimes called "loose space."[81] There's not a fixed definition of
what's appropriate there. Lack of clarity about what behavior is allowed in loose space creates a lack of clarity about what behavior

isn't allowed. **Loose spaces are spaces that let you get away with things.**

What do people do in loose space? We do things that break the rules—transgressive things. *Transgressive* simply means that: it breaks the rules. That could include illegal activities, crimes, dangerous or violent behaviors, but also includes behavior that is harmless but odd or simply out of place (by someone's definition). Walking a dog is transgressive if land is privately owned. Mountain biking is often transgressive on private property without the owner's permission or on public land where biking isn't allowed. Transgressive uses also include behavior that's legal for someone else, but illegal for you—underage drinking, pot smoking in states where it's not legal, illicit sex.

The line of legality becomes rather fuzzy (loose) in these spaces. Growing a tomato plant on the land just outside your property is transgressive but not illegal; growing marijuana there is. Dumping lawn clippings might not be transgressive but is illegal; dumping chemicals there is both.

The act of breaking the rules can be part of the allure of these spaces. **Some things are better done out of daylight.** Anything kids do out of sight of adults is a temptation in these spaces. Art often benefits from being transgressive, and loose spaces can be provocative sites for guerrilla artwork.

Loose spaces can be places to play, a provocative notion in this age of over-scheduled children and helicopter parents. A place to build a fort or a fire, a place to spray graffiti, a place to simply escape from the world for a while. These spaces make us uncomfortable because they are "wild" in this way, too: untamed, beyond society's rules. **Anything can happen in the blank spot on the map.**

A blank spot is an invitation, to anyone with a criminal agenda in mind but also to those who need a loose space to play. A blank spot is also an invitation to express yourself, to explore, to get lost for a while, or to make your own world. **Space with no rules can be exactly the opportunity someone needs to make the world anew.**

CHILD'S PLAY

Outdoor play is precisely the prescription for much of what ails a lot of kids these days, especially kids in cities, especially kids in households without many financial resources. Let's connect some dots:

Obesity   As of 2016, almost 20% of American kids from ages six to nineteen were obese, more than triple the percentage of the 1970s.[82] American kids are suffering at alarming rates from diseases of obesity, including those previously thought of as diseases only affecting adults. Poorer kids suffer from obesity at higher rates than those from more affluent homes, due to poor diet and other reasons, including a lack of active play that can burn off some soda and chips. Kids need a place to play in order to get that active play, and that place needs to feel safe enough and actually be safe enough to be appealing.

Too much screen time   Plenty of experts draw a line from the country's childhood obesity crisis and the amount of time kids spend staring at screens, whether computer, tablet, smartphone, or TV. One survey found that children ages five to eight spent nearly three hours each day looking at a screen on any device.[83] The connection between screen time and weight gain makes intuitive sense: if you're watching TV or on a device, you probably aren't playing tag or soccer. Less obvious is that screen time and sedentary lifestyles are in a chicken and egg relationship, in which it's difficult to tell which is cause and which is effect. The more you stare at a screen, the more sedentary you are, but the more sedentary you are, the more chance you have to stare at those screens. As a child becomes heavier and less fit, sedentary activities may be more appealing as well, so it's a positive (not good, but positive) feedback loop, too. This dynamic is bad, bad news.

Social media   Meanwhile, some of that screen time is social media time, and you don't have to look far to see the downside of social media for kids and teens. A better tool has never been created for bullying, and we have too many sad illustrations of that. About 15% of American teens reported having been bullied via social media in 2017.[84] Part of what makes online bullying so much worse than the old-school analog kind is that it is so inescapable. If you're always connected to social media, you are always in your bully's crosshairs. A place apart that's offline could be a lifesaver.

Nature-health benefits, Jr.   Kids get other benefits out of exposure to nature, a point thoroughly made by Richard Louv's books, including *Last Child in the Woods*.[85] Kids probably get similar benefits from exposure to nature to what adults get, including stress reduction, improved ability to pay attention, and enhanced creativity. Little people need these benefits just like big people do. "Vitamin N" is needed in the city as well as in the suburbs and rural areas.

I say "probably" because little of the nature-health research has involved children. There are good reasons for this: concerns about the ethics of involving children in studies and the greater red tape therefore involved in getting a study of kids approved. Nonetheless, it means we're not as sure about how kids might benefit from nature. Some of the benefits we see in adults logically are of even more value to kids, though. For example, childhood obesity is arguably more worrying than obesity in adulthood, so the greater outdoor activity associated with greater tree canopy could be more valuable to kids. Since kids' minds and bodies are still developing, health benefits like stress reduction could be even more valuable to them, too.

PTSD in inner city kids   Actually, that stress reduction benefit of exposure to nature may be needed **more** in the city than in the countryside or suburbs, because urban neighborhoods include some pretty stressful places to live or to grow up. Living in a neighborhood with a high rate of violence is stressful, even traumatic, considering the violence a person witnesses as well as that suffered by friends and family. For a vulnerable child, this is all the more true. For kids (and adults) in this kind of situation, stress reduction like that provided by exposure to nature is desperately needed. (More about PTSD and the inner city in Chapter 12: Public Health.)

Wild spaces are free   Perhaps obvious, but easy to overlook, especially for those of us in comfortable financial circumstances: access to urban wilds is free of charge, which makes them affordable to anyone, including people of very limited means. Lots of cures for this list of ills aren't free or anywhere near it. Even going to a city park can include bus fare or the expenses of owning and operating a car. Since urban wilds tend to be situated in or near the very distressed neighborhoods where household resources are the most limited, this can be a free resource close to home: a place to play, to burn some calories, to release some stress, and to nurture creativity.

Of course, wild places can also be dangerous places, not just because of crime, but also because of some of the elements that make them wild, like wildlife and obstacles to trip over. Not every kid should go wandering into any urban wild. But for wild spaces that aren't too hazardous, this can be just what's needed to counteract a host of problems for city kids.

WILDER PLAY SPACES

Those kids can do some cool stuff there, too.[86] Among people who study the role of play in childhood development, unrestricted play is seen as a considerable benefit. Wild spaces are not programmed for specific activities, so they encourage more creative play that originates with the child herself. Contrast this with a traditional playground, where the easiest activities are to slide on the slide, to swing on the swings, and so forth—to do, in other words, precisely what's programmed. Play in wild spaces is seen therefore as fostering imagination. This same lack of programming can make wild spaces much more physically challenging. On the face of it, you might read that as "dangerous," which could be the case, but they are also more challenging simply because they aren't programmed. A wild space is a blank slate. There might be trails you could follow, but there are also lots of other places you could walk or run, letting a child explore. Which way should you go? What's over here? Trees and rocks might be good for climbing, or they might not—you find out by trying. Maybe this rock is no fun to climb, but it makes a good house or fort or castle in pretend play.

This determination of "where should I go and what should I do there?" is a challenge itself. Experts report that this increased physical challenge promotes better agility in children. Of course, play in wild spaces, like other activities in natural areas, cultivates awareness of the natural world, too. For kids or most especially teens, wild spaces offer a place to test boundaries, to take risks. This can include destructive behavior, but these same places can also be a setting for solitude or to socialize with friends away from supervision.[87] Wild spaces allow you to shape the world to your taste, whether by destroying something or building forts.

Given all this, it's not surprising that a few intentional settings for play have been constructed that are wild in some way. Adventure playgrounds feature an imaginative, open program and are dynamic places. Adventure playgrounds allow children to build things and shape their surroundings, in the same way that wild spaces do, a creative activity that's markedly different from traditional swing-and-slide playgrounds. This building can be the literal kind, including saws and hammers, such as children experience at a wild public playground in Berkeley, California.[88] At another adventure playground in Wales, building happens every day with pallets and other found objects (sometimes called "junk").[89] Zip lines, lots of items to climb on and in, and even fire (!) are common components of adventure playgrounds, which got their start quite a while ago in Europe, just after the Second World War.

There's a contradiction here that merits highlighting: these innovative play settings, particularly in the United States, are primarily fee-for-use amenities used, therefore, by families that can afford to use them. Some facilities even require advanced booking, to ensure that there's enough supervision for the number of kids there.[90] This is quite different from the kids most likely to live near wild spaces in cities. Obviously, one benefit you pay for here is the assurance at some level that this is a "safe" wild, although some of these play settings do require a liability waiver. Parents likely are much more comfortable with the idea of their children playing in a wild setting that's controlled and used by many other kids (there's a clear overlap here with Cues to Care, discussed above). They aren't wrong, either, because while wilderness play areas may have more risks than traditional playgrounds, your child won't be running into the serious hazards that are real possibilities in many urban wilds—big scary hazards like chemical contamination or violent crime.

This points to a second contradiction: one of the elements that makes wild play so valuable is the need to spot and evaluate risk. When you use these skills, you get better at them, so a child who learns to manage some risk is a child who enters his teen years better equipped to handle more independence in a risky world. We want that. We want that as a society, not just as individual parents, especially because teenagers are notorious for exactly this shortcoming: managing risk poorly. Yet we don't love the idea of children in risky places. However, if you hone risk management skills in risky environments, it seems logical that the riskier the environment, the better the skills developed.

There's risk everywhere, if you look hard enough. On a traditional playground, you can fall off the slide (although we put shields on slides and ladders now to prevent this). You can jump off the swings at too high an elevation (although we put cushion-like materials under the swings to break your fall). If you really try, you can run smack into any piece of play equipment and knock yourself out (although many playgrounds have safety zones designated around play equipment in which you are not supposed to run). Everything about a traditional playground is done to minimize risk, yet there are still risks to be found by the determined kid. Wild-ish play settings include more risk, because they are more flexible and less rigid about what kids do in them. That same open-ended character that makes them more exciting and beneficial also makes them riskier, because we adults can't anticipate everything kids might do in them and paint safety zones and put cushions around them. It's a trade-off.

Is there a trade-off between risk and benefit in the somewhat sanitized wild of adventure playgrounds compared to riskier urban wilds as places for play?

This is not in any way to say that every urban wild is a good place for kids to play. Obviously some spaces are dangerous even for adults. However, that very determination, of whether this is a safe-enough urban wild, is risk management. Developing that skill, of determining whether this is a safe place for me to be, is a really good, useful thing. In fact, for many of us, "is this a safe place for me to be?" is a question we'll ask ourselves regularly over the course of our lives, long after we've entered adulthood. For too many of us who are female/not white/LGBTQ,* this is a question that can become life or death on any given day. That makes it a pretty important skill to hone.

There are good questions here, about access to wilder play spaces, proximity of those spaces to different groups of kids, and where the line really is between too dangerous and beneficially risky.[91]

▶ *What's the best urban wild for play?*

---

* That's most of us. Think about it.

A City Planning Typology of Guerrilla Art

Wild spaces are also good places for adults to play, in terms of creative expression of all kinds. **An urban wild is that longed-for place where you never need to pick up your toys or clean up your messes.** As such, wild spaces attract artistic expression of the rule-breaking kind. Creative expression in spaces shaped by neglect is many and varied, as depicted in the excellent book *Canvas Detroit*, by Julie Pincus and Nichole Christian.[92]

For our purposes here, the big question about this art and the neglected city is: why here and not somewhere else? To answer it, we need to look at it as city planners, not artists. Much of the appeal of guerrilla art is the lack of rules. To me, that's a defining characteristic. That same free-for-all character makes it difficult to break down these works into simple, discrete categories. Nonetheless, here's an array of ways to think about these artworks and their settings:

City as canvas   Borrowing somewhat from Pincus and Christian's book title, the neglected city and its wild spaces provide the backdrop on which to create your masterpiece. The sheer number of surfaces or venues for artwork in a neighborhood with widespread abandoned buildings and vacant land is difficult to comprehend. There's always another wall or building or open space. Of critical importance to artists of limited means (and isn't that every artist?) is that the canvas is free, or nearly so. Consider what's involved in getting approval and permission and so forth to paint a mural on the wall of a building that's currently occupied and in an economically healthy neighborhood. The hoops would be myriad, and if the owner hasn't approached you, the artist, to do the mural, the odds of you, the artist, being able to choose your own surface for the work and put your mural there are slim, indeed. Contrast that with painting on an abandoned building in a neighborhood with a high vacancy rate. It's simple, right? You, the artist, have complete agency over where you paint and what you paint and when.

City as kit of parts   Not only is the canvas potentially free, but the materials from which you craft your work can be, too. The neglected city is full of found objects waiting to be incorporated into the next work, objects that you and I might call trash, refuse, discarded household items, or scrap from building demolition. The Heidelberg Project is the classic example,[93] but there are far smaller works based on this idea. That could be as small as figures of animals or insects created from salvaged hardware like bolts and hinges, or larger multi-media pieces that hang on the wall, with found objects as just part of the materials. Again, this is not only compellingly cost-effective for artists working on limited budgets, but it also has an inherent ecological ethic, reusing what's been discarded and giving it new life.

The artist controls how obvious the previous life of these materials will be, and whether to make their reuse visible. This is an intriguing opportunity. You could mill a reused beam into lumber and build something out of it, and it could be indistinguishable from new wood to the casual observer. This could be an intentional message, or it could simply be a cheap source of wood. The same with metal, which can be reworked, melted down, recast, ad infinitum. Or you can use the materials as is, making their provenance as waste product plain. Your choice.

Highlighting a few discarded objects makes the ocean of waste we generate more visible. A message of redemption underlies found object art: that beauty and purpose can be found in the most unlikely of places. Yet a criticism of our wasteful consumer culture runs through it, too: look at all you can do with just an infinitesimal portion of what we discard.

Part of what we discard is materials from demolished structures or those awaiting demolition. The volume of construction and demolition debris is truly staggering. In 2014 I created a design studio project that prompted students to explore this aspect of infrastructure replacement. Interstate 81 runs directly through Syracuse on an el-

evated viaduct of approximately 1 1/2 miles in length. It is an inescapable presence, a growling low-slung mass of concrete and steel
girders, literally dividing the city into east and west. For a number
of years now, the city has been gripped with the debate of what to do
with 81, since the announcement that the current viaduct had come to
the end of its lifespan and would be replaced. Whether the new I-81
should be a tunnel, a higher brighter viaduct, or simply the dispersion
of traffic onto surface roads, the old viaduct is coming down. And that
means there will be tons—literally—of debris. Concrete and steel.
Reinforcement and hardware. Road signs, bolts, and guardrails. Lots
and lots of asphalt.

As the project brief said:

*Demolition and construction waste carries major ecological impli-
cations and should be minimized. This reality can provide an au-
thentic connection to place, and like most constraints, can set the
stage for inspiration...*

*Figure 3: The aging elevated viaduct of I-81 in downtown Syracuse,
seen from below.*

Interstate 81 is a defining element of the landscape of central Syracuse. Debate about the future of the aging elevated highway has focused on replacement vs. surface boulevard vs. tunnel or alternative routes. Any of these alternatives will require the dismantling of the current structure. What should happen to those pieces? What could they become in a site design, and how could they recognize the history of this divided heart of Syracuse? In this project we explore the pieces of the elevated structure as a design opportunity, and a chance to reduce the ecological impact of new development.[94]

Beyond ecological considerations, the project prompted students to consider the profound cultural ramifications of I-81 and the urban renewal project that created it. In a sadly common story, the highway was built over Syracuse's African-American business district, the redlined 15th Ward, displacing families and businesses. The highway then played the usual role in the twin scourges of the 20th-century American city: disinvestment in the center and suburbanization at the edge. What is the most appropriate response to the death of such a conflicted structure? Is erasure a kind of disrespect to the losses of those displaced by urban renewal? Regardless of an individual's view of I-81 in Syracuse, its life in the city spans a half-century, an era defined by this unlovely structure and its effects. Doesn't that deserve some kind of commemoration in the landscape?

Students rose to the challenge with projects that reused the piers and beams of the viaduct in new structures, as sculptures, and as fill to create earthwork forms. Proposed designs included sculpture parks for stormwater infiltration, sports facilities, a bike park, markets, and amphitheaters.

Transgressive edge of setting   Cities grow. That's our whole understanding of them. We imagine a city as full of excitement and energy, and as Americans, we can easily link that to the national myth of constant westward expansion, our old frenemy Manifest Destiny, the force of progress. In this context, a shrinking city characterized by signs of neglect is transgressive, even by its very existence. **Places like this aren't supposed to exist here.** This setting therefore is a natural fit to amplify the impact of work critiquing the forces that build and motivate growing cities. Capitalism, consumerism, conformity, the American dream: all of these are fair game. The exact same sculpture or dance has far, far more credibility and impact set in an abandoned factory than in a tidy gallery space.

In fact, the canvas of the neglected city can speak very eloquently on its own, semi-independently of the artist's work. It's built-in, and thus more powerful and visceral. The choice of site in this context is a substantial part of the genius of guerrilla art. Consider: the Heidelberg Project and other works riffing on abandoned housing stock would be so much less powerful outside Detroit. It's pretty easy to find an abandoned house, even in prosperous growing cities, but in Detroit, they mean more. Detroit became Detroit because it was home to disruptively innovative factories that drew workers from all over the world. They came for great wages in jobs that required a strong back and work ethic, but little in the way of education or training. With one of these magical jobs, you could buy a house, a car, and a college education for your kids. You could ascend into the middle class, and do it on one income while your wife made that house into a home (or conversely, while your husband brought home sufficient bacon). The house was central to this American Dream, and all those workers, with all those dreams, meant there were an awful lot of houses built: single family homes with a yard and a driveway for that car, next to other single-family homes, and on and on, street after street. It's what makes Detroit so notably sprawling, even by American standards, today—these houses, for those workers, and all those cars.

This is the meaning of a house in Detroit. If you were one of the countless African Americans who came north to Detroit to escape the oppression of the Jim Crow South, that house in Detroit came at the additional price of fighting through housing discrimination to overcome centuries of landlessness through segregation and slavery. This, too, is the meaning of a house in Detroit.

When those houses, those American Dream houses, become so worthless that they are reasonable fodder for artistic expressions like covering them with stuffed animals or cutting them into parts and appending them onto another (worthless) house, it means something. It means something because there are so many of them. An abandoned house there is not special. As they all rose together in a great wave of construction in Detroit's days as a city of unimaginable futuristic progress, so they all have fallen together into disrepair and disinvestment. Each house is worth so little because there are so many.

Yet each one of these houses was once someone's home, a cherished doorway to the middle class, the embodiment of success and security. It's not just an abandoned house; it's the death of a dream, the death of lots of dreams. And all of this meaning is there in the abandoned house in Detroit before you, the artist, ever adds that first stroke of paint or nails on the first found object.

Lack of supervision and regulation   In the neglected city, no one's paying too much attention to what you do, which makes it ideal for art you can't do elsewhere, such as work with elements of destruction or vandalism. The perfect example is graffiti art, straddling the line between vandalism and artwork. Here the setting is a major component of the work: it's transgressive and therefore striking to put graffiti in a gallery. It's transgressive and therefore striking, but in a different way, to put a vibrant mural with graffiti style and elements on the wall of a decaying school or gas station. You want to smash a building as part of your next work? No problem. You want to burn something down? Go ahead. To a certain kind of artistic mindset, the idea of no rules can be, well, like match to gasoline. There's no box of regulations and ordinances and permissions to fence your expression in.

Not everyone likes this kind of guerrilla art. You've probably already spotted some of their reasons. Guerrilla art highlights the decay and abandonment of the neglected city—the exact opposite of the perception that community organizers, economic development, and local government are trying to create. If you want new businesses to start in the vacant spaces of your neighborhood, and instead you get a group of people burning discarded mattresses and calling it art, you may be less than pleased, to say the least. It's not just that you don't want the mattress-burners there; it's that you see them as one more obstacle to getting those new businesses in. **The apocalyptic chic of guerrilla art is both what gives it such edge and what many people living and working in shrinking cities object to. Two sides of the same coin.**

That same ambiguity and duality inhabits the way that much of this artwork affects the visibility of elements of the neglected city. You didn't notice the abandoned house—until someone covered it with doll heads and stuffed animals. Making the signs of neglect more visible, including to outsiders, is a potent impact of this artwork. Whether that's a positive or negative impact is entirely dependent upon your point of view and what you are trying to accomplish. Little of this work is pretty or conventionally attractive. None of it matches your sofa. **It's provocative, and not everyone wants to be provoked.**

Guerrilla art can be like a flare sent up to call attention to the unbearable condition of the city and its rougher areas. It can also highlight the potential of an area in making all the excess resources— land, buildings, materials, space—visible. And just as it repels some people, it attracts others. Never underestimate the power of something cool. We've seen this in recent years in the perception of Detroit, a kind of post-apocalyptic swagger that makes a notable address for your event or studio or start-up. It's a tougher sell for smaller shrinking cities like Syracuse, but not entirely absent, and there's a long history of people, usually outsiders with money, often white outsiders, using a gritty locale to provide a cloak of authenticity for their business or creative endeavor. This can bring needed investment and new people into an economically devastated area—and it can start the cycle of gentrification. Ambiguity again. By capitalizing on the grit of an urban neighborhood, you destroy that grit and drive out the people who've endured so much to stay there.

SMALL START-UP BUSINESSES

The same aspects that make the neglected city appealing for creative endeavor can make it appealing for creativity of a different kind: starting up a small business or company. This makes sense, because in some ways, starting a business or other enterprise is just another kind of creative endeavor. **The same freewheeling atmosphere that promotes creativity channeled into art can promote creativity channeled into entrepreneurship.** The same affordability in premises and materials can be helpful, too.

The line between entrepreneurship and artistic endeavor can blur, like in a short-lived venture in Syracuse that made furniture from timber salvaged from demolished buildings. Elsewhere, the accumulated layers of paint from paint shops in auto factories, called "Fordite" or "motor agate," is the rather celebrated centerpiece of some enterprising jewelry business.[95] And of course, there's any number of businesses specializing in the careful disassembly of abandoned buildings that enables any of this kind of thing. The architectural salvage and deconstruction business forms the foundation of these other creative and entrepreneurial endeavors.

The same edge and authenticity that attracts artists can attract entrepreneurs and give their efforts instant credibility. This "credibility by location" extends to an ecological vibe and a social justice mood, deserved or not. For the right kind of business or product, this boost in reputation and style can make all the difference between viability or ruin.

In a roundabout way, several of the same characteristics that make a city shrinking or an exemplar of urban neglect also make it a promising location for a shoestring start-up. A lack of municipal regulation or oversight can be beneficial early on. Low property values mean cheap rent, not just for business premises or manufacturing space, but also for employees who might not be making as much money with your little company as they would with a bigger, more established competitor. Economic decline means there's plenty of available labor force, sometimes a surprisingly skilled labor force, especially if your start-up needs the kind of skills that recently vanished industries used.

Local folks are glad to have you and your business there, and that can manifest itself in all kinds of benefits. Sometimes the people in whatever power position matters to you at the moment are noticeably pleased to have your enterprise there. State and local governments try all kinds of incentives to recruit new employers in economically moribund areas. **Somewhat ironically, these same cities characterized by neglect and disinvestment can be really generous in terms of financial incentives for new businesses.** These incentives often take the form of not doing something, such as tax abatements or credits, because that's more feasible for a cash-strapped city to do.

It's hard to be successful with a start-up anywhere, but there certainly are people who do it, even in the apparently unpromising environs of the neglected city. Some of the Rust Belt's bigger cities make an appearance in recent lists for most start-up growth, including Cleveland, Indianapolis, and Columbus (Ohio).[96] Chicago shows up elsewhere, of course, as do Pittsburgh, Cincinnati, and Milwaukee.[97] Detroit has a start-up scene, complete with multiple incubators and coworking spaces.[98] These are all large cities, and that's not an accident: to make it onto these lists, you need a lot of activity, and there's naturally more activity where there's more people. But there's start-up activity going on in smaller cities, too, that won't make it onto these lists. Any town with a large university, particularly if it is strong in tech or engineering, has some kind of start-up energy happening. One asset the Northeast and the Midwest has in abundance is big universities like these.

Looseness, or the lack of clearly defined purpose and ownership or rules, can be a real asset. Coupled with the low costs of living or starting an endeavor in places plagued with neglect, looseness can provide enough room to get up to things. Some of those things become play, or art, or start-ups based on someone's bright idea. But all these characteristics, this same looseness, has a downside, too. Again, there's enough room to get up to things. Some of those things aren't so friendly.

CHAPTER 6

THE SCARY CITY, CRIME, AND FEAR

A CONTRADICTION

Everybody knows cities are the worst places to live—full of crime and pollution, scary people who aren't like us (regardless of who "us" is), corruption, the whole vice-and-mayhem package.

Everybody also knows cities are the best places to live, the sites of the best civilization has to offer: culture, entertainment, excitement, the hot new restaurants.

Which "everybody" are you with? I hear truth in both descriptions. Cities are in fact both good and bad, and we see them that way.

At heart of this duality are the topics covered in this chapter: crime, fear, and social disorder. In our imaginations, a city is a place where you can get away with anything. Whether that's good or bad depends on who is doing the action and what they are trying to get away with. "Social disorder" is this idea: that here is a place where the rules don't apply, or where they are so weak that you can—probably—get away with actions and behaviors that would bring Authority down upon you elsewhere. It's the opposite of social cohesion, or a lack of cohesion.

One reason cities are this place to us, at least in our imagination, is that they allow greater anonymity. A person lost in the crowd is less accountable for her actions than one known to everyone she sees.

Another reason for this perceived lack of rules is the type of space encountered in cities, and that's what we'll discuss here.

FEAR, NOT CRIME

What do we know about cities—urban environments—and crime? If I ask a group of people this, the responses could include a bunch of other things "everyone knows":

- that there is more crime in cities and therefore your chances of being a crime victim are greater there.

- that not all cities are equally dangerous, and not all parts of an individual city are equally dangerous—that there are "good" areas and "bad" areas.

- that poor neighborhoods are more dangerous or that neighborhoods occupied by higher percentages of the resident minority group (African Americans, Latina/os of any sort, any immigrant group) are more dangerous.

- that it's safe enough during the day, but not at night.

- that a few local spots are known to be dangerous—the neighborhood you'd never park your car in, the park you were warned about when you moved to town, the place or places of the last crime sensationalized in the news.

- that it's really up to crime victims and their decisions about how to act or where to be or what to wear.

A scholar might sum up these comments as asking what part of risk should be attributed to an individual in a given environment and what part should be attributed to the environment itself.

This representation of what "everyone knows" about crime in urban environments—drawn from my discussions with classes over the years—is surprisingly misleading. **It's mostly about fear, not crime.***

Fear and crime are not the same thing. Fear is looking over your shoulder as you walk down the dark street at night toward your car, your steps quickening, your keys in your hand. Fear is deciding not to park there at all, or not to go without a friend, or to leave before dusk. Fear is telling your girlfriend or daughter not to go to the city on her own.

Crime, on the other hand, is the mugger actually accosting you on that street, your purse in his hand, the gun in your back. Crime is the broken car window and the missing items when you get to it.

Crime, in other words, is the actual event, while fear is our perceptions or expectations about the possibility or likelihood of those events. They may seem similar, but in fact they aren't the same. Sometimes they diverge in surprising ways when we talk about urban environments.

CRIME, NOT FEAR

A number of jobs ago, I was a landscape architect in Indianapolis. I worked downtown at a firm that didn't have its own parking provided, so I usually parked a few blocks away on the other side of a well-to-do neighborhood of renovated historic homes. I parked there because it was free—unrestricted on-street parking—and I never worried about walking through that neighborhood. When I worried was when I went to various project and construction sites around the city, often in the poorer parts of the city or to old brownfield sites and vacant lots.

---

* And in case you didn't notice, most/all of those assertions are wrong, or illogical, or prejudicial, or racist, or usually misogynistic, and/or indefensibly callous. Just because it's what "everyone knows" doesn't mean you should trust it or believe it.

A basic truth about being a landscape architect is that you frequent pieces of land that are unused, unkempt, and not currently occupied by anyone doing anything legitimate in the light of day, because your business is turning those pieces of land into something else, and these are the kind of parcels that are about to become something else. So as a twenty-something white woman in landscape architectural practice, I frequently found myself asking that litany of fear-based questions: is it safe to park here? Is it safe for me to walk here? Is it safe for me to be here at all?

I didn't ask myself those questions about the neighborhood next to the office in which I parked my car, but I should have. It was there, in front of one of those high-priced gentrified cottages that I was robbed at gunpoint in broad daylight one afternoon, as I walked to my car on the way to a meeting.

The neighborhood where I was robbed was not "dangerous," but it's where I was robbed. All the places I went for projects were "dangerous," because I feared them and my coworkers feared them* and my family would have worried about me visiting them if I had been foolish enough to tell them about it.

This is one anecdote, one woman's experience on one afternoon in one city. Like any single anecdote, it proves nothing. It does illustrate how fear and crime can diverge in terms of urban space. **Just because you fear a place does not make it actually dangerous.** Sadly, the converse is true as well: **just because you feel safe in a place does not make it actually safe.** They are different things.

We see this in neighborhood crime rates and maps of crime incidents in comparison to the reputations of different urban neighborhoods. In Syracuse, Thornden Park, a large area of rolling hills and pockets of woodland adjacent to campus, has a terrible reputation as a

---

* More accurately, my coworkers feared them a little, but probably less than I did, because my coworkers were mostly white men. Gender matters tremendously in this discussion, as does race.

haven for rapists and other criminals. Yet crime statistics, at least for the years I taught there, revealed the neighborhood of student housing next to the park, where my students felt relatively safe, to be home to more crimes.

This mismatch isn't unique to Thornden or to Syracuse. A number of explanations can be spun for this mismatch between places we find scary and those that are genuinely dangerous, including biased reporting, uneven publicizing of crimes in various places, and plain old racism. We are all subject to the tendency to remember and believe new information that fits the way we already see the world,* so if you already think a given neighborhood is dangerous—including because of the race or ethnicity or socioeconomic status of the residents—you're more likely to remember and believe accounts of crime incidents that happen there.

All these explanations may be true, at least for some places, some times, but what about the urban environment?

Does the urban environment play a role in this mismatch between fear and crime?

That question stated differently is this:

▶ *What kinds of urban environments are scary?*

▶ *What kinds promote crime?*

▶ *Are the two kinds of urban environments the same?*

---

* This is called confirmation bias, and it's everywhere, including in the way you yourself see new information: Jeff Stibel, "Fake News: How Our Brains Lead Us into Echo Chambers That Promote Racism and Sexism," *USA Today*, May 15, 2018, available at: *https://www.usatoday.com/story/money/columnist/2018/05/15/fake-news-social-media-confirmation-bias-echo-chambers/533857002/*.

A Great Place for a Crime

What researchers know about urban environments and promotion or discouragement of crime is that yes, it can make a difference. If you've heard of this at all, you've heard of Jane Jacobs, most likely her "eyes on the street" idea.[99] If this is new to you, in summary: public spaces, like streets, are safer when there are more people around to see them. This casual surveillance gives us the sense that we can be seen by others, so we shouldn't do anything bad, and that nothing bad will happen to us, because someone will see it. Even more reductive version: busy places are safer places. It's regular people, not security forces or cops, who are doing the surveillance.

Also along these lines is a more elaborate set of basic principles, called Crime Prevention Through Environmental Design, or CPTED.* CPTED originated in the 1970s, primarily through the work of C. Ray Jeffery[100] and Oscar Newman,[101] building on the work of earlier thinkers like Jacobs. As an architect, Newman focused more closely on the role of the built environment and on practical applications to real places, so in this book, our sympathies lie more with him as well.

The big idea here is that safe communities are those that allow residents to control the areas around their homes. Like Jacobs' classic "eyes on the street," control of the area includes being able to see who's coming and going. Control also includes the feeling that the area near your home belongs to you, if not in a legal sense, in an emotional or psychological one. If an area belongs to you, you tend to notice what's going on in it and who's there. You're very likely to challenge strangers in a space that belongs to you, or at least notice them and pay attention to their behavior.

We know this without being told. For example, if I told you to walk into your neighbor's front yard, lie down and take a nap, would you do it? Of course not—because that yard belongs to them, and it

---

* Pronounced "sep-ted."

would be really weird for you go lounge there, unless you are really good friends with your neighbors.

Napping is not particularly threatening, but what if I told you to go over and peer into their windows, and try to open one? I'd expect that not just your neighbor would notice you were there, but some of your other neighbors might, too. Someone would be very likely to challenge you or at least ask what you are doing. Your neighbor's front yard belongs to him, even if he's just renting. But consider doing similar behavior in places someone "owns" but does not actually have legal title to: a private office. Someone's desk at work or school. The hallway immediately outside your apartment door. All of these spaces belong to us, so we certainly notice people there, even if we don't confront them.

That apartment is a good example, because it's more similar to public housing, which has been a focus of CPTED application. Conventional public housing, more or less by definition, is not owner-occupied. It can be very impersonal and institutional in design, too, which means residents can feel like they "own" nothing beyond their front doors. Many CPTED strategies work to counter this exact issue: to make the space outside your front door or your building feel like it belongs to you and your immediate neighbors. If these strategies work, you and other people will treat that space like your neighbor's front yard in the example above—like it belongs to someone else.

In recent years, CPTED has suffered a bit from its association with Broken Windows (see Chapter 5—Places No One Cares About) and its critics—guilt by association. Others have criticized it for over-promising, saying that crime **deterrence** is more accurate than crime prevention. This is a fair point, since like all interactions between the environment and human behavior, the environment can't force anyone to obey the law. It just makes it more likely. Some of CPTED's basic principles have long since escaped the label of CPTED and assimilated into the general toolbox of urban design.[102] That tends to be the ultimate test of success of design movements: your principles just become part of "how we design," and cease to be known as their own thing. (You can find examples of the same phenomenon with sustainable design, which used to be niche indeed.)

A GREAT PLACE FOR FEAR

When we talk about environments and crime and safety, it's critically important to draw a sharp, clear line between actual crime incidents and the fear of crime. Fear of crime is about perception—whether we perceive a given urban environment as conducive to crime or ourselves as vulnerable to crime within it.

An interesting twist on this division is the perception of criminals as to the suitability of a particular urban environment as a setting for crime. If you or I, as potential crime victims, perceive a particular place as a mugging waiting to happen, it has no real impact on our chances of being mugged, because as the victim, we don't make that crime happen. Yes, you can blame the victim,* but realistically, there is no action I can take that will magically produce another person with the desire to rob me or cause him to take the actions to rob me.

In this sense, the victim or potential victim's perceptions don't matter. On the other hand, the criminal or potential criminal's perceptions matter very much, because he must decide to commit the crime, or the crime does not happen. **The criminal has the agency here, meaning that s/he decides whether or not a crime happens.**

One assumes that the suitability of a particular place, including the likelihood of being observed, of getting away, and of getting close enough to the victim to perpetrate the crime, matters quite a bit to the criminal in deciding whether to pick this moment, this person, and this place for the crime. Even if unconscious, this decision is key to whether the crime happens. An enlightening study a few years ago examined this by surveying a group of thieves and hearing them de-

---

* If you think blaming the victim is morally defensible. It's not.

scribe in their own words how they used dense vegetation to aid in their crimes, including to hide in before and after the crime, and as a place to dump unwanted stolen items.[103]

The thieves' assessment of suitability of different places for plying their (criminal) trade shows how we are all alike in some ways: the general run of people (which includes far more potential victims than thieves) rate the same kind of environments as dangerous, aka perceived as scary.

What kind of environments are scary? We find environments threatening in which we can't see very far, because of views being blocked by objects like tall, dense vegetation. We are particularly unnerved by narrow passages, such as trails or pathways, with dense visual screens on either side. We find signs that others do not maintain or value a place threatening, such as unkempt vegetation or peeling paint or litter. Lack of familiarity with a place is threatening to us, meaning that those of us raised in an urban environment find rural areas more threatening, and vice versa, and that every place is more intimidating when it's new to you. Generally, the presence of other people makes us more comfortable with environments we'd find threatening alone, assuming those other people aren't threatening themselves. It's worth emphasizing that "threatening" is perhaps the ultimate in subjective judgments, when we apply it to people. Whether I see you as threatening likely says as much about me as it does about you, perhaps more. In addition to the obvious connections to race, ethnicity, age, and gender, a person's individual background and experiences can matter in this perception as well. But, generally speaking, more people are better for feeling secure, and fewer people makes us more wary of an environment.[104]

In urban areas, these characteristics tend to be found in a particular type of land—an urban wild (more about those coming up in Chapter 7—Accidental Nature).

STUDYING CRIMINAL MISCHIEF AND TREE CANOPY

After the point above about the thief/rapist/assaulter having total agency over whether a crime is committed at any particular place or time, you could be forgiven for thinking this idea of environmental characteristics having any kind of consistent relationship with crime rates is nonsense. If it's all up to the thief, it's got nothing to do with the trees or lighting or the wholeness of windows, right?

You'd think. But associations between environmental characteristics of various sorts and crime rates are real, not just happenstance, because that's what statistics, in essence, tell you: the relationship you see between these two variables is not mere chance, but a genuine relationship. When you see that same relationship between, say, canopy trees and crime rates, borne out in study after study, you can be confident there's something real going on there. So what's going on?

In a nutshell, more trees, less crime. More explicitly, a host of studies have found lower crime rates in areas with more tree canopy or more trees.[105] Some studies measure vegetation in a broad sense, like in legal parcels designated as "park" in tax maps, which obscures any detail about the kind of vegetation in question. But other studies are more detailed, specifying canopy trees, street trees (which are almost always canopy trees, so that they don't block drivers' views), or mowed lawn with scattered canopy trees. The association with fewer crime incidents is, like many nature-health effects, small but statistically significant. For example, one of the studies I just cited found in part an association between a 10% increase in tree canopy and about a 12% decrease in crime.[106] It's small—but it was significant, statistically speaking. It should go without saying here that if you are the person who doesn't become a crime victim, a small benefit is well worthwhile in your view.

So that's it: more trees, less crime. Except when it's more trees, more crime. That's what we see if the "trees" in question are low shrubby ones that block the view into an area and, for good measure, appear unmaintained or weedy. At this point there's several words that should have become red flags: "shrubby," "unmaintained," "weedy." You see where this is headed.

It seems likely that there's a point where the negative effects of weedy and shrubby take over from the good effects of trees, from a human behavior standpoint. Trees are good, until they become too overgrown. Overgrown vegetation is bad, until it grows to the point where it becomes tree-like.

▶ *Where's the tipping point, and what happens around it?*

Unanswered questions like this are good starting points for studies. So I studied this, in 2013 and again in 2014, aided by a few assistants. We compared tree canopy coverage and crime rates in Syracuse, focusing on non-violent crime, especially criminal mischief. The headline is that things seem to change around the threshold of 40% tree canopy coverage. Where there was less tree canopy, we found what we expected: that more tree canopy was associated with more crime incidents, likely reflecting the weedy understory vegetation pervasive in the city. But for spots with more than 40% tree canopy coverage, even more canopy was associated with fewer crime incidents. Why? We speculated that where canopy is dense, there's enough shade to reduce understory brush, which provides less cover for unsavory activities. Is that the only possible explanation of these results? Of course not. But they do support the big idea here: that neglect matters in how it shapes the urban environment, and with it, our lives.

In all the ways we interact with urban environments, the question of people brings significance to the exploration of neglect in cities. Who cares what neglect does if no one is there to be affected? If neglect falls in the forest and no one hears it, does it make a sound? Nonetheless, we're not the only ones living in the neglected city. There are other creatures among the *Homo sapiens*, and neglect bears on their health and prospects, too. Sometimes our interests align with theirs, and sometimes, they don't.

MORE ABOUT THE CRIMINAL MISCHIEF—TREE CANOPY STUDY

My studies of crime incidents and tree canopy, mentioned above, are one instance of neglect changing the rules about what we think we know about how cities work. These focused on the influence of weedy understory vegetation and how that subverts the established "more trees, less crime" finding. Any finding is only as good as the study that produced it, and in the case of preliminary studies like these, there's not a published record of how the study was conducted. So if you want to know more about that criminal mischief-tree canopy study, here it is:

We studied criminal mischief incidents in 2010 and tree canopy, as reflected in LiDAR data*, for the city of Syracuse at the parcel level. We chose criminal mischief to study rather than all crimes because it is a low-level, non-violent crime, more or less encompassing vandalism.

Why criminal mischief? We speculated that the transgressive behaviors encouraged by overgrown or unkempt areas would be seen in criminal mischief, because that crime category is in essence transgressive behavior that has crossed the line into illegality—and

---

* LIght Detection And Ranging, a type of remote sensing which bounces lasers beamed from airplanes to measure the height of whatever is on the ground, essentially. More detail from NOAA here: "What Is Lidar?" National Oceanic and Atmospheric Administration, February 26, 2021, available at: https://oceanservice.noaa.gov/facts/lidar.html.

been caught at it. We chose Syracuse as a study site because of the city's wealth of overgrown and unkempt parcels and its high rates of vacancy and abandonment relative to the city's small overall size. If a relationship existed between tree canopy and criminal mischief, it would be most likely to be detected where there was a lot of both elements—somewhere like Syracuse. Unlike many cities, Syracuse also had LiDAR data for tree canopy available for a recent year (2010).

Recognizing the well-established relationship of more vegetation—less crime, we expected to find exceptions to this general rule in neighborhoods characterized by vacant land, abandoned buildings, and overgrown ruderal vegetation. These exceptions might involve criminal behavior that is non-violent in nature, and therefore more closely related to the transgressive use of "wild" spaces than the social and psychological benefits of exposure to nature.

More simply, we hypothesized that:

Incidents of non-violent crime would be not associated or positively associated with greater percentage of tree canopy cover in postindustrial urban cities.

Or:

More tree canopy, more crime, sometimes.

A lengthy process of methods development followed, as tends to happen with exploratory studies. Initial study focused on city parks and included pavement repair data, but the final inquiry focused on vacant land, partially driven by the availability of complete data with matching years. Using GIS (Geographic Information System, software for spatial analysis), we identified all tax parcels classified as "vacant" in 2010 in the city, over 3000 individual parcels. We then calculated the percentage of tree canopy cover for each parcel, using 2010 LiDAR data. We geocoded all reported nonviolent crimes, including criminal mischief incidents, in 2010 using public data provided on request by the city police, then selected all crimes within one block (0.1 mile) of at least one vacant parcel. We then analyzed these data for correlation between the percentage of tree canopy and the number of crimes. We did separate analyses for criminal mischief alone and for all nonviolent crimes, which included a list of drug-related offenses as well as arson, prostitution, and thefts that don't include personal interaction between the thief and victim.

We found something surprising: crime incidents did indeed rise with percentage of tree canopy, but only to a point. That point was around 40% tree canopy coverage, for both criminal mischief incidents alone and for all nonviolent crime. For parcels with more than 40% tree canopy coverage, higher percentages of tree canopy were associated with fewer crime incidents.

It's easy to poke holes in any study. This was just one city, chosen for its distinctive shrubbiness and high rates of vacant land. As an exploratory study, this was designed to fish for evidence of a suspected relationship rather than to test the general presence or strength of that relationship. And these are just preliminary findings.

Still, though—what's happening at that 40% tree canopy point? I suspect it's about shrubbiness or blight. You'd expect that in a study like this one, designed to find the point where the crime-encouraging influence of overgrown weediness intersects with the crime-discouraging influence of canopy trees and neatly mowed lawn, you'd see the opposite curve. That is, that more tree canopy means less crime up to a point, then even more tree canopy means more crime. That's the opposite of what we found.

One possible explanation is that the shrubbiness of Syracuse means that vacant parcels with 80% or more tree canopy coverage are not just covered with canopy trees, but also with dense thickets of buckthorn and other tall shrubs, presenting a solid wall of prickly vegetation to any person passing by, regardless of the legality of his or her intent. **It may simply be physically difficult for a person to enter these parcels, and thus, they are home to fewer crimes.**

Another possibility is that up to a point—40% tree canopy coverage—a higher percentage means more understory vegetation and thus more crime incidents. Beyond that point, the tree canopy becomes thick enough to hinder the growth of understory vegetation, because of shade. With less view-blocking understory vegetation, you see crime rates drop.

How do we find out? We do more studies that are more definitive and less exploratory. To be continued...

PART III

NEGLECT AND URBAN NATURE

CHAPTER 7

ACCIDENTAL NATURE

Picture Abandonment

Imagine standing at your front door. Picture the house across the street—neatly mowed lawn, a tree shading the sidewalk near the street, a row of evergreen shrubs along the foundation on either side of the front door. It's an unremarkable scene, but now imagine the house across the street is abandoned, for whatever reason. No one tends to the yard or house. It goes wild.

Nature will take back your neighbor's land, but not through some romanticized return to a world without humans. Instead, the successional growth will be heavily flavored with invasive exotic species, the hardy survivors of urban environments. *Wild*, but not *wilderness*, with its connotations of untouched nature never sullied by human contact. It will be a different kind of wild. It will be an accidental urban wild. We've mentioned urban wilds in passing several times, but here we think about them more, in the foreground.

Imagine the wild yard after one week, then after a summer of neglect, then after a year or five years or ten. As trees grow up and the house falls apart, how does your view from your front door change? How does your view of the neighborhood change? Do you still want to live there? Do you worry about your property's value or whether you could sell your home? Do you worry about vermin or vagrants more? Or do you see more birds and wildlife from the impromptu nature preserve across the street? Do you enjoy the wildflowers and lush shrubs as the seasons change? And however you react, do your other neighbors and the passers-by on your street share your reaction?

▶ *How does this new wildness change the neighborhood and the way it is seen by others?*

REASONS FOR WILDNESS

Far from being merely hypothetical, this scenario is repeated countless times across urban areas in the United States and other postindustrial countries. Vacant land and abandoned buildings are abundant in shrinking cities. But urban wilds aren't confined to cities that have lost manufacturing. Many growing cities also have pockets that have lost population or lost investment that paid for maintenance and upkeep. Thus wildness is not solely a postindustrial phenomenon.

Other factors contribute to wildness in our cities as well. Climate change is resulting in warmer temperatures and higher rainfall in some areas. And climate change benefits some species, even while it imperils most others. Poison ivy benefits, growing faster and larger, and becoming more potent.[107] Many introduced species that are already invasive, like purple loosestrife (*Lythrum salicaria*), benefit, too, perhaps because they are already the most rapidly adapting species around.[108] So the composition of urban wilds also is changing, with more poison ivy and deer ticks, which in turn changes how we perceive wild areas.

Our preferences, via changing trends and tastes, shape urban landscapes toward a wilder city as well. Organizations like the Audubon Society and National Wildlife Federation promote wildlife habitat in cities, through "wild yard" and "backyard habitat" programs. These are great programs—but they also increase the amount of vegetation and wildlife in cities, not just increasing their diversity of species. More subtly, backyard habitats affect societal norms about the man-

Figure 4: Dow Prairie at the University of Michigan Arboretum, in Ann Arbor. Definitely wild and definitely intentional, and in the center of the city.

agement of landscapes, making a less-maintained (and thus, more wild) landscape more acceptable.

This same ecologically minded trend toward creating habitat in urban areas shows up in parks and public spaces, resulting in less mowed lawn and more areas of meadow or other successional vegetation. We see it in a changing view of the role of parks, too, from gardens or recreational facilities to wildlife preservation and green infrastructure. Less maintenance is less maintenance, regardless of the motivation, which suits anyone looking to cut costs. (And the deficit continues to design...)

Speaking of green infrastructure, its increasing role in cities is making them wilder, too. Green infrastructure includes rain gardens, green roofs, and other installations that use natural processes to manage stormwater, rather than just funneling it all into pipes and treatment plants.[109] What green infrastructure does—manage storm water, improve air quality, reduce urban heat island—is definitely necessary in urban areas, because climate change and public health. Nonetheless—more green infrastructure in cities means more vegetation and wildlife. More wild.

Just like with changing tastes about wildlife habitat, the increase in green infrastructure influences societal norms about landscape maintenance, making wilder landscapes more acceptable. These changing norms influence the maintenance of transportation and utility corridors, which provide not only larger areas of land but also do a lot for ecological connectivity. When such corridors are no longer mowed regularly, they can really increase urban wildness. Changing social norms may also encourage those responsible for larger industrial or commercial parcels to mow less and let succession take over more, making even more land quasi-wild. These last two examples are significant, because they push urban wildness beyond vacant and underused land into other land use types. This adds substantially to the total acreage of urban wild. It also can produce urban wilds in cities that **don't** have large amounts of vacant land. Urban wilds for everyone.

A Typology of Urban Wilds

Vacant Lots

More commonly, though, urban wilds are vacant lots that have fallen out of maintenance, meaning that no one mows them regularly. These vacant parcels become covered in tall grass and weeds, then gradually shrubs and trees colonize them. The lot often contains relics of its past use as well, like discarded cars, trash, or ruined walls and structures. With this type of urban wild, the wildness is tied to the ambiguous ownership and to the low value placed upon the land.

Figure 5: Vacant land gone wild in urban Syracuse

Ambiguous Ownership

A related type of urban wild is land where jurisdictions or ownerships overlap, making it unclear who bears the responsibilities of ownership. You see this at the edge of parcels where the exact location of property lines is unclear, or where multiple parcels come together. This also happens where multiple authorities, such as a park department, an electric utility, and state department of transportation, all have responsibility for the same land. It's everyone's responsibility, so no one actually takes ownership of it.

Figure 6: Wild vegetation at the property line, further complicated by the adjacent utility corridor.

Messy Private Land

Urban wilds also include land in known, unambiguous public or private ownership that is covered in unmaintained vegetation. This can include privately owned land, like that of businesses or residences, that is allowed to grow wild in the back or side yard. This is often tied to a low standard of landscape maintenance overall in a neighborhood, so that an unkempt backyard does not stand out or attract particular notice. It can also be tied to relatively low or falling property values, where landlords or owners no longer see property maintenance as a worthwhile investment.

Figure 7: Not vacant, but still wild: an urban sidewalk in Syracuse, adjacent to a privately owned and well-used parking lot belonging to several local businesses.

Utility/Transportation Corridors

Public land can become an urban wild in the same way, and for the same reasons. Those utility and transportation rights-of-way and corridors mentioned above are good examples of this. The maintenance of power line corridors or freeway rights-of-way may be driven by cost, on the face of it, but these areas are closely maintained in some areas and allowed to grow wild in others. Something drives that choice. Part of that something is perceptions about what local people will notice or tolerate.

The visibility of such corridors from public thoroughfares may play an important role in these decisions, too—if no one sees the corridor, does it matter if you mow it? These corridors may be periodically mowed or cleared of brush for reasons other than aesthetics as well, such as access by vehicles or wildfire prevention.

Figure 8: A wild utility corridor in urban Syracuse. The vegetation here is primarily invasive Phragmites.

Messy Public Land

Public park and school properties can become wild due to budget constraints, because landscape maintenance and mowing is an easy cut to make in tough times. Mowing is a sneaky expense in maintaining property. It's not expensive to mow once, but it's a small expense that hits you every week or so during the growing season. It's easy to put off, but you only get away with that for a few days before it becomes so much harder to mow that the next mowing takes more work than usual and therefore costs more, too. It's deferred maintenance in miniature. Parks and schools have plenty of full-sized deferred maintenance, too. The crumbling pavement, mossy walls, and peeling paint add to the atmosphere of disorder created by the overgrown vegetation, and it seems less and less important to mow the lawn.

Figure 9: Elmwood Park in Syracuse

Brownfields

Postindustrial cities and postindustrial areas in other kinds of cities tend to have a different kind of urban wild: brownfields. A brownfield is land that was previously occupied by an industrial use or other use that is suspected of contaminating the soil, such as a gas station or dry cleaner. Not all brownfields are contaminated, but it's the possibility and/or perception of pollution that matters here. A brownfield is dirty land in need of redemption. Accordingly, they are rarely maintained. The legal status of brownfields is often in limbo, as investigation and litigation regarding what's in the soil and whose fault it is and who should pay can drag on for years. Programs abound to encourage re-development of brownfields. The added complexity of navigating these programs and regulations can make redeveloping brownfields more difficult, and certainly makes redevelopment take longer than building somewhere else on "clean" land.

Figure 10: Overgrown gravel pit, near the city limits of Syracuse

Brownfields are often larger parcels than these other urban wild types, which can make them more significant ecologically. Interestingly, the larger size of the parcels means that brownfields may have less impact than you'd think on area maintenance standards and perceptions of an area. There may be little road frontage or similar places where a brownfield is visible to passers-by.

Brownfields also stand apart from these other wild types in that they often occur outside of the distressed inner-city neighborhoods where the other types are most common. Brownfields happen where industry or railyards happened, and also where extractive uses (like gravel pits and mines) happened. This tends to be near other industry, or along rail corridors, or along bodies of water. Brownfields can be present right in the center of cities, where older factories or mills were once common,[110] but they tend to be farther from the center, more out of sight. Brownfields can indeed be so large that they determine how urban or rural the character of adjacent properties is; a house next to a 100-acre brownfield is hardly urban.

Eco-landscapes

Finally, remember that green infrastructure and those backyard habitats we discussed? They make a final type of urban wild that transcends land use or ownership. These eco-landscapes are the result of a bunch of positive, needed changes in how we see landscapes.

Figure 11: An overgrown rain garden.

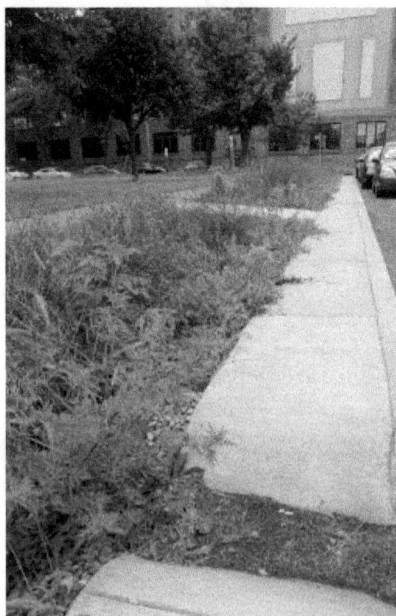

This brings me to an important point: while we distinguish between these different types of urban wild, legal and land use categories only matter to humans (and not even always to us). Natural systems and wildlife "see" the world differently, and these boundaries don't exist to them. We may look at a neighborhood and see a patchwork of residential yards, parkland, utility corridors, and overgrown vacant land, but a fox sees only several acres of continuous tree canopy and forest edge. To an insect, there is no difference between your beloved backyard perennial bed and the brownfield down the street, if they contain the same plants (and they might—see Chapter 12—Public Health).

ACCIDENTAL WILDLIFE

Urban wildlife is the heart of urban wilds. The sight of a deer or coyote or even feral pig* running across a city street expresses the disorder and dissolving of boundaries that urban wildness connotes in the strongest possible terms. This disorder, the feeling of untamed and potentially dangerous nature encroaching into the very areas where we imagine nature to be the most dominated, is both exhilarating and unnerving. The sense of mystery in places we thought were readily knowable repels and lures simultaneously.

There's always been wildlife in cities—rats with the plague, pigs eating garbage in colonial America, stray dogs prior to the advent of dogcatchers. How does chronic underfunding affect wildlife? More urban wilds means more wildlife, both in quantity and variety. The quality and species complexity of the vegetation within those wilds may matter, too. Increasing urban tree canopy, an increase in understory vegetation, and growing species diversity within that vegeta-

---

* Don't think it can't happen. One example from Utica, New York, in 2012: Steve Hughes, Nov. 8, 2012, "UPD shoots 200-pound wild boar in East Utica; 2nd on loose," *Utica Observer Dispatch,* November 8, 2012, available at: *http://www.uticaod.com/article/20121108/news/311089822.*

tion (e.g., not all the same kind of tree) could all have an impact. Abandoned or vacant buildings and structures can provide habitat as well.

URBAN WILDS AND WILDLIFE

One way to see urban wilds is as novel ecosystems, as newly formed native communities adapt to massive disturbance, including large proportions of exotic invasive species. Wildlife in urban wilds can also be a mixture of native species that tolerate human presence and disturbance and introduced species that thrive on urban conditions.

Urban wildlife evokes stronger responses from the public than vegetation, possibly because we see wildlife as more "wild" and therefore less suitable for the city. People frequently fear wildlife, worrying about attacks or diseases. Because most people don't readily recognize individual plant species as invasives and out of place, plants can pass as belonging in urban areas. Only a botanist or environmentalist will notice them. In contrast, pretty much anyone can spot a deer in the city and wonder exactly what is going on.

On the whole, cities are bad things for wildlife. More buildings, people, and pavement means less species diversity and less wildlife overall. Yet some species thrive in city conditions. Sometimes urban or suburban conditions around the edges of cities actually support greater numbers of a given species than were present in estimates of pre-settlement numbers in the same area. Some of these are creatures of the woodland edge, like white-tailed deer. Others, like raccoons, thrive on food sources inadvertently provided by humans, such as trash and pet food. Still others are species that arrived with people, then became feral, as is the case with dogs, cats, and pigs. There are also the ever-present companions of human settlement—pests such as rats and cockroaches.

An interesting twist falling somewhere between these other categories is animals that do better in cities because city humans treat them better than rural humans do. One expert on urban coyotes notes that since we killed off wolves and cougars from most of the country, coyotes' chief threat is people, namely hunting, trapping, and poisoning. These are all well-established traditions in rural areas, but rarely done in urban areas.[111] By being where we don't expect them, coyotes have been able not just to survive in cities, but thrive.[112]

LANDSCAPE MANAGEMENT

The dynamic between human use and care of developed land and wildlife populations is interesting and sometimes contradictory. Contamination or "spoiling" of sites can benefit wildlife in some ways, especially when the notoriety of a site keeps people and new development away. The site of the Chernobyl nuclear disaster is a well-studied case of this, especially famed for the (possibly mutant) wolves that have prospered in the now-abandoned site.[113]

It's all well and good for those radioactive wolves, but sites of terrifying nuclear disasters are few and far between. What about wildlife closer to home? This same dynamic is probably at work on a much smaller scale somewhere near you. Many urban brownfields are preserved in part due to this—the sense that this is a dangerously contaminated place best left alone. The sites of smaller disasters and tragedies can have this effect, too, but it has to be something big enough or frightening enough to be remembered and widely known among the public. An ordinary housefire won't do.

If you grew up in a town with an abandoned house all the kids thought was haunted, that house's overgrown yard was preserved by this kind of fear, in part. I used to live in a town with a major pharmaceutical plant bordered by a large area of former houses, made uninhabitable by groundwater pollution from the plant. The company bought up the houses, tore them down, and surrounded the whole thing with chain link fence, but they couldn't get the public roads through it closed, so you could drive through and look at the sidewalks to nowhere...and the rabbits and deer thriving inside the fence. This kind of spooky site can be a benefit to wildlife, because that prickly feeling on the back of your neck and that uneasy gut feeling of danger affect you and me, but not insects or birds or trees. Sure, contamination of any kind can be deadly to any living organism, but the fear—the public perception of a site as dangerous or haunted by the evil of past events—affects only humans. Sometimes this can leave room for wildlife and nature. Fear is a pretty good preservative of space for nature. In a roundabout way, we can end up benefiting from our fear of these sites, because the de facto natural areas they become provide us with ecosystem services, just like any other non-spooky natural area (see Chapter 8—The Price of Nature for more about this).

Less disruptive changes in how humans manage landscapes influence wildlife diversity and presence in urban areas. Take tree canopy. While tree canopy coverage has decreased in US cities as a whole over the past decade,[114] canopy coverage in most of the urban Northeast now approaches 30%. This increase in tree canopy can be correlated with the re-establishment of various bird and mammal species within urban areas. In a rough sense, the more tree canopy coverage, the more and bigger animals are present.[115] This is especially intriguing because increasing urban wildlife is not generally considered, certainly not as a primary objective, in urban forestry efforts.

Similar phenomena may be observed on urban waterways where water quality has been successfully improved. As the water becomes cleaner, more wildlife move back in, sometimes to the consternation of city residents, particularly with larger animals like beavers.

BUILDINGS AND STRUCTURES

Abandoned buildings and other structures can provide habitat for wildlife within cities as well, especially for larger mammals and for feral animals like dogs. While frequently accused of providing refuge for pests like rats, abandoned buildings can also function startlingly well as shelters for stray dogs.[116] Many homeowners know firsthand how welcoming other small mammals, such as squirrels, can find any open nook in a building. Beyond buildings, structures that are allowed to fall into disrepair can provide nesting or denning sites, or simply cover for hunting or hiding from predation. (For more about this, see Chapter 12—Public Health.)

Perhaps the greatest asset to wildlife from abandoned buildings and structures is the repellent force they exert on humans—fear as preservative, again. The lack of human interference or presence around a vacant building may be more beneficial to wildlife than any shelter or habitat directly provided by the structure. If crumbling structures are perceived as dangerous themselves or as likely sites of dangerous behavior by others, they can become an oasis for wildlife within the human-dominated city.

PEOPLE AND WILDLIFE

We're ambivalent about living with wildlife in the city. Some see wildlife as an asset, a little restful nature or bucolic beauty in the city. Others see danger, nuisance, or simply an inappropriate rural concern not expected to be a part of city life. Of course, this response varies with the species. Everybody loves songbirds; not many love large flocks of crows or starlings. Foxes may be tolerated, but coyotes usually aren't. Rabbits are cute and cuddly—outside your garden—but deer get a mixed reception. We see this play out in communities struggling with too many deer.[117]

Our ambivalence about deer pales in comparison to conflicts over feral dogs and cats, beloved pet species gone wild. Some see feral dogs as frightening and dangerous, while others want to rescue them. Defenders of wild birds favor elimination of feral cat colonies,[118] while others seek to redeem the cats as pets. Pet owners may (correctly) see both as carriers of disease and dangers to their own pets.

It's difficult to quantify the benefits of the presence of urban wildlife, but we shouldn't dismiss them. These fall into the cultural category of ecosystem services (described in Chapter 8—The Price of Nature). Residents may receive health benefits from wildlife watching, reducing stress and refreshing fatigued cognitive abilities (which you remember from Chapter 4—Wild and Healthy). The presence of wildlife can even change how we see our local wild areas, evoking feelings of stewardship and motivating us to protect or improve them as habitat.

DISEASE, FEAR, AND WILDLIFE

Fear of disease lurks behind a number of concerns about urban wildlife. We know certain species, such as raccoons, skunks, and bats, as carriers of rabies or other fearsome diseases. Other species, like deer, are maligned as being linked with increase in other disease vectors, such as deer ticks carrying Lyme disease.

Lyme and other scary insect-borne diseases have been in the news a lot recently. Lyme is about ticks, but also mice and deer, and definitely about increase in suitable habitat for all of them. Lyme is also about increase in specific kinds of vegetation—tall grass and weeds or brush—that facilitate ticks biting humans. It's not just more trees or more lawn, and not just more tall weedy herbaceous vegetation—it's that **in places where humans touch the vegetation**. Example: the interstate right-of-way (ROW) can be overgrown and lousy with ticks, but you won't get Lyme driving by. You won't even know the ticks are there, and if there's mice and deer, the whole tick life cycle can chug along nicely replete with Lyme, and never infect a person. If, on the other hand, that interstate ROW is also home to a network of bandit mountain bike trails, or is used as an outlaw playspace for neighborhood kids, or contains a homeless camp, there's a great chance of Lyme infecting people, because the ticks now have the chance to get on the people. It's not just the vegetation and it's not just the use of the space by people—it's both together. (More about much of this in Chapter 12—Public Health.)

THE UN/WELCOME INVASIVE SPECIES

When we talk about nature in cities, we talk about invasive species, sooner or later. This is largely because invasives, as the toughest, most opportunistic things around, are easy to find in challenging urban sites. But invasives also matter to discussions about ecological function of landscapes and how we interact with and perceive those landscapes. If you want to explore these topics, you need a baseline of knowledge about invasive species, both plants and wildlife.

Talking about invasives means getting comfortable with several overlapping terms. Their meanings are similar, but not the same, and it's important to know the differences.

- "Invasive"—an organism that spreads rapidly and is difficult to control, therefore crowds out other species and limits ecological diversity. Invasive species may be native or introduced.

- "Invasive exotics"—plants, animals, or other organisms that are not a native part of an ecosystem and spread in an invasive manner. Usually when people talk about invasive species, they mean invasive exotics.

- "Feral"—a domesticated species (usually an animal) that has become wild, such as feral pigs or cats.

- "Naturalized"—similar to "feral," but used more frequently to describe plants that have escaped domestication to become wild, such as dandelions or Queen Anne's lace.

The Problem with Invasives

Invasive species crowd out other species and limit ecological diversity, which impoverishes ecosystems. This happens through simple physical displacement, such as garlic mustard (*Alliaria petiolata*) outcompeting native woodland wildflowers, or indirectly through eliminating food sources or other vital resources necessary for a native species to thrive. For example, pastures and lawns in the United States are primarily composed of cool-season grasses, introduced and naturalized long ago. These grasses are primarily of the running type, meaning that they create uniform stands and fill in gaps—exactly what you want in a lawn or pasture. In contrast, native warm-season grasses are primarily bunching in their form, meaning that they grow in clusters with gaps between them. Native grasslands also contain a diversity of plant species—not just grasses, but also forbs (wildflowers) and other plants we'd likely characterize as "weeds." This creates a network of sheltered spaces in meadows, which provides ideal conditions for the chicks of the bobwhite quail (*Colinus virginianus*). These chicks struggle in cool-season meadows, which has diminished the population of bobwhites. It still looks like a meadow, but the biodiversity is lessened by the replacement of the native grasses by the invasives.

Invasive species have other ways of changing their environment to make it less suitable for other species. Alder buckthorn (*Rhamnus frangula*), an invasive exotic large shrub rampant in the Northeast and Midwest, changes the pH of the soil around it as its leaves decay. Another large invasive shrub, Amur honeysuckle (Lonicera maackii), leafs out very early in the spring and holds its leaves very late in the fall, making the ground around it far shadier than native shrubs do. This changes the suitability of the ground underneath the honeysuckle for various native ephemerals and herbaceous plants.

Some invasive species, including diseases and pests, prey on other desirable species. Well-known examples of this are Dutch elm disease (*Ophiostoma ulmi*) and chestnut blight (*Cryphonectria parasitica*), both of which arrived from overseas and decimated tree canopy in the United States by virtually eliminating American elms (*Ulmus americana*) and chestnuts (*Castanea dentata*), respectively. More recently, the emerald ash borer (*Agrilus planipennis*) arrived in the United States. Despite efforts to contain it by restricting the movement of infected wood, the borer is spreading and continuing to kill several ash species, most especially white ash (*Fraxinus americana*).

White ash and American elm both illustrate the overlapping ecological, economic, and social impact that losses due to invasive species can have. Both these tree species were widely planted as street trees in cities. In fact, the common street name "Elm Street" indicates how widespread this use was and how elms defined the identity of a street corridor. Although several other tree species have been promoted as replacements for the lost elms, none of them truly duplicate the majestic character of the American elm, which is still mourned by those old enough to remember them. In the post-elm period, ashes were a particularly popular choice for street trees, sometimes (unwisely) used throughout neighborhoods as the only street tree. Whole neighborhoods have been deforested by the ash borer, such as the ones studied by Donovan et al. in 2013.[119]

How This Happened

Many naturalized plants, such as broadleaf plantain (*Plantago major*) and garlic mustard, were brought by immigrants from their home countries as useful garden plants or crops. Others were imported as ornamentals, and promoted and sold by the landscape industry before their invasive potential was realized. This situation is complicated by the variety of climates across the United States, meaning that the same species may be a tremendous problem in one area and a well-mannered garden plant in another. Garden ornamentals gone wild include purple loosestrife (*Lythrum salicaria*) and privet (*Ligustrum* spp.). Animals, too, may be introduced intentionally, then adapt too well and become invasive. European starlings (*Sturnus vulgaris*) and house sparrows (*Passer domesticus*) are two examples of this phenomenon.

Other invasive species arrive by accident. Ballast water in ships is a known conduit for this, bringing zebra mussels (*Dreissena polymorpha*) and other aquatic invasives. Norway or brown rats (*Rattus norvegicus*) probably stowed away on the ships of early European settlers, the same way they got to Europe from their native China. A host of problematic pastureland weeds likely arrived in hay brought from Europe to feed livestock.

How any invasive arrives is complicated by the lag time between when a new exotic species is introduced and when it begins to become difficult to control. This population growth curve means a species is present at low levels for years, then suddenly begins rapid spreading and growth. Eventually the species' growth plateaus, and we say it has naturalized. Species in the middle part of this curve, where it slopes sharply upward, are most often the ones targeted by control measures. Those at the beginning of the curve often go undetected, or seem to be easily controlled. Those that have plateaued are ones like dandelion (*Taraxacum officinale*) or Norway maple (*Acer platanoides*)—probably impossible to eradicate regardless of their cost or negative impact. With these species, the battle has been lost.

WHAT DO WE DO NOW?

The best way to control invasive species is not to import them in the first place. But it's not easy to predict what species will become invasive, and of course, many invasives are introduced unintentionally as well. Once they're here, what can you do? Control measures include quarantines, such as that in place for emerald ash borer, and preventative removal of host species from the leading edge of an infestation, as is being done in some places with ash trees. Occasionally predators are imported from the invasive's place of origin to control the invasive, but this can easily backfire when the predator itself becomes invasive.

In terms of an individual piece of land, invasives may be removed by landowners, volunteers, or other stewards of natural areas. This can include manual removal (e.g., pulling weeds), chemical pesticides and herbicides, and deliberate removal or extermination of invasive animals. The reintroduction of natural processes like fire can rebalance ecosystems by favoring the native organisms that co-evolved with those processes over invasives. This kind of management-based approach can be the most successful, while mechanical removal on a small-scale tends to be impractical for large infestations. It can work for individual properties or particularly sensitive areas, however, as long as a vigilant steward is in place to monitor regrowth or re-infestation.[120]

INVASIVES IN THE WILD CITY

Invasives form a substantial proportion of the nature present in urban areas. Conditions common to urban areas can inhibit or kill native species, creating voids and empty ecological niches for invasives to fill. Sometimes urban conditions create more favorable conditions for invasives. These urban conditions include disturbance by humans and materials generated by humans (like trash or dog food), compacted soils, disturbed hydrology (either wet or dry), contamination and pollution, low soil fertility, and urban heat island. A major but often overlooked urban factor is the removal of topsoil as a customary part of site development, leaving the developed site with infertile subsoil. This helps make urban soil an extremely challenging environment for plants, along with soil compaction, contamination, foreign materials, and poor drainage or droughty conditions. Peter del Tredici likens the level of disturbance typical to urban sites to that caused by glaciation.[121]

"Urban glaciation" underscores the major advantage of urban invasives: they grow and survive, if not thrive, where other things do not. **They thrive on neglect, in leftover or forgotten spaces, requiring neither human care nor civic investment, merely tolerance.** The level of intervention required to restore native ecosystems or to establish other desirable vegetation is out of reach in many urban areas. This is especially true in cash-strapped postindustrial shrinking cities, but also true in other less affluent urban neighborhoods. Even where sufficient funding is available, time and energy are still limited. Restoring urban ecosystems on a large scale is simply not a high priority in most areas. **We therefore face a likely choice between this "cosmopolitan urban vegetation" and no vegetation.** Given the many established nature-health benefits in the city, we may be far better off welcoming the invasives. At any rate, the impracticality of eradication of urban invasives means that they will be with us in urban environments for the foreseeable future. This is especially true in wilder cities, where we'd be well served by learning to maximize their benefit to us.

CHAPTER 8

THE PRICE OF NATURE

WHAT'S IT WORTH TO YOU?

"Ecosystem services" is not a sexy term. Neither is it intuitively clear. The idea behind the term, however, is simple, and of fundamental value to all of us: an ecosystem service is something nature does for you.

The term "ecosystem service" comes from a strategy to make us better value the essential benefits provided by intact natural systems by putting a price on them—making them compatible with monetary and other accountings. There are four categories of ecosystem services,[122] into which you could put some topics we've discussed in previous chapters.

Provisioning services are any kind of product you can extract from nature, like food, but also clean drinking water, wood products, and any kind of fuel. Regulating services keep the natural world humming along in a way that makes this a fit environment for humanity. This includes filtering air and water, the breaking down of wastes of all kinds, pollination of plants, and the infiltration of flood waters. Importantly, this also includes sequestering carbon and other natural climate-regulating services. Supporting services are somewhat similar, but they keep the ecosystem itself running, rather than keeping the environment fit for us. Items in this category include the hydrologic cycle and soil creation. Last on the list is "cultural services," a fuzzier category, into which are put all intangible benefits we derive from ecosystems. This is a broad range, from inspiration to recreation, and encompassing all the cultural, artistic, and spiritual activity based in nature. That's an enormous range: from cave paintings to fairy tales about big bad wolves to artists working today.

A common denominator here is health. The relative functioning of natural systems in cities affects residents' health through disease, heat island effect, water and stormwater, and air quality. Those nature-health benefits from Chapter 4—Wild and Healthy? Not here. Nature-health benefits are not usually considered ecosystem services, although they sort of loosely fall into cultural services as non-tangible benefits. Why the omission?

The bottom line with ecosystem services is money: how to quantify and monetize what functioning ecosystems do for you, so that you can balance them against other financial concerns. Health benefits, without question, matter to the bottom line. If you've somehow missed it, healthcare is expensive, both paying for the care itself and paying for the insurance to cover the care. The blood-pressure-lowering benefit of spending time in a forest is worth a lot, and it's pretty easy to put that into dollars and cents—what does medication cost to lower your blood pressure? The financial tally of nature-health benefits rises much higher if we consider avoided costs as well. That's the cost of the heart attack you didn't have because you lowered your blood pressure by being in that forest. Some estimate these nature-health services would add up to as much as any other ecosystem benefit, if they were assessed in the same way in the same procedures.[123]

Nonetheless, ecosystem services do include an enormous list of benefits provided to us by the natural world. This chapter investigates what other services the natural systems of the neglected city provide for residents, beyond those already discussed. Natural systems that are able to function fully provide benefits in a number of ways, a powerful incentive to protect and restore such systems, beyond a simple love of nature or land. The reverse is often true as well: dysfunctional natural systems result in costs for people. These costs might be monetary, but could also be based in health or community cohesion or a number of other public goods. We might think of these as ecosystem disservices.*

HOT TOWN

Let's start with heat island effect. A simple idea: cities are hotter than the rural areas around them. It's not your imagination: it really is hotter in the city. This is due to the massive amount of thermal mass present in a city's pavement and buildings, and to the lack of green spaces and unpaved ground because of all that paving and all those buildings. Heat emissions from within the city, particularly tailpipe emissions and heat expelled by air conditioners, also raise the temperature in the city.

Excessive heat is a sneaky killer, not one that scares us much, but deadly all the same, killing about 600 Americans each year.[124] Given the rising temperatures of the world overall and the near-constant record setting for warmest month or year ever,[†] excessive heat is worth worrying about. As the world gets warmer, the cities will, too. In a way, cities' heat today is the worlds' heat tomorrow, like a window into a hot, hot future.[125]

Heat island also diminishes quality of life for the most vulnerable. The closer you live to the center of the city, the more impact the heat island has on you, since you are surrounded by more of the hotter area. This means that inner city neighborhoods are more affected by heat island. In general, inner-city neighborhoods are also home to

---

* There's a few other definitions around for "ecosystem disservices," but this is how I'm using it throughout this book.

† 2018, 2017, 2016, and 2015 are all on this list. See "2018 Fourth Warmest Year in Continued Warming Trend, According to NASA, NOAA," NASA Jet Propulsion Laboratory, February 6, 2019, available at: *https://climate.nasa.gov/news/2841/2018-fourth-warmest-year-in-continued-warming-trend-according-to-nasa-noaa/*.

poorer residents, so the greatest effect is where people have the fewest resources to mitigate it. In particular, the lack of air conditioning or the lack of willingness to run air conditioners due to expense is more common in poorer neighborhoods. This sad situation is exacerbated by people being afraid to open windows because of crime, especially at night, when the air is at its coolest.

Vegetation, particularly shade trees, can counteract heat island by providing shade and through the lowering of air temperatures immediately around the plant because of water vapor released through the plant's leaves. However, in general, poorer urban neighborhoods have fewer trees than their more affluent counterparts,[126] so again, heat island hits the poor harder. Finally, some residents are less able to tolerate heat because of their physical conditions. This includes the elderly, and perhaps some disabled or chronically ill residents as well. These same characteristics may also make these residents more likely to live in less affluent neighborhoods, multiplying their vulnerability.

STORM/WATER

Natural systems in cities provide a substantial yet subtle benefit in the management of water, like rainfall and snowmelt, and amelioration of flooding. It's hard to appreciate this until it's gone. No one thinks, "Wow, this is so fantastic—it's raining and my house isn't flooded with four feet of water!" unless their house was previously flooded with four feet of water. **We take for granted the freedom from floods.**

Yet messing with natural systems is a really effective way to produce flooding. Excess water needs to go somewhere. When ground is porous and not covered with impermeable materials like paving or buildings, excess water can soak into the ground (infiltrate). This is the best solution, because it creates the least disruption, but it also serves to recharge groundwater, and we all want that, because groundwater provides one-quarter of US water supplies.[127]

However, the ground can only absorb so much, so in bigger storm events, where does the water go? In a natural landscape, excess water can run downhill into streams, then into bigger streams, then rivers, and eventually into the ocean. When there's too much water in the streams, flooding occurs, spreading out over low-lying floodplains. This allows the water to infiltrate into a greater area of soil, and slows down the floodwater, minimizing damage. Flood waters deposit soil and other material they carry, which replenishes the soil of the floodplain. When you restrict this flooding in one place, through channelized streams or levees, for instance, you make it worse somewhere else, because—again—the excess water has to go somewhere. **You displace flooding; you don't fix it.**

We learned this fatal dynamic through catastrophic floods like those along the Mississippi River in 1993 and the Missouri River in 2019, but similar dynamics are at play in urban watersheds. Because water can't infiltrate through paving and buildings, excess water collects in the street and floods it. To stop this, we channel stormwater through gutters and pipes and eventually into urban streams and rivers. Water runs faster through these systems than it would over undeveloped ground, and none of it infiltrates (unless your pipes are leaking, with that crumbling infrastructure), so more water eventually reaches the stream or river, and it's going faster when it gets there. More pavement and less permeable surface makes this dynamic worse.

This cumulative impact on urban watersheds diminishes water quality. When rainwater runs over undeveloped ground, especially through vegetation, some of the material carried by the water is filtered out. In contrast, water running over pavement tends to pick up pollutants, which aren't filtered out by pipes, so all the pollutants and other stuff the water picks up ends up in the urban stream. This lowering of water quality is detrimental to wildlife and ecosystems, but also bad for anyone drinking the water downstream. Water systems are forgiving, so a little impact doesn't make a noticeable difference. We tend to think, then, that this impact can go on forever at any magnitude; that the bill will never come due, but of course, it does. **One place isn't a big problem; every place is a tremendous problem.**

Remember the point about the speed of water being faster through the pipes and without floodplains to allow excess water to spread out? This faster water wears away soil through erosion, and can be a real danger where watersheds have become much less permeable in recent years. Erosion is serious—it can undercut structures and paving and foundations. We tend to think of erosion as no big deal—one of the many slow but sure processes that humans are bad at seeing as dangerous. **Don't underestimate erosion: erosion + time gives you the Grand Canyon.**

All of this is fairly intuitive to understand. The trouble is that most people (people who aren't civil engineers) never think about it. What's not as intuitive to understand is that vegetation in urban areas improves stormwater management, and some types of vegetation do this better than others. Vegetated land absorbs water, slows the speed of what it can't absorb, and improves the water quality of runoff through filtering. Generally, the larger the plants are, the more of these benefits happen, and the more dense the plants are (meaning more plants per acre or square foot), the more of these benefits happen. Plants, too, need water, so they take up some of the water, leaving less to be absorbed into the soil or to run off. Trees in particular slow runoff and diminish its overall amount because trees have a lot of surface area, with all the leaves and branches. It takes more water than you would think to coat all of that surface area. Thus less water reaches the ground under trees (a phenomenon you've lived if you've ever taken shelter under a tree during a rainstorm), and what does reach the ground is delayed, providing more time for other water to be absorbed first. All that surface area also lets more water evaporate before ever reaching the ground. Denser plantings filter water better because more water touches more plants as it runs through.

Runoff Isn't Sewage

The stakes are raised on all of this by the antiquated nature of the pipes into which runoff often flows. It used to be common to channel runoff into the sanitary sewer system (where the sewage goes). These are called, logically enough, combined sewers, in contrast to having separate sanitary and storm sewer systems. Having combined sewers means that all that stormwater runoff, which is clean compared to what you're flushing down the toilet, gets treated at the sewage treatment plant just like sewage, a waste of money and resources. It's also a waste of stormwater, which could be infiltrating into the ground and recharging the groundwater instead of going into any pipe.

The really dire problem with combined sewers is that in a big storm, they can overflow, because there's so much more stormwater going into the system than normal. That overflow typically goes directly into urban watercourses without being treated, so that's sewage—plus the stormwater—going into the stream or river, and that's very, very bad.*

I probably don't need to elaborate on why it's bad to have raw sewage pouring into your rivers and streams, but it's worth noting here that this, again, is a dynamic where carrying capacity is relevant: a little sewage in a big river is OK, or at least you won't notice any ill effects. But more sewage is worse. As populations grow, there's more sewage, but also more stormwater as more land is paved. This kind of increase in impermeable surface can change combined sewer overflows from a rare event that can be absorbed without much ill effect, to a common event that is an intolerable hazard. It's also worth noting here that raw sewage in water is a really effective opportunity for infectious disease, including some of the biggies like cholera.

---

* It's not quite that simple, because it's not just the amount of rainfall in the storm, but also the amount of water already in the system before the storm. This is the basic dynamic, though.

MORE OXYGEN, LESS CARBON DIOXIDE

Functioning natural systems, especially trees, in urban areas are either great for air quality or not so great, depending on who you ask. Without question, when natural areas replace pollution sources like factories, coal-fired power plants, or congested highways, air quality wins. However, it's less clear-cut about the overall impact of natural systems on a per-tree basis, and what's known about this is mostly about trees.

Trees, like all green plants, absorb carbon dioxide and release oxygen, which improves air quality for everyone who breathes. This is really the headline here: More trees, more oxygen. Another headline here is that trees, like all green plants, sequester carbon, meaning they take it from the atmosphere and hold it, keeping it from contributing to the greenhouse effect. Plants (and other living things) are largely made of carbon, so as a tree grows, it incorporates carbon into its branches and leaves and roots. This carbon comes from the carbon dioxide trees take in during photosynthesis. Trees are especially valuable in removing carbon from the atmosphere because they live for decades, even centuries. Even after a tree's demise, its leaves and roots can be incorporated into the soil around the tree, keeping more carbon tied up and out of the air (and improving the soil). The carbon in the tree remains stored in any lumber from the tree until it decays or burns.[128] This can be a very long time—witness centuries-old buildings made of wood, or even the books in your library.* If you're fighting climate change, reduction of carbon in the atmosphere is the name of the game.

---

* If you're reading this chapter in an old-fashioned paper book, those pages you're holding are sequestering carbon, removed from the atmosphere by a tree cut and processed long ago. So don't burn your book.

Respiratory Problems and Trees

What's not to like about urban trees? Well, pollen and mold. Anyone who suffers from mold allergies—and there are a lot of us—can tell you that trees are great places for mold. Anyone who suffers from pollen allergies—and there's an awful lot of us, too—knows that pollen from various tree species is a very potent allergen.

Allergies matter, affecting over 50 million Americans and costing more than $18 billion each year.[129] More sinister: asthma has long been recognized as being a bigger problem for inner city kids than other kids (although there's new debate about the influence of poverty and race/ethnicity in this versus urban environmental factors[130]). When you have asthma, worse air quality is a problem. All respiratory diseases and disorders are aggravated by the environment of poor urban areas, especially poor minority urban areas, with proximity to pollution sources and disamenities, like freeways and railroads and factories. Other factors are lifestyle ones that disproportionately affect poor folks in cities, like lack of exercise among people who work multiple jobs or live in high-crime areas and can't afford gym memberships. Smoking rates and poor diet in food deserts also come into play. More pollen and mold turns up the heat under this situation. It makes the problem worse and/or more urgent. So pollen and mold aren't trivial, or at least they aren't if it's your kid who can't breathe.

Trees may actually compromise air quality in certain places where people are likely to be, such as underneath the trees along a sidewalk. The science is not settled, but instrument readings taken in this position show that the levels of particulates can be higher there, probably because the tree blocks air circulation, keeping all the pollen and filth there for you to breathe under the tree.[131]

Smog and Tree Canopy

Viewed more broadly, though, trees do a lot for urban air quality when it counts by lowering the temperature that critical few degrees on the hottest days. Ground level ozone, the villain responsible for air quality alerts and action days, is more of a problem on hotter days. Ozone, the primary component of smog, is formed when two gases produced primarily by factories, cars, and industrial solvents react in the presence of heat and sunlight. To prevent this reaction, you can reduce the amount of these gases, nitrogen oxides (NOx) and volatile organic compounds (VOCs), as the implementation of the Clean Air Act did, but we've only reduced them so far.[132]

As the political appetite for climate action and/or regulations to protect health and the environment wanes, there's less of a brake on the production of these gases—bad news for breathing people like you and me. Weather matters in the production of ground level ozone. Hotter temperatures mean more ozone, and in an unpleasant doubling-down, the hottest days are also often accompanied by calm conditions. This allows the ozone that forms to hang around and build to high levels.[133]

By reducing the temperature, particularly in urban heat islands, trees can lower dangerous ozone levels. A 1998 study found that a Los Angeles with more tree canopy could reduce temperatures by about 3° F on the hottest days. That doesn't sound like much, but it's more than half of the temperature boost caused by the region's heat island.[134] A few degrees can make a big difference, especially when you consider that climate predictions and observations about rising temperatures are generally in terms of a few degrees.

Trees and Other Air Pollution

Trees also remove other pollutants from the air, absorbing some particles through leaves via openings called stomata. Other particles simply stick to the tree, and are thus removed from the air you are breathing. The amount of pollutants removed by trees can be impressive: up to 15% decrease in one hour in urban areas fully covered by tree canopy.[135]

To me, the controversy about the impact of trees on urban air quality doesn't stand up to broader assessment. There's a lot on the plus side as you look over this list. Respiratory health issues in urban areas are no joke, especially given their implications for serious health conditions like diabetes and heart disease and their disproportionate burden on poor urban communities. However, it's hard to argue this outweighs the substantial good done by these other pathways, which also benefit those same urban dwellers.

WILDLIFE HABITAT CONNECTIVITY

Remember urban wildlife? It provides us with both ecosystem services and disservices. Which one largely depends on the type of organism and how we feel about it as urban neighbor. Disease transmission, damage to property, injury to us or our pets, and influence on populations of other creatures all weigh in the balance. That final point could be control of an undesirable creature through predation by another creature, such as urban coyotes reducing rat populations. Or it could mean an increase in an undesirable creature due to the presence of another creature, such as more ticks due to more deer and mice. Wildlife can really enhance the enjoyment urban dwellers receive from viewing nature out their door. This enjoyment and observation goes to restoring fatigued directed attention and/or relieving stress. In addition, the promise of seeing wildlife or signs like tracks can motivate city dwellers to spend more time outdoors in nearby nature, providing the whole package of nature-health benefits.

Zooming out, wildlife in cities reflects larger habitat connectivity, beyond the city boundaries into the surrounding countryside. For bigger animals, this can be regional or even multi-state scale.

Habitat connectivity involves the size of patches of suitable habitat, and how well those patches connect to other habitat patches. When these patches are too disconnected or too small, we say the habitat is fragmented, and wildlife suffers. Fragmentation can make wildlife populations less resilient to disturbances, including things humans do, natural storm events, and weather variations. Sources of food are fewer, as is the amount of each source. Potential mates are fewer, so populations can become inbred. When anything goes wrong, it is more difficult to get away from it.

FRAGMENTATION AND CLIMATE ADAPTION

Habitat connectivity across regions and states becomes more and more important as the planet warms. In the natural climate changes of the past, different species adapted by moving north or south with their preferred climate conditions. They could also adjust by moving up or down in elevation or east to west with rainfall levels. But this adjustment needs time, and our human-created climate change is moving faster than any previous natural change. It's tough for species to move quickly enough to adapt.

THE SIXTH EXTINCTION

Habitat fragmentation is a critical barrier at a mega-critical moment because people who study these things have been screaming for a while now about the dire threat of an ongoing mass species extinction. A landmark study in 2017 summed this up: "...beyond global species extinctions Earth is experiencing a huge episode of population declines and extirpations, which will have negative cascading consequences on ecosystem functioning and services vital to sustaining civilization."[136] Strong language, especially by the standards of dry academic papers.

It's warranted, though, by the paper's findings, that it's misleading to look only at the rate at which species are going extinct worldwide, which could prompt you to conclude that that we humans are getting better at sharing the planet. Rather, the authors analyzed data from 1900 on, considering the overall numbers and geographic ranges of a wide variety of wildlife. This broader analysis revealed massive carnage: nearly half of the animals they studied had lost more than 80% of their range. Thousands of species had lost population, with a third of those being ones not considered endangered. Compared to other periods in Earth's history, the **rate** of extinctions in our time is higher than you'd expect, an ominous sign.

Numbers like these lie behind talk of whether we have entered the sixth extinction, following five other periods when most of the life on Earth died off. You might take comfort in the knowledge that this has happened before, until you find out that the last mass species extinction was 65 million years ago. And yes, that's what killed the dinosaurs, making way for mammals like us.[137] Most of the previous five extinctions are attributed to climate change events, not our human-created climate change, but earlier natural events.[138] This one is on us, through our own warming and weirding of the climate.

CONNECTIVITY AS ESCAPE ROUTE

One small effort that might turn out not to be small at all is to provide connected habitats, which allow an escape route for species. Cities form roadblocks or gaps in connectivity, with land development a major cause, perhaps **the** major cause, of fragmentation. How much natural habitat remains in a given city, its tree cover and the quality of that tree cover, whether its waterways are allowed to flow unimpeded and lined with naturally occurring vegetation, even whether green space exists within the city at all—all of these determine how big a gap a city creates in connectivity and for which habitats, and which creatures it affects. **Just as the abundance of vacant land and**

unmaintained vegetation of the wild city make it a more attractive habitat for wildlife, so they make the wild city a more connected habitat for wildlife on the move. As the planet warms, this function of the wild city will become more and more important, perhaps even standing between certain species and the eternal void of extinction.

DISEASE: A BIG NEGATIVE

Mass extinction is dramatic, but for my money, emerging infectious disease is the most frightening topic here. It's the final item on our list of ecosystem services—or in this case, a disservice.

The basic dynamics are these: Warmer, wetter weather creates more favorable conditions for disease vectors, like mosquitoes and ticks, as well as creating more favorable conditions for their habitat and their hosts. At the same time, warmer winters allow diseases and disease vectors that have previously been restricted to warmer areas to move northward. Warmer weather can also increase the rate at which mosquitoes themselves become infected by disease, and make infected mosquitoes more likely to spread the disease. So it's more of the diseases we already had, plus new diseases that we always considered tropical. Between 2004 and 2016, diseases transmitted by mosquitoes, ticks, and fleas more than tripled in the United States. But wait—it's worse than that: experts agree that these diseases are underreported.[139] Tropical diseases like dengue fever and Zika could reach decidedly un-tropical latitudes like Alaska by 2080 or so, according to studies based on the expanding range of the species of mosquitoes that carry these diseases.[140]

Before we move on, let us note that infectious disease in warmer wetter cities is also about water—standing water, flood water, dirty water. This should ring some bells from the earlier section concerning Combined Sewer Overflows (CSO). Sewage + water is a bad combination in terms of infectious disease. Warmer wetter cities provide opportunities for water-borne disease, diseases like cholera and ty-phoid. Not much is as scary as that.*

OTHER VICTIMS

All this is also true about diseases that affect plants, animals, and other organisms, including crop plants and livestock—bird flu, any-one? The stress of climate change, particularly warmer temperatures and less dependable moisture, exacerbates these plant diseases' im-pact. Stressed plants are less able to cope. Climate change can make a particular region more hospitable to diseases or pests, which often act as disease vectors. For example, the woolly adelgid, a tiny insect that kills hemlock trees, has been kept out of more northern areas by its inability to tolerate cold winter temperatures, but it's expected to spread northward as warmer winters take the brake off its population.

More wildlife in cities can boost disease rates through diseases spread by animals, to humans (like rabies) or to other animals we care about (rabies again, but also distemper and a variety of other pet diseases). In all discussions of wildlife as disease vector, the specific species involved matter tremendously. All wildlife isn't bad. Not all creatures carry rabies, and even some that do are not very effective at spreading it to you or your beloved pets. For disease to be transmitted, there has to be a pathogen present **and** there has to be a pathway for transmission. Just as you cannot get Lyme disease from driving by a field full of ticks, your dog cannot get rabies from watching wistfully through the window as a raccoon ambles through the yard.

---

* For some bonus terror, we could talk about the overuse of antibiotics and the result-ing emergence of antibiotic-resistant diseases, or about anti-vaccine sentiment and how it has damaged herd immunity in this country.

THE AMBIGUOUS WILD

Last note: natural areas in cities are habitat. They are habitat for all sorts of things, and basic ecology teaches us that an intact ecosystem includes predators that act as controls as well as burgeoning populations of prey. That's true, sort of, for degraded urban ecosystems as well. In the utility corridor behind your house, there aren't wolves or cougars—probably—but there very likely are foxes or feral cats. The foxes might be native—gray, yes; red, maybe[141]—but the feral cats certainly aren't, yet they are probably doing exceptionally well in that corridor all on their own. Yes, you love your kitty, but Kitty is just fine without you, and Kitty will rapidly produce a legion of descendants that will decimate songbird populations all around your yard. Kitty and company also catch and eat mice and other little critters that abound in urban areas. So even though Wild Kitty isn't native, she's helping keep a lid on those mice and rats in the urban wild behind your house. And we want that. We want that, in part because of disease transmission via rats and mice. Diseases like bubonic plague, carried by fleas on rodents, which you'll remember for killing 60% of 14th-century Europe.*

Non-infectious disease can also be affected by the wilder city. Asthma and allergies are exacerbated by poorer air quality, including more pollen and more ozone from warmer, wetter weather. Diabetes, heart disease, and the many other diseases of obesity are, as we all know, best fought with exercise, in tandem with nutrition and other

---

* More at *https://www.cdc.gov/plague/history/index.html* (Centers for Disease Control and Prevention, National Center for Emerging and Zoonotic Infectious Diseases (NCEZID), Division of Vector-Borne Diseases (DVBD), "Plague," July 23, 2020) and a reassuring side note: bubonic plague is, incredibly, now readily treated with common antibiotics like streptomycin. As long as it's diagnosed correctly and early, it's simply not a problem, and can be cured with a drug you can buy for $4 at your local pharmacy. And that, friends, is why science is awesome.

behavioral changes. So, anything that makes you more likely to exercise helps with these, and anything that makes you less likely to exercise contributes to their increased spread and severity. Weather conditions as well as the attractiveness of outdoor spaces and our perceptions about their safety can make a big difference in this. More about this kind of thing coming up in Chapter 12—Public Health.

Urban nature is at the heart of neglect's impact on the city. It's a decidedly mixed bag, and a lot of the good points about urban nature have a subversive edge to them that makes us not quite trust them. The bottom line is that sometimes nature in the city is just like nature anywhere else, and sometimes nature in the city is a real problem. The benefits are pretty good, though, and importantly, they tend to be exactly the benefits we city-dwellers most need. To evaluate the pros and cons, we need to adopt a broader view, looking at the neglected city as a whole: nature, people, and built elements.

CHAPTER 9

PORTRAIT OF THE NEGLECTED CITY

PUTTING IT ALL TOGETHER

Each of the aforementioned effects of neglect is pretty easy to understand, examined individually. It's always easier to comprehend things broken into components: because that approach makes the complex much simpler.

But cities are nothing if not complex, and that is as true when we look at them through the lens of neglect as it is in any other case. Simplification comes at a cost, though. The danger of looking at complex phenomenon in this one-by-one manner is that you miss interactions. You can be lulled into believing you understand it all when actually you understand only the basic building blocks and not the structure they comprise. You cannot readily isolate the influence of one factor and study it all alone, being confident that what you see is real and that the conclusions you make are valid. **In real life, everything acts on everything else.** Things are messy and complex.

Or, brought to bear on the topic at hand:

▶ *How do the foregoing effects of neglect interact with each other?*

▶ *How do they affect each other?*

NEGLECT PILES UP

The most basic interaction is that phrase I keep repeating: neglect piles up. Effects of neglect do not happen in isolation, but instead happen in the same places. Since they happen in the same places, people who live in those places are affected again and again. The accumulation of neglect's effects hits those residents the hardest.

Why does neglect pile up? Neglect piles up because old buildings and old infrastructure tend to be located in the same neighborhoods, because of the way neighborhoods are developed and built over time. Neglect piles up because in the absence of gentrification or other disruptions, neighborhoods tend to house poorer and poorer residents as their building stock ages, a phenomenon sometimes referred to as "filtering." In general, poorer residents also have less political power and certainly less economic power, so as the neighborhood building stock ages, the political and economic power of its average resident declines. Neglect also piles up because disorder encourages more disorder, an idea close to the legitimate roots of the controversial Broken Windows idea. Where properties are abandoned or unmaintained, other property owners and residents have less incentive to maintain their own properties, especially once the value of their properties begins to decline.

NEGLECT LOVES COMPANY

Neglect may also pile up because of **how the different effects of neglect act on one another**. With multiple effects of neglect present in the same neighborhood, the stage is set for them to interact with each other. These interactions could include both cases where effects exacerbate each other and those where they counteract each other.

Buried Streams

Cases of exacerbation are easier to bring to mind. Buried urban streams can be a good example of this. When a stream is buried in a city, it's often because it's become noxious to the people around it, either because of flooding or pollution or both. Remember that it was not that long ago that urban waterways were used as open sewers for all manner of refuse, from industrial wastes to plain old sewage. The prospect of that running by your home or business is unappealing, to say the least, even if your home or business is one of the polluters.

It also was not that long ago that we did not understand the relationship between water pollution, particularly with sewage, and disease. Once that relationship was understood, putting the stream out of reach underground seemed to many like not just a good idea, but a public health imperative.

We now know that it's much more imperative to public health not to dump sewage and other nasty things into streams at all, and that burying the stream tends to cause trouble sooner or later. Buried streams are of course ecologically devastating. Flooding elsewhere in the watershed tends to worsen, particularly downstream where water comes blasting out of the pipe like a firehose. Water quality definitely suffers when water runs through a pipe instead of being filtered by plants and other organisms in a natural stream bed.

But buried streams can cause problems for the properties directly over the culvert—the very place "protected" by the culverting process in the first place. Buried streams have the problems of all buried water pipes. They are hard to maintain, and no one sees when they leak. **If you learn nothing else from this book, learn that everything falls apart sometime.** Leaks spring, and since no one notices them, they grow. They are able to go undetected even longer than leaks in water or sewer pipes because no one notices a difference of pressure at either end of a buried stream.

Moving water erodes soil, and eventually that eroded soil causes sinkholes along the corridor of the buried stream, and then all hell breaks loose. Water is the enemy of structures, and water underground is a particularly insidious enemy, because, again, you can't see it. You can't see it, that is, until your basement floods or your foundation cracks or the cracks in your basement walls begin to weep. Wet basements, cracked foundations, and cracked walls are all trouble for buildings, so you can trace the path of some buried streams by the problems of the buildings built over them.

Buildings with problems are harder to maintain, and if those problems are persistent, they can soon seem not worth maintaining, so it's Broken Windows again—neglect breeds neglect, and the buildings over the buried stream get a head start on neglect. Other kinds of property neglect follow, as landlords and residents find they can't keep up with the never-ending stream, so to speak, of problems. The paint peels. The lawn grows. The soffits and eaves fall apart, and squirrels or bats move in. The property values fall, and despite the cheaper price, these are unappealing properties to buy. Abandonment isn't far away.

Meanwhile, the same eroding subsoil weakens the foundation of the underground utilities and roads that serve these properties. A rigid linear object, like a pipe or a road, is particularly vulnerable in places where there's a gap in the material below it. Sooner or later, it will crack. Those utility and road failures add another layer of neglect. And all of this from the decision to bury the stream.

OFFSETS

Compelling though the buried stream example is, there are cases where **effects of neglect can offset each other**. One effect can mitigate the negative impact of another effect. Part of what keeps us from seeing this mitigation is that we don't consider that a negative effect can have some beneficial impact. Seeing these benefits requires a deliberate effort to evaluate the impact of effects, even if their overall presence seems unquestionably negative. **If we look at outcomes, these surprising benefits come into view.**

Pavement Disintegration

Case in point: crumbling pavement. Pavement cracks—it's what it does.* More accurately, the concrete and asphalt we routinely use for streets and sidewalks in American cities in this century crack—it's only a matter of time. The cracks occur because of frost-heave in the Snowbelt, and from temperature extremes (especially extreme heat) and traffic loads elsewhere (and also from problems with the structural material below the pavement).

Leave a crack alone, and it grows. Let enough cracks grow large enough—that's deferred maintenance—and eventually the cracks win and the pavement crumbles. Your asphalt or concrete begins to resemble gravel. This may be unsightly, but gravel has one distinct advantage: it's permeable, meaning that rainwater can flow through it and seep into the soil below it. Permeable pavements are all the go these days because they allow this kind of groundwater recharge. They also help prevent flooding by letting water seep in a little bit everywhere, instead of funneling it into a few places that are increasingly too small to handle our climate-change-enhanced storm events and precipitation. So if your flood control systems are also suffering from neglect, your crumbling pavement is actually helping offset the neglect in flood control by allowing more infiltration and reducing run-off. It's making the flood control system closer to adequate, kind of less failed.

---

* To paraphrase Frank Lloyd Wright, who famously replied to complaints about roof leaks in one of his buildings, "That's how you know it's a roof": of course it cracks— that's how you know it's pavement.

We also care about stormwater runoff from pavement because of the demand it places on combined sewer systems, where those exist, and as previously noted, those exist in a lot—more than 700—of cities in the United States, primarily in the Northeast and Midwest.[142] They are more likely to exist in neighborhoods with older buildings and older infrastructure, because neglect piles up, so they may well be co-located with—underneath—that crumbling pavement. (To remember what CSOs are and why we care, look back at Chapter 8—The Price of Nature.)

What does this have to do with crumbling pavement? Well, the smaller the amount of stormwater entering the combined system, the better. Remember that the way combined sewers are fixed is to build a separate system to handle the storm water, and divert runoff from catch basins and so on into that separate system instead of into the sanitary (formerly combined) sewer. All that extra pipe is really expensive, and the digging up of roads all over the city to install it is guaranteed to irritate your constituents. There's substantial incentive to "fix" combined sewers in a different, less invasive way: decrease or eliminate the stormwater running into the combined sewer by allowing the stormwater to infiltrate directly into the ground, instead of putting it into any kind of pipe underground.

That simple strategy has allowed Syracuse to avoid construction of an additional wastewater treatment plant, an expense this shrinking city could ill afford. Mandated by court order to adopt a third strategy to fix CSOs, adding wastewater treatment capacity for every drop that flows into the combined sewer, Syracuse has instead become a national leader in sustainable stormwater management through its award-winning Save the Rain program, which uses rain gardens, bioswales, and other green infrastructure to increase infiltration of stormwater—just like that crumbling pavement.[143]

BENEFIT BY NEGLECT

Pavement that's disintegrated enough to become permeable to rainwater performs this same function: allows rainwater to pass through the pavement and infiltrate into the ground below, instead of being collected into a combined sewer or causing flooding somewhere downhill. It increases on-site infiltration and decreases runoff. It performs this valuable function not just cheaply, but without any expenditure at all (although someone pays—see costs of failing infrastructure, above). **Maybe most importantly, pavement failure happens on its own schedule, without needing permission from or action by anyone.** No amount of government indifference or dysfunction at any level makes any difference here. Or rather, in a contradictory way, that inaction and apathy is what allows the pavement to crumble. It takes lack of action, not action taken, to make this change. And lack of action is something we can always summon. In an age of deep political polarization and lack of will to spend on mundane maintenance, the importance of this can't be overstated: neglect just happens on its own. Things fall apart. In this case, when they fall apart, they offset CSOs. **Benefit by neglect.**

Want another example? Take overgrown rights-of-way (aka urban wilds) full of photosynthesizing, air-cleansing, temperature-lowering vegetation lining congested urban highways, and doing all that better than a neatly mowed right-of-way would. Or feral cats, which are often associated (perhaps incorrectly) with abandoned buildings and vacant land, acting as a predatory cap on rats or mice, and all the diseases they carry. Grimmer yet, how about residents of neighborhoods with high heart disease rates[144] (as poor inner-city neighborhoods tend to be) walking more because city buses are too infrequent, too unreliable, or simply don't show up?

This kind of trade-off doesn't make failing systems or neglect good, nor does it absolve anyone from the responsibility of letting the failures happen. Grandma should be able to ride the bus, and feral cats are bad news for biodiversity, wild birds, and beloved house cats. But a thorough look at the benefits does contribute to a realistic, complete portrait of what happens when neglect piles up. Some you win. Once in a while.

Where Does Neglect Pile Up?

Where does all this neglect-offsetting-neglect happen? **What kind of urban neighborhood sees failing systems overlap?** Where is neglect likely to pile up? It's probably the neighborhoods with the oldest average buildings or housing stock, especially if those neighborhoods haven't been gentrified. Because of filtering, these are also likely to be among the poorer neighborhoods in the city, and because the United States (still) has pronounced racial economic inequality,[145] you can expect that a lot of those poorer neighborhoods are also majority African-American and/or Latina/o.

If your city has neighborhoods developed in the floodplain of a watercourse, those are likely spots for neglect to pile up, because of the additional strain that regular floods and saturated soils places on infrastructure and buildings. There's a decent chance that those poorer neighborhoods are also the ones in the floodplains, because historically floodplain development held cheap housing for people unwelcome in other, higher neighborhoods or unable to afford anything better. Frequently, this began as temporary cheap housing, sometimes mere shanties, that evolved over time into permanent, but still modest, homes.[146] The building stock improves; the ground stays low. The soil type of floodplains and stream corridors can play a role, too, if it's more erosive or less suitable for construction.

These previous examples assume that neglect piles up where there's some kind of inherent physical characteristic in the environment that makes structures there more prone to failure or more difficult to maintain (two sides of the same coin). But clearly there can be factors that are all about how people relate to each other that determine where neglect accumulates—social, political, and economic factors. Simply put, things get fixed where people complain to officials about them. The opposite is also true: things don't get fixed where no one complains to officials about them being broken. This is especially true in cities where resources are scarce and there's a lot of broken stuff to fix.

It's whether anyone complains, but it's also whether those complaints are deemed worth listening to by officials who can make a difference. This has obvious implications for power structures and differentials in a given city. Suffice to say, if a particular neighborhood is full of people whose opinions matter to officials, stuff gets fixed, generally. But if you're in another neighborhood, well, maybe not.

NEGLECT AND THE URBAN ENVIRONMENT

What does all of the preceding mean for the urban environment? The portrait painted by our examination of effects of neglect is this:

A place with many abandoned buildings and many that are in disrepair. Streets are potholed and riddled with cracks, as are sidewalks. Any rainstorm produces flooding, perhaps at street intersections if not in the houses or yards around them. Anytime there's a power outage, it seems to happen here, and other utilities have more failures here than you'd expect. While some of those happen out of sight underground, repairs to them and the delays and inconvenience they cause are readily visible. Where repairs are put off, there may be barriers or traffic cones around severe potholes, sinkholes, or other hazards caused by failing infrastructure. There's a lot of litter, including larger discarded items like furniture and cars.

The neglected city feels unsafe, even if it isn't, and part of that feeling of threat is due to overgrown vegetation that seems to be everywhere. The large number of vacant lots really contributes to this sense, with tangles of shrubs and weeds obscuring everything within them. These wild sites are home to wildlife you don't expect to see in the city, like deer, foxes, and coyotes, as well as wildlife that's always somewhere in the city, like rats and feral cats. There's plenty of graffiti around, too.

Is this a place you know? If you recognize this portrait, think about where it is within the cities you know. Think about who lives there. Then think about who doesn't live there. **Someone's bearing the burden of this neglected environment, and someone's getting away without feeling any impact at all from it.**

▶   *Aren't they?*

Figure 12: A collection of images from the Neglected City

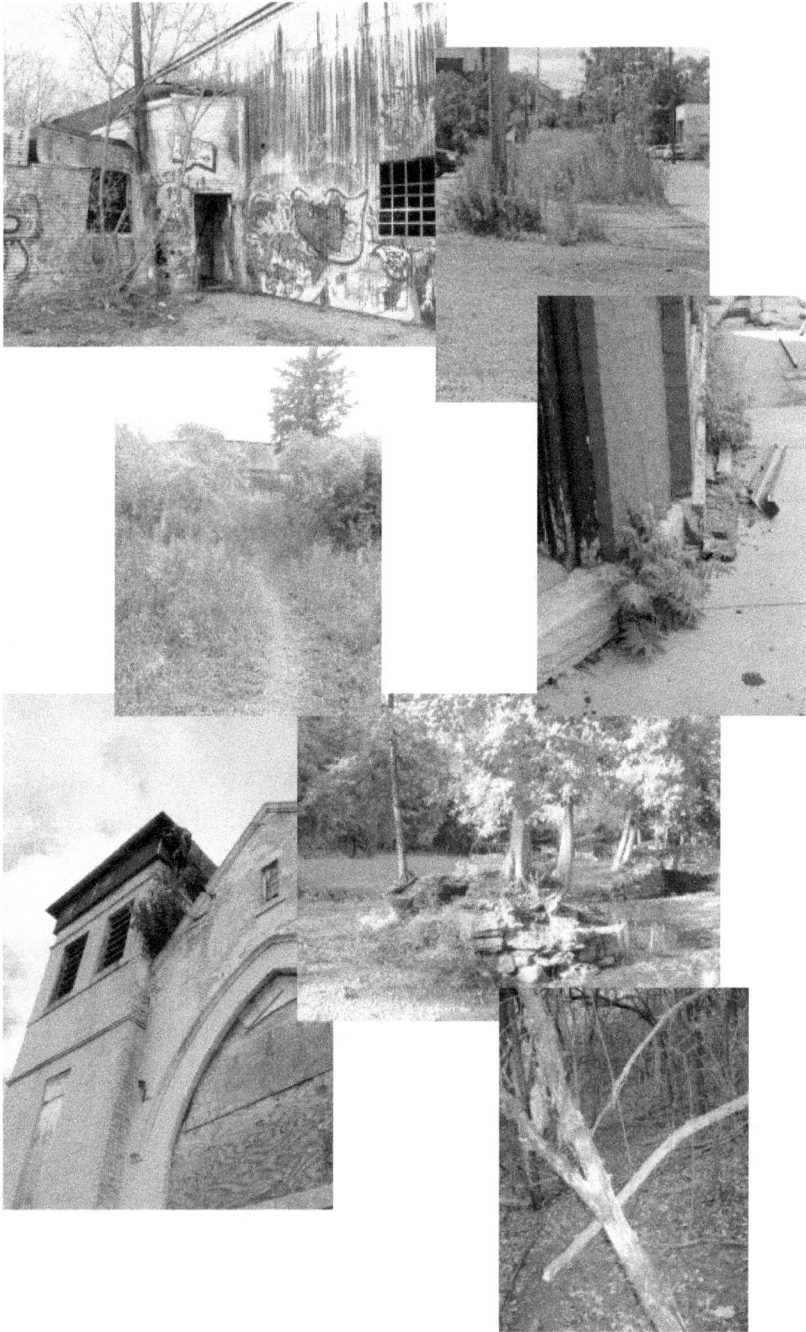

DEFICITS DESIGN WHERE?

If your neighborhood has no abandoned buildings or vacant lots, and your street has never seen a graffiti tag or water main break, what does urban neglect mean for you?

▶ *Does neglect shape the city as a whole, or do deficits only design the most unfortunate of urban locales?*

COMMUNITY

Yes, it affects us all. It affects the rest of us in the city because we exist in a community with the rest of our city. That community exists in the sense of moral obligation toward our fellow human beings, particularly those less fortunate than ourselves, particularly if they are less fortunate because of the advantages we ourselves enjoy. It affects us because what hurts the most vulnerable of us hurts us all.

MUNICIPAL CONNECTIONS

That community also exists in some more concrete ways. Different parts of a single city share a tax base and a municipal structure, and in that way, conditions in the most dire parts of the city weigh down the rest. Infrastructure such as water systems and electrical lines are a network, so failures in one part of the system adversely affect the rest of the system. This is particularly true for systems, like water supplies, that were built in the oldest parts of the city first, then extended bit by bit to newer parts. This tree-like form means that a break (a failure) in the oldest part could compromise or even knock out service to everything up the tree, even the leafiest affluent neighborhood.

REPUTATION

We also share a reputation as a city, the way people in other parts of the state, the nation, and the world think of the place we live. Not every part of Detroit is a post-apocalyptic wasteland, but to people outside Detroit, that's their image of the entire city. Not everyone in Nashville plays guitar, but that's what we think of. These reputations matter because we are a mobile nation in a global economy. A lot of people, especially people with enough money to make a difference in the fortunes of your city, have a choice in where they live, work, and travel, and they can pick your city or not based on these reputations. Neglect and its effects matters to reputation. When I tell you that Syracuse had more than one water main break for each day of 2014 and again in 2015,[147] what do you think of the city? Would you move your business there? One of the deadliest aspects of the power of reputation is that it does not happen in real time—reputation lags behind reality. Thus, although conditions in Detroit are actually quite a bit better these days, it's still the poster child for urban decay.

Lots of examples of neglect are cases where maintenance deferred means bigger expenditure down the line, with the other option being complete failure of the system in question. In this case, we all end up paying more in the end because we didn't fix the problems in the beginning in the most problematic places. **All of us pay in the end**.

ECOLOGICAL COMMUNITY

We also live within larger ecological systems that transcend the scale of the city. The ultimate example of this is the planet and climate change, which is coming for us all, but there are smaller scale ecological systems, too. Money always gives you more options, but in general, nature does not care how much money you make or what your house is worth. To name a few examples: flooding, wildfires, infectious diseases spread by "wild" agents, air quality problems, any sort of pollution or contamination that moves, damage from invasive species. **We are connected in this because nature does not pay attention to the boundaries between neighborhoods or between municipalities.** On the plus side, that is also true in regard to ecological benefits, so that nature-health benefits and ecological improvements or health can spread across human-made boundaries.

WE SHARE THE BAD AND THE GOOD

The other benefits of neglect we've discussed can act this way, too. We remain connected even when what's spreading is good. Better health and less violence in our city's most disadvantaged or crime-ridden neighborhoods benefits all of us, including by costing us less in emergency health care and law enforcement. Poor kids nurtured by creative places to express themselves and play outdoors grow into more productive, healthier, happier members of society, who can contribute in ways that benefit us all.

Cities rise and fall together. You can only cheat the devil for so long before someone has to pay. The bill always comes due. We all benefit when the people most at risk are less at risk, and we all suffer, eventually, when we ignore or exploit the plight of the most vulnerable. The same is true of countries. We rise or fall together. We can fix what's wrong or bear the cost. Anyone who tells you we can ignore the problem and dodge the bill is lying or foolish or both.

When you look at it through this broad lens, you see how neglect is not just a shaper of poor neighborhoods or Rust-Belt cities, but of nations, through our priorities, our people, and most especially our shared ecological health. Climate change is a direct threat to the world, only varying by how soon and how dire the impacts are or will be where you live. Neglect impacts a series of larger issues that we face here in the United States as a nation, many of which, like climate change, are not just American concerns, but global ones. Through these we'll see how neglect affects not just the residents of the most neglected urban environments, but all of us wherever we live, too. We'll also edge closer to the question about whether neglect is ultimately a net positive or net negative for our cities. Read on.

PART IV

CONNECTIONS TO LARGER ISSUES

NEGLECT MATTERS TO THE ISSUES THAT MATTER

It's impossible to ignore that this country is overdue for a reckoning about the big issues that threaten our livelihoods and our cohesion as a nation, if not our survival. There are a lot of monsters under the bed. We need to talk, and we need to act, and what we need to talk about and act on is inequality, public health, and climate change. Neglect and the environment it shapes bear on each of these.

INEQUALITY

Inequality—racial, social, economic—is continuing to grow in the United States, as the wealthiest of the wealthy leave the rest of us behind. The thumbnail sketch of inequality and neglect is this: inequality is bad, it's getting worse, it's affecting most of us, and its relationship with neglect is clear.

What matters relative to economic inequality is that as wealth is more and more concentrated into fewer hands, there are fewer chances for those hands to invest some of that wealth into urban environments. Take the recent question of what city a dominant online merchant will choose as its hub. One or two cities win big with this, but as StuffByMail grows ever larger and more powerful, other cities will lose as the smaller companies located within them lose out to StuffByMail. If StuffByMail drives 1000, or 10,000, or 100,000 local stores out of business, that's 1000 (or 10,000, etc.) local stores that are no longer keeping the lights on and the paint job maintained on 1000 streets in 1000 cities. Each local store was not investing much into its city, but it was invested across 1000 cities. It was decentralized investment. Instead, we have a lot of wealth and a lot of potential investment going to the few chosen cities where StuffByMail locates. In a way, it echoes worsening inequality itself, where the few at the top win big, and the rest of us go home empty-handed.

A second point about inequality regarding neglect and urban environments is that neglect isn't distributed evenly across urban areas, but rather is more pronounced in areas with lower income and fewer resources. The average resident of those areas also may be more affected by neglect, for good or ill, because s/he has fewer resources (mostly money) with which to cushion her/himself against neglect's effects. That average resident may also be more impacted by neglect's effects because she's unable to leave that neighborhood, no matter how difficult conditions become, especially where affordable housing is in short supply. Racial discrimination in housing, which is very surely still a thing,[148] also curtails options for residents of color. And again, those residents in more neglected neighborhoods are quite likely to be people of color, particularly African-American or Latina/o. **When people of color and/or poorer people are more affected by neglect and its impacts, that's inequality, too.**

This gets more complex when we consider those benefits and costs to residents of neglected environments. When we talk about neglect's negative effects, it's the same old story of the same old places and people getting screwed—absolutely worth exploring, absolutely unsurprising. But: what about the occasional benefit from neglect's effects? Do neglect's positive effects also accumulate disproportionately to those same places and people who usually lose out? If so, that could provide counterpoint to one of the most dominant American narratives of the age. If neglect is actually countering inequality, even in a small way, it's big news.

▶ *Could neglect actually favor some of the most have-nots in our increasingly unequal society?*

Public Health

Some of the highest-stakes benefits and costs of neglect fall into the arena of **public health.** Here the effects of neglect are more balanced, good vs bad. You should care about public health, because 1) we're the public, and 2) public health is about avoiding epidemics and death and misery, and we all want that. Public health focuses on societal measures and interventions. It's more about the averages and how to push those averages in the direction of the angels, rather than how to beat those averages through your own access to medical care or miracle cures. As such, public health is of great interest to those concerned about the welfare of all of us who aren't the 1%. It's also of great interest to people who want our nation to be able to invest in things like roads or schools or national defense, rather than fighting preventable diseases or paying the price for preventable deaths.

Things get murky talking about neglect and public health. The ambiguity of neglect's effects, particularly urban wilds, is key here. That same urban wild that harbors ticks and mosquitoes and other agents of infectious disease gives someone access to nearby nature, in the everyday dose that lowers stress and improves focus, and all the health benefits that go along with that. Infrastructure failure, too, is a public health concern, when the infrastructure failing is that which safeguards our health, safety, and welfare, little niceties like clean drinking water and sewage treatment. And again, since neglect piles up and this is all happening more in poorer neighborhoods than others, all these public health impacts are happening where people have the least resources to mitigate impacts or the most exposure to the benefits, and perhaps the most to gain from them.

CLIMATE CHANGE

Climate change looms behind public health concerns, and again, the ambiguity of urban wilds and other effects of neglect are on display here. Mitigating the effects of climate change and adapting to what we can't mitigate could be where the balance shifts toward benefit over cost in terms of neglect's impact on residents. **More vegetation is more vegetation, and when you're fighting a battle to sequester carbon, vegetation is an important weapon.** Plus, urban trees do a lot for us in this arena—lower temperatures, provide shade, clean air, slow down flooding—and more vegetation probably gives you all those benefits, too. All this happens more in the very places most likely to be hammered by climate change, so it's where you need it, naturally.

A less obvious interaction between neglect and climate change: climate change is, at heart, a demand that we change our ways to those that will spew less greenhouse gas into the warming world. Changing your ways means doing things differently, including things that take a lot of space, like transportation (29% of 2017 GHG emissions) and housing (5.2% of 2017 GHG emissions) and agriculture (9%, likewise) and industry (22%, same deal).[149] All that "doing differently" requires space to happen, and neglect provides space. All those vacant lots, all those abandoned buildings, all those overgrown wilds: all potential sites for something new, the new somethings we need to do right now, and in a big way, to stem the unfolding catastrophe. **The biggest benefit of neglect could end up being the space it's cleared in our cities for what we need to do next.**

EVERYTHING AFFECTS EVERYTHING ELSE—
FORTUNATELY

Nothing happens in a vacuum. Certainly nothing in cities does, and the interactions between these topics are clear. The biggest interaction between inequality, public health, and climate change is this: they are all dire and worsening, and if neglect affects them, we need to know how and where. These topics place neglect at the center of the most urgent conversations we need to have and the actions that must follow from those conversations, as soon as humanly possible. If you want to solve these problems, you need to know about neglect, most especially because if you want to solve these problems, you need all the help you can get. **Neglect can offer you a hand, when it's not slapping you down.** The trick is to get the help without the slap.

CHAPTER 10

CLIMATE CHANGE

IS THE NEGLECTED CITY A RESILIENT CITY?

Climate change is the key question of our age, the ultimate bottom line. Confronted with a challenge that threatens the very existence of humanity, we have to ask how this challenge affects everything, and if it doesn't seem to affect it, whether it should.

▶ *What does neglect have to do with climate change?*

We begin with the foundational assumption—which is really a foundational fact—that the world is warming. Our climate is changing; has changed already; is poised to continue to change.
Consider:

- The three warmest years in the 138-year record were 2016, 2015, and 2017, in terms of global averages, at this writing. The global average sea surface and land surface temperatures for 2017 were, likewise, the third warmest on record.[150]

- But don't forget: individual years can go up and down in average temperature without meaning there's a long-term warming trend. NASA has a handy analysis of this, from 1880 to the present.[151] This analysis shows just such ups and downs; 1940–1945 were rather warm years, while 1947–1951 were cooler. But the overall line from about 1910 goes up, and up, and up some more.

• This same upward curve echoes the long-term trend in natural disasters, from 1980 to present. This is true for both the number of disasters and their cost in damages (adjusted for inflation), which makes sense, since more disasters are generally more expensive. NOAA's National Centers for Environmental Information—formerly known by the more climate-y moniker of National Climatic Data Center (NCDC)—looks at this all on one graph, including hurricanes, wildfires, droughts, flooding, winter storms, and other severe storms and freezes.[152] It's a one-stop shop for all those kinds of disastrous weather events, and that's the best way to look at them. Cost of damage isn't a perfect way to assess disaster severity over time, but it does allow consistent comparison between, say, a monster hurricane and a devastating wildfire.

The big story on all these data is that they match predictions about the impact of global warming on our climate. We're seeing it happen, right now in front of us. Nonetheless, it's easy to find people—that is, pundits and politicians—who are eager to convince you that climate change is a theory, that it's not proven, and/or that there's nothing we can do about it. These claims are politically charged, and in the dark magic of our times, that makes the facts that we just saw politically charged. But they remain facts.

CLIMATE IMPACTS BY REGION

Before we go any further, it's worth remembering that despite the name, global warming doesn't just mean that every place gets hotter, and neither does it mean that effects are the same worldwide, aka globally. Climate change will change your weather in different ways depending on where in the world you are. Impacts will vary even within the United States, from region to region. Many, if not most, of these changes are already being observed. This train has already left the station.

Northeast

The pre-Trump EPA had a great summary of these effects by region on their website, now available (for now) as an archived version.[153] Even more detail is available in the National Climate Assessment's 2014 report.[154] Simply put, it's hotter everywhere. In a bit more detail, they say that we'll have a warmer Northeast; that we already do, in fact. Climate change is bringing more intense and frequent heat waves to the Northeast, as well as much more rain during storms and more frequent storms. EPA notes there's already been a staggering increase of more than 70% in the amount of rainfall during storms in the region, as measured from 1958 to 2012. So, for the Northeast, the weather ahead looks hot, wet, and stormy.

Midwest

The Midwest is already seeing warmer temperatures, in terms of average annual temperature. Ominously, this trend has picked up steam, in recent decades, compared to the rate of rise observed since 1900.[155] Besides heat, the Midwest is expected to continue to see wetter winters and springs, an impact that's already bumped annual precipitation by 20% in some areas.[156] At the same time, summers in the Midwest are expected to be drier (and hotter, of course). In some ways, this wetter-yet-drier trend could balance out, but in other ways, the Midwest's extreme climate becoming even more extreme is very bad news in terms of stress on systems. Those systems include infrastructure, agriculture, and living things. Like us.

Southeast

The Southeast is also hotter than it used to be, especially during the summer, which pushes the already hot and humid season into more dangerous days. There will be more hurricanes and stronger hurricanes, a trend already observed from the 1980s to the present.[157] Rainfall in the Southeast is trickier to predict because it might be wetter like the Northeast or drier like the Southwest. We've already seen examples of both possibilities in the South's weather, in terms of more rain during storms but also some severe droughts. So: hotter, stormier, and wetter or maybe drier.

Great Plains

Predictions for the Great Plains, between eastern and western regions, seem to be a mix of the predictions for those neighboring regions. Hotter, naturally, with warming already being felt, especially in the summer. But the big story in the plains will be about water. Hotter summers mean you need more of it, and the southern plains are predicted to see drier summers and more droughts. The northern plains are predicted to see more precipitation in winter and spring. Much of the Great Plains depends on the High Plains Aquifer for water, so the real question is how these hotter-drier-sometimes-wetter changes will balance out underground, and therefore at the tap.[158]

Southwest

Predictions get really dire for the Southwest. Perhaps this isn't surprising, since the Southwest is already a difficult climate in which to live, to generalize broadly about a wildly varied region. Again, water is the big story, and that's where all the trends converge: warmer temperatures, especially in the summer and fall, are already being felt and are predicted to get worse, perhaps by as much as 10° F of average annual increase by 2100.[159] Droughts are already a feature of life in the Southwest, but they are expected to be longer, drier, and more frequent. Snowfall in the mountains is what sustains the region through these droughts, and that, too, is bad news: less snow, especially in late winter, and earlier snow melt, already seen in the recent decades. All this spells trouble for the region's growing population. It also spells wildfire, another hazard that's part of life in the Southwest, that's already more common than it was historically, and that's predicted to increase even more as climate change worsens. So the forecast for the Southwest is hot and dry, dry, dry. And also smoky. And occasionally on fire.

Northwest

The Northwest is, like everywhere else, already warmer, and predicted to grow warmer still, particularly in the summer, with increases similar to those predicted farther south. Also like the Southwest, the Northwest has already seen a reduction in snowpack, both because of less precipitation overall and less of what falls falling as snow. This is in line with predictions for future declines in rainfall, up to 30% less rain in the summer, yet more rain during storms.[160] Some might welcome a bit less rain in this notoriously damp region, but here, too, increased wildfires are a worry. In a sentence, that leaves us with warmer and drier, overall.

On the Coasts

It's worth a mention here, too, that sea level rise is a part of the future for all the coastal areas of the country. Rising seas are of particular concern for Hawaii and other US islands in the Caribbean and Pacific. Anyone on an island ought to be intensely focused on rising sea levels, because the proportion of coastline to inland area is, obviously, higher on an island. In addition, our islands tend to have their infrastructure concentrated in low-lying areas near the coast: exactly where it's most vulnerable to rising seas.[161] Sea-level rise can also threaten drinking water supplies, more of a worry because of the natural isolation of islands. But sea-level rise is already a worry elsewhere in the United States, particularly along the Gulf Coast and the Atlantic Coast. Some areas, like coastal Louisiana and Chesapeake Bay, are seeing greater sea-level rise—up to 8"—already because of subsidence on land.[162] Lower land, higher water.

How much the seas will continue to rise is a matter of great debate and frequent revision, as polar ice continues to melt and break off, sometimes in ways no one predicted. Most predictions are in the range of one to three feet—that's feet, not inches—by 2100, but the timeline of that rise and its exact amount is up for debate. Regardless, take a look at a map by elevation of your favorite coastal city, and you can appreciate just how much area is within 3' of sea level. Also consider this: over 50% of the US population lives in coastal areas (including the Great Lakes).[163] A large amount of our infrastructure is also located along the coasts. This is especially true of energy infrastructure, and especially true of the Gulf Coast. And the final point to consider in this section is just two words: storm surge. When we talk about climate impacts by region, we need to think of the coasts as sometimes part of their larger regions, and sometimes as a region unto themselves. The outlook for the coasts is really one word: higher.

So climate change in the neglected city? It depends on where that city is, and especially how close to the coast it is, but the forecast for everywhere is change, not for the better.

CLIMATE IMPACTS BY CITY

Let's unpack what a warmer world means at the scale of the postindustrial city. In this case, where our postindustrial city is in the world or the country matters, because climate change impacts will vary—are varying—depending on that level of geography. They also are varying according to finer scale geography in some cases, such as flooding, in that cities lower in elevation and adjacent to bodies of water are more vulnerable to flooding. We focus here primarily on the postindustrial areas of the United States, the Rust Belt, and the Northeast. Some have characterized this region, the northeastern quadrant of the contiguous United States, as a "winner" in climate change, because of water. As droughts intensify and the temperature rises in the western United States, the Great Lakes and other surface water of the East becomes more valuable and attractive. In addition, climate change will increase precipitation in the East, so it's a wetter world for us. Negative impacts of "wetter" include flooding, somewhat obviously, but also landslides and structural collapses, erosion, and more.

NEGLECT AND CLIMATE

In a backhand way, **failing infrastructure** is a boon to climate action, because a large portion of our infrastructure, as it is today, enables greenhouse gas emissions. Transportation alone comprises 29%[164] of US GHG emissions; that transportation at this writing is nearly all fossil-fuel powered, since even electric vehicles may be plugged into power from a fossil-fuel-burning power plant. The private automobile is the villain here, with some aiding and abetting by tractor-trailer transport in place of shipping by water or rail, both of which are more benign in terms of GHG emissions. If the roads crumble, there's less driving. **We make a choice about future GHG emissions, and thus humanity's future, by what transportation infrastructure we rebuild.**

In a similar somewhat dystopian vein, the **crumbling electrical grid** is a boon to climate action, because electricity generation is 28%[165] of US GHG emissions. No power, no 28%. This is misleading, though, because when the lights go out, what do we do? An increasing number of us fire up generators, which run on diesel or gasoline. If it's cold, many of us light kerosene space heaters or fireplaces or woodstoves, all of which emit GHG as well. These little distributed power and heat sources can be more efficient than the big power plants, or they can be less efficient. They can run on fossil fuels or renewables. Diesel-powered generators, in particular, are notorious for their emissions, despite being the mainstay of blackout resilience.[166]

It's a false choice to think it's simply power from the coal-fired plant or nothing. It's actually power from the coal-fired plant or the decentralized alternatives people turn to when the power goes out, and that is less simple. Contrast this with transportation, where the most popular option—private cars—is also the dirtiest, and the alternatives—bicycles, walking, mass transit of any sort, boats and ships—are all greener. Power is difficult to call.

Regardless, the answer to climate change is not to roll us all back to the 14th century, or at least that's the answer we very much want to avoid. The answer is to change how we live to a carbon-neutral way, and weather the inescapable impacts of climate change as best we can.

▶ *How can neglect help with these efforts, the change to carbon-neutral and the adaptation to unavoidable impacts?*

▶ *Does neglect hinder these efforts or make the impact of climate change worse?*

NEGLECT HELPS US FIGHT CLIMATE CHANGE

Surprise! Neglect can contribute much more to climate action than you'd think. This includes straightforward mitigation of climate change's impacts, as well as adaptation to the impacts we can't escape.

Vacant land has the potential to be a climate savior, through vegetation that sequesters carbon. From this perspective, the more overgrown the urban wild, the better, because greater mass of vegetation is just more carbon sink, even when that vegetative mass is below ground, like roots. Roughly, bigger plants are better. Meadow-like tall grass and forbs are better than lawn; shrubs are better than meadow;* trees are better than shrubs. Individual species vary in their effectiveness as carbon sinks,[167] but that's a good rule of thumb.

All the benefits of urban trees come into this account as well: cleaner air, cleaner water, slower water during flood events, and reduced temperature. These are potent tools to mitigate or adapt to climate change. Vacant land also fights climate change impacts in its permeability to stormwater because vacant parcels are generally not paved or covered with buildings. Where pavement or buildings exist on vacant land, they are rapidly disintegrating, so if it's not permeable today, it could be tomorrow or next year. Permeability fights flooding, which is a major hazard from more extreme and frequent storm events and from increased rainfall. Besides the direct damage to life and property from flooding, floodwaters also increase infectious disease risk from waterborne and mosquito-borne illness, so permeability indirectly fights these, too. That's a lot of benefit from a vacant lot.

But wait: there's more. Vacant lots and other urban wilds can make the city more livable for wildlife, and that reduces or mitigates habitat fragmentation for various creatures. Habitat fragmentation and loss of connectivity have become a more urgent problem as the climate changes because various creatures can't move out of habitats that have become too warm, wet, dry, or extreme for them. **The wild city is not the roadblock to wildlife movement that the manicured city is.** This might seem minor, but plenty of people who know about these things are very worried about massive extinctions of species due to climate change. Cities wildlife can move through are important in fighting mass extinction (for more about this, see Chapter 8—The Price of Nature).

Abandoned buildings are negative for the local environment of neighborhoods (environmental lead, asbestos, etc.). **But: every aban-**

---

* Probably—prairie plants have incredibly extensive root systems, but most of what you find growing on a vacant lot is not native prairie plants.

doned building is a chance to rehab an existing structure in place of new (greenfield) development. That is far more environmentally sustainable than demolishing the old building and building new. The savings here re: climate come from the resources required to produce construction materials, including wood and concrete, but also the resources required to ship them from quarry or sawmill to building site. It adds up. Materials from demolished buildings also go somewhere, generally to a landfill, which also comes at a climate cost, and again, there's the energy required to haul them there, too. You can put a lot of new materials and energy into rehabbing an old building before you break even with new construction, climate-wise.

Table 4: Ecological/climate benefits of urban neglect[168]

Sequester atmospheric carbon
Improve air quality
Reduce ground-level ozone (smog)
Improve water quality
Reduce flooding and combined sewer overflow events
Increase groundwater recharge
Reduce urban heat island effect
Reduce cooling need
Reduce resources used to replace/repair infrastructure (heat stress)
Promotes denser development by making city more livable*

...Except When Neglect Makes Climate Change Worse

Just when you thought neglect was all positive for climate change, it's not. Here's the other side of the argument, ways in which neglect's effects contribute to climate change or make its impacts worse.

---

* These benefits are actually attributed to trees or urban forests by these sources. It's an open question whether "wild" shrubby or weedy vegetation has more of these benefits, less of them, or the same amount as trees do.

Infrastructure repair or replacement requires fossil fuel inputs in materials, transportation, and construction, as well as hauling away debris. This is the same argument, more or less, as the one about fixing up abandoned buildings vs. tearing them down. It's still more sustainable to rehab/repair existing infrastructure than to build new, like with buildings. But with infrastructure, the need is to maintain services, not add new ones. It's about maintaining the status quo, not replacing growth with a lower-carbon alternative. Without neglect, the infrastructure wouldn't be failing at all, and there'd be no need to rebuild it, just routine maintenance. In any case, the less material and energy you have to expend, the better for the climate (and for your budget).

Vacant land may exacerbate rates of or **spread of infectious disease due to climate change**, because the overgrown urban wilds provide additional habitat for some disease carriers like ticks and mosquitoes. However, this isn't clear-cut, because urban wilds may also provide additional habitat for larger creatures, like possums and bats, which prey upon those same disease carriers. Best guess is that there is a dangerous middle ground between too manicured for any wildlife to thrive and so wild that predators thrive, too. The verdict about vacant land's impact on infectious disease may rest upon how much of the average vacant parcel is in this dangerous semi-wild condition

Indirectly, neglect may encourage people to live outside the city, because of the ways it makes the city less livable, like perception of crime, actual crime, fear about falling property values, and systems not working. Living in more densely populated areas—cities, more or less—is one of the best, most potent strategies to fight climate change. It's about changing a whole lifestyle, rather than just details here and there, so it makes a big change, and it changes some of the biggest climate villains, like transportation. It also generally means we live in smaller spaces that take less materials to build and less energy to heat and cool. **So if neglect makes the city less appealing as a place**

to live for those who have a choice about where to live, that's a problem in terms of climate.

Table 5: Ecological/climate costs of urban neglect

Fossil fuel required to rebuild infrastructure
Increased infectious disease
Discourages people from moving to urban core

HELPING MOST WHERE NEED IS GREATEST

It's not just whether neglect helps or hurts in the fight against climate change. It's **who** it helps or hurts, or whether it helps or hurts everyone equally. Since this bridges from the physical to the social, it's helpful to travel along geography from one to the other.

Therefore:

► *Does neglect affect all parts of the city equally?*

Some negative impacts of climate change affect us all equally, such as the loss of diversity of species due to those mass extinctions. Some affect all of us, but affect the poor more, like power outages from storms and failing infrastructure. On balance, though, the poorer you are, the worse it is, because you can't insulate yourself through wealth and what it can buy, plus your housing is more likely to be in a place that's more vulnerable to various disasters, because that vulnerability is reflected in property values.

Part of the question here is whether everyone in the city as it is, sans neglect, bears equally the brunt of climate change. The answer to that is a clear "no." If you can't afford air conditioning, or you can't afford to run the air conditioning you have, you suffer more from extreme heat. Reminder: people don't just sweat in extreme heat; they die.[169] That's disparity in impact according to socioeconomic status. People also cool down their homes by opening windows, but if you live in a high-crime neighborhood, or at least one in which you fear crime, you tend to leave the windows closed. This is especially a problem with older residents of urban neighborhoods. Who lives in high-crime neighborhoods? On average, they tend to be people of lower socioeconomic status, and in many places, they are also neighborhoods populated by anyone who's the other: African Americans and Latina/os, but also immigrants of any stripe. That, too, is disparity.

When extreme weather events and increasing precipitation cause flooding, whose neighborhood floods? When FEMA redraws flood maps and requires property owners to purchase flood insurance, who is it that can't pay? To the extent that neighborhoods on floodplains tend to be lower income neighborhoods—and they do—that's disparity, again.

Any public health problem associated with climate change, like those infectious diseases, but also allergies to increased pollen, or breathing difficulties due to greater ground-level ozone, all affect those who can't afford access to regular health care more than those of us with a regular family doctor. Again, this is disparity favoring the wealthy and punishing the poor, but health care access is also geographic, meaning that in some places access to health care is poor even if you have the money. Anyone without good access to health care is poised to bear more of the costs of climate change.

If we add neglect into this, an interesting dynamic emerges, because neglect, on balance, is more clearly present in those same poorer, more vulnerable neighborhoods. **Whatever neglect is doing in terms of climate change, it has the potential to do more of in these disadvantaged places.** In the ways neglect exacerbates climate change's impacts, it will make it worse in these neighborhoods that are already poised to suffer more. But take another look at Table 4, the one about how neglect mitigates climate change's impacts or helps us adapt to them. These benefits should also be most in play in these same poorer, more vulnerable neighborhoods: exactly where the need is greatest. **What matters most is how to leverage neglect's effects to provide the most benefits while dodging its negative effects.**

ROOM TO REBUILD

In every discussion about climate change and every plan about how to handle it, the common thread is change. We must change how we live. We must change how we move around, how we move stuff around, and how we make and grow stuff. If you come to climate change action from architecture and engineering, you immediately see that all this change requires space to happen.

If you don't come from these fields or similar ones, you might not be used to looking at the world in spatial terms. In that case, consider your home, your street, and the place you work or go to school. Each of these buildings or streets takes up a certain acreage of land. If you live and work or study in an urban area, it's likely that when you look around, you don't see much land that's not occupied by buildings or pavement or intentional green spaces like parks. That's because neighborhoods in cities are typically completely developed in terms of land area, a state we refer to as "built out." To build anything new in a built-out area, something old must come down.

We need room to build a new world, simply stated. The best place for that space is close to where people live, because it's fundamentally more sustainable to produce what we need close to where we live, thus eliminating the need for much transportation, and also making our systems more resilient to the various disruptions of climate change. **Available space, close to where people live...this sounds a lot like the vacant land characteristic of neglect.** Room to rebuild, brought to you by neglect.

In a way, neglect can also create space for rebuilding in less literal ways. **Systems that don't function create an opening for new systems to replace them.** It's an easy argument to win, compared to wanting to replace something that ain't broke. Infrastructure failure creates opportunities to rebuild better, in a more sustainable way.

PUERTO RICO'S NEXT POWER SYSTEM

A great example is, as I write this, the plans flying around about re-building Puerto Rico's decimated electrical system as a resilient net-work of interconnected microgrids powered by clean fuels. At pres-ent, most of the lights are back on in Puerto Rico, finally, after the longest blackout, at nine months, in US history. But there's general agreement that the patched-up grid is fragile and ripe for devastation at the hands of the next hurricane (and they roll through regularly). In the wake of the island's flattening by Hurricanes Irma and Maria in 2017, proposals for how to rebuild the power system better have come from all quarters, resulting in 53 submitted comments/plans from var-ious institutions and companies.[170] These included at least one plan to replace the island's grid with interconnected microgrids, generating power from solar and other renewables, storing it when needed, and using it all within an individual neighborhood or district. Although the microgrids would normally work together, each would be capable of continuing to run when others went down. This is resilience in a nutshell.

Normally, the big barrier to adoption for systems like this is cost, but the island has astonishingly high electricity costs: current rates are about twice the average rate in the mainland United States.[171] This is partly because more than 90% of the island's electricity is generated with imported fossil fuels, especially oil, a common feature in power systems on islands.[172] The island's pre-storm power lines were also in terrible shape, due to years of deferred maintenance, according to the US Department of Energy's report.[173] This kind of failing system—wobbly grid and high prices—is ample incentive to develop alterna-tives, and Puerto Ricans have done just that on their own for years. A sunny Caribbean island is an obvious candidate for solar generation, if not wind and that from running water or waves, so people had set up their own solar cells as defense against unreliable central power. This accelerated after Maria, with the Puerto Rican government officially recognizing and legalizing these small private microgrids in May 2018.[174]

As I write this, the path ahead seems obvious, and for once, cost-effective even in the short term: lower electricity costs, make the system more reliable, and make it more resilient to hurricanes by moving the island totally to interconnected microgrids powered by solar and other renewables. But—nothing is certain. The Department of Energy wants generation from natural gas, which would require massive upgrades in island import infrastructure to allow its importation from the mainland.[175] Island government has a stated goal of only 30% renewable generation, and is actively moving for privatization of the island's state-owned power system.[176]

Given the longstanding reputation for corruption in island government, this is less than encouraging. Even FEMA money for rebuilding is prohibited from replacing power facilities with anything better than what they were pre-hurricane. So we'll see. But regardless of outcome, the opportunity to do something better is unquestionably there, a door opened by tragedy and failing systems, and a dash of climate change.

FAILURE FORCES YOUR HAND

Neglect also can create space for rebuilding in the way we make decisions. Or the way we don't make decisions—the way we put action off and are hamstrung by gridlock and apathy. You can limp along for years with a sub-optimal system, knowing you could do better but never doing it. If you aren't maintaining that system, though, you are inviting the system to make the decision to act for you. Eventually, that decision will be made—when the system fails. **Failure means you have to act.** There's impetus to action, breaking the inertia of decades that has given us crisis-level deferred maintenance. **Once you need to rebuild, you might as well rebuild it right.** This is particularly glaring with electricity and transportation, but it's also in play with building stock.

BUILDINGS AND GHG EMISSIONS

This is really counter-intuitive, because we're used to expecting technology to save us from climate change. Surely, therefore, we must need the latest and greatest breakthroughs to make an appreciable difference in how much energy we use and the size of our carbon footprint. Right? Well, yes and no. Technology and innovation may well end up saving humanity, but we can do quite a lot to shrink that carbon footprint right now, with the technology we've got.

Residential and commercial buildings created about 12% of total US greenhouse gas emissions in 2014. This is primarily due to heating, but doesn't include air conditioning, many appliances, or anything else powered by a plug in a wall outlet. All of those indirect GHG emissions from electricity generated elsewhere but used in buildings contributed another 10%, approximately. So that's 22% total, in 2014, coming from buildings.[177] That's a national average, but buildings play an even larger role in GHG emissions in our largest, densest cities. A whopping 67% of New York City's 2015 GHG emissions came from buildings, including the electricity used within them, far outpacing transportation at a still-substantial 30%.[178] Although this figure includes institutional buildings as well as residential and commercial, it underscores how much more of GHG emissions in New York City come from these land uses, compared to agriculture, for example.

Twenty-two percent may not sound like that much. But consider that the top GHG emissions villains in the United States, as of 2014, made up 30% (electricity generation, including that used in buildings), 26% (transportation), and 21% (industry), with commercial and residential properties (without their use of grid electricity) coming in at #4 (12%).[179] For perspective, the US commitment to the Paris

Agreement under Obama was to reduce GHG emissions by 26–28% below 2005 levels by 2025.[180] So the amount of GHG emitted by our buildings is an amount worth considering.

HEROIC WEATHERSTRIPPING

Perhaps more importantly, reduction in GHG emissions from our buildings is available not just through existing technology, but through common and rather mundane technology. The US Department of Energy estimates that efficiency improvements can save individual property owners up to 30% on their energy bills.[181] That includes really low-tech stuff like weatherstripping and insulation. Simple stuff that also makes your house quieter and keeps out critters. And saves you money. For a little more money, you can upgrade your windows and outdated appliances, like refrigerators. These, too, pay off in numerous ways. New appliances cost more up front, but pay off in savings in energy while also usually doing the job better.

We can also get reduction in GHG through conservation, which is simply using less. For the most part, we know how to conserve energy, although education does have a role to play. But we often see it as too much trouble or not the cool thing to do or simply something we shouldn't have to be bothered with as Americans. More so than these other energy use reduction strategies, conservation is about people's behavior—everyday, habitual behavior involved in lots of small tasks. And that gets into the realm of motivation and peer pressure and status-seeking. In other words, why people do or don't adopt conservation practices is complicated, beyond what we're discussing here. Let's just say that we know how to do a lot more than what we actually do on a daily basis, and if pressed, we could do more.* If we

---

* A revealing aside about conservation is that its image in the American public is partly a function of fashion. We've had a long, long run of it being unfashionable, from the oil embargo and Jimmy Carter in his sweater in the 1970s to the rise of

did, it could add up. A 2008 study estimated that Americans implementing the six most effective personal conservation measures—all about how you drive and with whom—could cut our individual energy consumption by nearly 18%. Adding in the three next most effective personal conservation measures—changing your lightbulbs, adjusting the thermostat, and washing clothes in cold water—lowered individual energy consumption even more, for a total of up to 26%.[182] That's a lot, and it doesn't even include actions that require up-front investment. This is all just changing your behavior, like turning the washer from "hot" to "cold."

A final point about the value of existing technology and conservation measures is this: they are proven, and thus much closer to foolproof. Work as an architect for a while, and you see that every shiny new technology, no matter how cool and innovative, has a huge potential flaw: it's new, so it's unfamiliar in terms of how to install it and how it will perform. In construction, everything new has a higher risk of failure or other problem, simply because it's new and therefore less tested. Weatherstripping and insulation are about foolproof as it gets.

Room to rebuild is a big player in whether neglect will hurt us or help us as we fight climate change, and struggle to adapt to what we can't fight. It's a wild card. **It's what we make of it.**

SUVs. But not that long ago, conservation was not just fashionable, but normal, to the generation that lived through the Great Depression of the 1930s and the war effort of the 1940s. Like I said, we know how to do it. We just don't.

CHAPTER 11

INEQUALITY

Inequality Is a Massive Problem

For a country that prides itself on the declaration that "all men are created equal," the United States is remarkably beset by inequality. *Inequality*, in this case, refers to economic inequality, or in simple terms, who has the money and who doesn't. You may be tempted to be relieved that this isn't about racial inequality or gender inequality, but not so fast, because those are involved, too. Money is power, not the only kind of power, but an enduring and important one. Don't for a second think that race and gender aren't involved with this.

According to the latest figures available:*

The richest 1% of Americans received over 21% of total annual income.

The poorest 90% of Americans received just over 50% of total annual income.

The poorest 60% of Americans received a mere 27% of annual "equivalence-adjusted" aggregate income.

* "Income" is money coming in over a certain period of time, while "wealth" is savings + other assets. "Equivalence-adjusted" considers household size and composition to produce a fairer measure. All figures are 2014 data from Drew DeSilver, "The Many Ways to Measure Economic Inequality," Pew Research Center, September 22, 2015, available at *https://www.pewresearch.org/fact-tank/2015/09/22/the-many-ways-to-measure-economic-inequality/*.

There it is in black and white. Plenty of smart people see this inequality as an urgent and serious threat to the country, but unfortunately, plenty of people in positions to make decisions see it as not a problem at all, and are in fact right now making decisions that are furthering this divide and continuing to concentrate wealth in the hands of the wealthiest at the expense of everyone else. The current administration didn't invent inequality, though—people have been sounding warnings about it for some time, at least since the early 2000s. Income inequality has waxed and waned over the years, with some notable peaks in the late 1800s (the Gilded Age, before the modern income tax)[183] and then in the 1920s. What you need to know is this: the gap closed greatly during the post–World War II expansion. You need to know this even more, though: that gap between the very rich and the rest of us is now larger than it has been for about a century.[184]

This is extremely bad, because it's a fundamentally unstable social situation, and because it's wrong, and because it makes most of us worse off at the expense of an even better life for just a few. You look at these stats and statements about inequality for a while, and it starts to feel less and less like this is a country founded on the idea of equality among (white male) citizens. It feels even less like that when you look at how economic inequality breaks down by race:[185 186 187]

In 2016, the median income of African Americans was only 65% of the median income of white Americans.

Also in 2016, the average white American family had a staggering 13 times the wealth of the average African-American family.

Even higher-income Hispanic Americans earned only 65% as much as higher-income white Americans, also in 2016.

And by gender:[188]

> American women, of any race or ethnicity, earn an average of 79 cents for every dollar earned by men.
>
> The gap is even larger in terms of wealth: American women, of any race or ethnicity, own only 32 cents for every dollar owned by men.

These disparities multiply each other, too, so that African-American and Latina women earn even less compared to men's earnings.

NOT SOMEONE ELSE'S PROBLEM

Inequality is a big problem. But is it really our problem, we who concern ourselves with urban environments and people?

Yes.

Yes, absolutely, it is our problem. Conversely, if you care about inequality and social justice, you need to care about physical space and cities, because they are linked. Issues of justice and physical space lie at the heart of power, privilege, and marginalization in our cities.

Issues of justice and marginalization often are seen as peripheral by the environmental design fields of architecture, landscape architecture, and interior design. The presumed neutrality of the built environment makes its role in expressing and perpetuating bias and inequality covert. We don't think to ask whether the status quo of the built environment is favoring some while working against others, because we assume it's neutral. This allows that bias to work in the background, unquestioned, which makes it potentially even more powerful.

These two truths taken together point to a realization: the built environment very effectively preserves inequality over time. Even as societal values evolve, we don't consider making the built environment into a more level playing field, because we insist on seeing it as neutral, if we notice it at all. It takes deliberate action to change the built environment, though. It doesn't just evolve on its own. For better roads to provide access into underserved neighborhoods, someone has to build the roads. For safe pedestrian routes to allow those without cars to have equal access, someone needs to build those pedestrian routes. It's not just construction that needs to happen, either. It's design and permitting and planning and funding, too. In other words, it's a lot of work by many people, and none of it happens by accident.

Shaping the built environment includes navigating issues of inequality, whether the shaper is conscious of that task or not. Ignorance of this role likely leads to missteps and lost opportunities to create more just cities and more equality of life opportunities.* When we study the built environment without including bias and inequality, we miss a major part of the story.†

HISTORICAL ROOTS

In terms of urban areas, inequality is not merely that someone has more and someone else has less, or more accurately, that a few people have a whole lot more and everyone else has less. It's that those people with less tend to be the same people who always get less, and that's been the case for a long time. This is not merely a coincidence, of course, but both cause and effect of the historical compounding of advantage and disadvantage. What I want to convey with no misunderstanding is that this is not at all like a fair match, as in "some you win." This is a rigged game.

---

* I presented a few examples of rethinking common landscape architecture design projects to better serve Latina/o communities in the rural Midwest in my previous book, *Immigrant Pastoral*. S. Dieterlen, *Immigrant Pastoral: Midwestern Landscapes and Mexican-American Neighborhoods* (London, UK: Routledge, 2015).

† And the story misses us, meaning that environmental design professions are predominantly white and male, and even more so in positions of power.

Two particular villains deserve specific mention pursuant to this rigging. **Each generation does not start from zero in terms of wealth**. We get a leg up or a handicap from those who came before us in our families, not just our parents, but their parents, and their parents, and the generations before that. Wealth extends across generations, and so does its lack. Very clearly, some of us are born to tremendous financial advantages, things like property, investments, and corporations, as well as familial connections and famous family names. Just as clearly, some of us (most of us) are born lacking all of those things, and perhaps with some negative "gifts" from previous generations—debts, bad reputation, traditions of abuse and need. This can stretch back centuries, to the original settlers of the continent and more.

Consider for a moment those around Jamestown in the 1600s who owned large pieces of land or shipping interests, and consider how those assets might have appreciated and grown over 400 years. Now consider that there were also many people in this country from the 1600s who amassed no wealth or assets, because they could not. They were forbidden from accumulating assets because they were themselves someone else's assets: slaves. Slavery continues until the Civil War, but then a lot, most, former slaves remain in abject poverty due to the sharecropping system for another hundred years or so. It's really not until the Civil Rights movement in the 20th century that most Black Americans get a fair shot at what's supposed to be a level playing field economically. And you remember how we started out talking about income inequality building to historic levels currently? That begins in the 1960s as the trend that takes us to today.[189] Take another look at that figure above about income inequality by race. Not much of a coincidence, is it?

REDLINING

It's worse than that, though, because that second villain I mentioned also targeted African Americans, as well as Latina/os and to an extent, other minorities. **Redlining** explicitly shaped urban environments to penalize non-white residents and to favor white residents, and it did it through government instruments in the real estate market. In a nutshell, starting in the 1930s, the federal government decided to encourage Americans to own their own homes rather than rent. A major vehicle for this was insured mortgages provided by the government, via the Federal Housing Administration. Whether a lender provides a mortgage is dependent upon the lender's assessment of the risk that they will not be repaid. With FHA insuring mortgages, far more of them became a good risk, and home ownership soared—except that not everyone was equally served by FHA.[190]

Housing discrimination is typically full of subtlety and innuendo, the kind of thing you know in your gut is wrong but have trouble proving. Not so with redlining. The practice got its name from the red lines drawn around any non-white neighborhoods, in a system that classified neighborhoods according to their suitability for FHA loans. The criteria used to classify the neighborhoods were explicitly racial: the definition of neighborhoods to be coded "red" included "undesirable population or infiltration of it."[191] No subtlety there.

Not only did this mean that white Americans could get government-insured loans that non-white Americans could not, but it also meant that if you wanted to buy a home in a redlined neighborhood, you couldn't get a mortgage from any traditional lender. People were driven to sub-prime mortgages with usurious rates and blatantly unfair terms, often resulting in the forfeit of the property for a single late payment.*

---

* This is called a land contract or contract-for-deed, and they're still around and still pretty nefarious. More on that and the similar rent-to-own scheme in

For many (white) Americans in the middle decades of the 20th century, the purchase of a family home was fundamental to their ascent into the middle class. That one purchase gave them not only their largest asset with the promise of appreciation over time, but also a place for their kids in suburban schools, and the lifestyle of the suburbs—affluent, fresh and new, wholesome... and white. Black Americans (and Latina/os) were excluded from this because they were excluded from the lending programs.

Redlining's legacy still shapes our cities. The cycle of disinvestment that spawned neglect was cemented into place by the redlining system. Schools, building stock, local businesses, even street trees were hurt by redlining and the disinvestment it assured. To look at inequality in the United States today without looking at redlining and urban environments is missing a truly fundamental part of the construction of inequality in our society and why it is so very enduring.

IMPACT ON RESIDENTS, AND WHICH RESIDENTS

Analyzing the city by neighborhood, region, or other geographic unit helps break down a staggering problem—inequality—into more manageable bites. But it can also obscure that inequality is about people: who is affected by neglect, and whether we're all affected to the same

---

Alana Semuels, "A House You Can Buy, But Never Own" *The Atlantic*, April 10, 2018, available at *https://www.theatlantic.com/business/archive/2018/04/rent-to-own-redlining/557588/*.

For more about their history, impact over time, and the rest of the racist real estate bag of tricks, see T.-N. Coates, "The Case for Reparations," The Atlantic, 2014, available at: *https://www.theatlantic.com/magazine/archive/2014/06/the-case-for-reparations/361631/*.

degree. We might assume that these effects from neglect would all be negative. Except—as we look more closely, that easy assumption doesn't look so air tight.

▶ *What kind of impact does neglect and the environment it shapes have on urban residents?*

▶ *Do urban residents benefit in some ways from the environment underfunding shapes?*

A more sophisticated version of these same questions is how the cost or benefit of living in an environment shaped by municipal neglect is distributed among residents.

▶ *Does everyone within a given city bear the same proportion of the negative impacts and the positive impacts, or are some people hurt or helped disproportionately more?*

▶ *If this help and hurt is not evenly distributed, how does it break down geographically among areas of the city?*

▶ *How does that relate to different demographic groups, such as racial minorities or those of lower socioeconomic status?*

Continuing on in sophistication, we might ask whether this differential help/hurt is zero-sum, meaning that the people who receive more benefit (or less harm) do so **because** others in their community receive less benefit (or more harm). Does what helps me hurt you, and vice versa? Given the long history of city core disinvestment and simultaneous suburban investment, it's particularly compelling to investigate whether a particular city's suburban residents benefit more from the environment of neglect than its urban residents do. It would be a little subversive yet satisfying to find that the reverse is true: that in this dynamic, unlike so many others, residents within the city core are actually better off than those in the often-wealthier suburbs.

NEGLECT BY NEIGHBORHOOD

If we think about social justice and urban neglect, we have to wonder whether there are inequalities in how different residents of the same city are affected by neglect or experience it in their daily lives. If neglect affects some residents more and some less, the next question is whether this difference falls along demographic or socioeconomic lines. If neglect affects minority residents more or poorer residents more, that's inequality. Because our cities remain quite segregated by race, ethnicity, and socioeconomic status, a good place to start with this question is to see whether neglect has more or less impact on different neighborhoods within the same city. This approach makes sense as well because urban neglect, in our exploration, makes its presence known through characteristics of the built environment. It's a phenomenon of physical space.

▶ *Does neglect affect individual neighborhoods differently within the same city ?*

Let's take a look. A table is a good way to summarize this and readily compare different areas of the city with each other.

Table 6: Effects of neglect by neighborhood

Effect of neglect	Variable by neighborhood?	Where most severe	Effects positive or negative
Failing infrastructure	Yes, depending on system	Central city Floodplains	Mostly negative. Some benefits
Abandoned buildings	Yes	Inner city Poor neighborhoods Redlined neighborhoods (these are often same places)	Negative
Vacant land	Yes	Inner city Poor neighborhoods Redlined neighborhoods Along watercourses and railroads (industry)	Mixed
"Wild" vegetation	Yes/no (depends on impact of vegetation)	Inner city Poor neighborhoods Redlined neighborhoods Along watercourses and railroads (industry)	Mixed
Wildlife	Yes	Inner city Poor neighborhoods Redlined neighborhoods Along watercourses and railroads (industry) Affluent neighborhoods Suburbs	Mixed
Loose space	Yes	Inner city Poor neighborhoods Redlined neighborhoods Along watercourses and railroads (industry) Along transportation corridors (road)	Mixed

A Subjective Interpretation of the Table

Redlining's long shadow falls across Table 6, too. Notice that every effect is logically more severe in redlined neighborhoods, except for failing infrastructure. Failing infrastructure, too, is likely present in those neighborhoods, because all central city neighborhoods are likely to have a lot of crumbling infrastructure, especially those that have not experienced any kind of gentrification and that lack political power to direct scarce municipal resources to their potholes and water mains. Since infrastructure problems unfold over decades, a historical lack of power would logically tend to make those problems worse.

What else do we see in that table? Vacant land, wild vegetation, and loose space in large part depend on one another for their geographic distribution, because they are the same areas within the city, i.e., the same collection of parcels.

A fair amount of the logic used here in the "where" determination rests upon history, not so much current conditions or forces. Like redlining, but also floodplains. Old industry can create these conditions through contamination, leaving vacant buildings or land, as a disamenity, all of which can be about what happened, say, 1890–1960, and not directly about the last fifty years. This means you don't want to place too much blame on anything current, including the current residents or even current city government.

Neglect Affects Some Neighborhoods More...

Big conclusion #1 from the table: **it's by and large the same type of area getting hit most severely by effects of neglect.** You could layer these conditions and see subsets of sets—floodplain areas along transportation or railroad corridors in disadvantaged central city neighborhoods that were redlined. So, no. **It's not affecting every place within the shrinking city equally, and that means it's not affecting every resident of the shrinking city equally.** Note, however, that

Figure 13: Parts of the city: An illustrative section

From city center to city edge

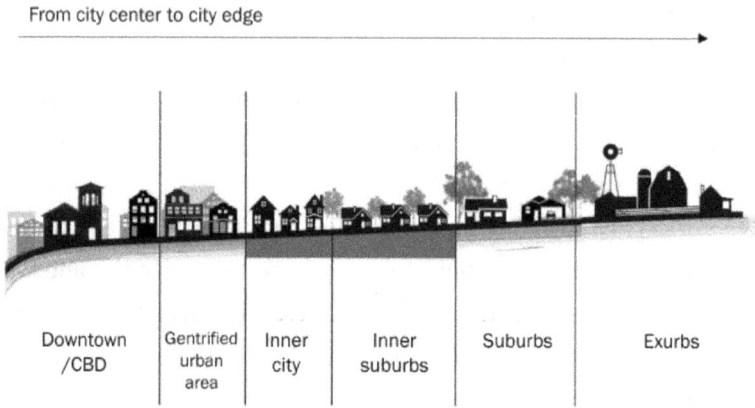

| Downtown /CBD | Gentrified urban area | Inner city | Inner suburbs | Suburbs | Exurbs |

some effects of neglect do impact areas other than these, so it's not that wealthier, higher, whiter, and/or newer neighborhoods get away scot-free.

...BUT NEGLECT'S EFFECTS ARE BOTH BAD AND GOOD

Big conclusion #2 from the table: **The impacts of neglect on these most-neglected neighborhoods are a mix of good and bad, but there's more negative impacts.** Any weighing of negatives and positives attributable to neglect will be subjective and thus, will change according to who does the weighing. This is a situation that should raise a red flag and wave it vigorously about needing the people actually impacted by decisions to be the ones whose subjective assessment matters. As a creative, outdoorsy environmentalist, I may value green space for recreation and habitat and loose space for creative expression highly enough that I'm willing to accept lower property values and the perception, if not the reality, of increased crime. A person of my parents' generation might see that differently, that fear of crime and property values outweigh all else, and who cares about birds and bunnies?

The slipperiness of that last paragraph is not an evasion, but an open door. Nothing here is cut and dried. **This means there is an opportunity to put your thumb on the scales of that weighing of good vs. bad.** You can maximize the positive and minimize the negative—if you can only figure out how to do that.

TREES AND INEQUALITY

Various studies have found that when other variables are controlled for, more affluent neighborhoods tend to have more tree cover, and their residents have more access to nature and green space generally than residents of poor urban areas.[192] As a notable study among these announces through its title, "trees grow on money."[193]

Reasons for this disparity are less clear. The studies tend to be focused on documenting the relationship—the what—and not on causation—the why. Some common explanations are that wealthier residents can afford to install, irrigate, and maintain more trees, and can afford to replace them if they die. This is particularly relevant in more arid parts of the nation. Some also note that street trees planted in the public right-of-way along streets and sidewalks are better maintained and replaced faster in wealthier areas, even when municipal authorities do the maintaining instead of property owners.

This bias can have unexpected twists, however. I've heard working designers say they've been told by inner-city residents that they don't want street trees. Some saw the trees' inevitable damage as just more emphasis on the city's apathy about their neighborhood. It's less sensational but more common for costs associated with street trees to be borne by the owner of the adjacent property. These can include cleaning up fallen leaves and branches as well as paying for replacement of sidewalks broken by tree roots pressing against them. Even where property owners are not in fact responsible for these costs, people may believe that they are.

WILD VEGETATION AND WILDLIFE

What about wild vegetation—should we expect its impact to be uniform across the city? No, for the simple fact that spontaneous vegetation is largely the result of lack of maintenance, such as mowing, and maintenance costs money or takes time. Therefore, areas with lower income are likely to have more unmaintained vegetation, other than canopy trees. Spontaneous vegetation also characterizes certain types of land, such as vacant lots and brownfields. These are likewise more common in poorer neighborhoods, as we discussed. Vacant land also is common at the edge of cities, where new development tends to happen in a leapfrog pattern, leaving "wild" parcels to be filled in later.

Wildlife likes urban wilds, but wildlife also likes canopy trees. It depends on the creature in question. Canopy trees are generally more common in more affluent areas, thus creating a contradiction. Wildlife is where habitat is, and where food is, and where water is. Canopy trees create habitat, but so does spontaneous vegetation. For some species, derelict structures provide the ideal home. Some urban wildlife may be more common in more affluent areas, where the abundant landscaping provides the ideal home. Deer are the oft-cited example of this, but this may be true for other creatures as well. Suburban yards can look a lot like forest edge habitat with fewer predators, to a deer or raccoon or possum. This diversity is why the Wildlife row in Table 6 includes most, or maybe all, of the city.

The differential impact of urban wildlife in the Neglected City is therefore rather contradictory. It's likely the case that it depends on the species or type of species—insect, mammal, bird—that one focuses on. We may say generally that the Neglected City has more area within it that is less dominated by humans, and therefore has more opportunities for wildlife to flourish in whichever niche best suits it. This is not a clear implication for one part of the city to have more wildlife, but it's also not a clear implication that the impact of all wildlife is positive or negative. So, we conclude that wildlife's impact on different groups within the city varies. To be continued.

SEGREGATION, STILL

The geographic areas of the city most likely to be affected by neglect are areas that are less affluent, less white, built longer ago, or all three. There are exceptions, but it's generally possible to characterize neighborhoods in this way because residential neighborhoods in the United States tend to be segregated by socioeconomic status. This sounds harsh and somewhat un-American stated baldly like that. It's what property values and zoning do, though, and we're used to talking about them. Segregation or residential concentration by race is more uncomfortable to talk about. Yet it's still very much with us. There are plenty of studies and data confirming this.[194]

You know this intuitively as well. Think of a city you know well, one with some racial diversity. Ask yourself where the Black neighborhoods or the Mexican ones or the [insert minority here] ones are. If you've got an answer, that city has perceptible residential concentration by race (or Latina/o ethnicity)—you've just perceived it. A city without any segregation or residential concentration would be one in which a person of whichever racial or ethnic group is equally likely to live next to a person of any other racial or ethnic group. This means if I'm white, I'm just as likely to have an African-American neighbor as if I'm African-American myself. That is rarely the case in American cities. As a white person, I probably live in a neighborhood that is about 80% white, on average. About 50% of African Americans and about 40% of Latina/os live in neighborhoods without any white residents.[195]

Add to this that within the United States, race and socioeconomic status have an intertwined relationship, and it makes that question about geographic areas of the city more complex. "Intertwined" means that non-white residents, especially African-American and Latina/o residents, are more likely to be poor than non-Hispanic white people are. Yes, there are plenty of poor white folks. But the averages are far lower for non-white groups. As of 2017, real median household income in the United States was just over $61,000 per year. For non-Hispanic white Americans, that number was higher: over $68,000 per year. For Latina/os,* it was quite a bit lower: about $50,486 per year, and for African Americans, it was lower still: about $40,258 per year.[196]

A final wrinkle is that all these factors—race/ethnicity, socioeconomic status, residential concentration—can all work together. This interaction varies in severity from place to place, meaning that in some cities, if you are poor and not white, you are very, very likely to live among only other people who are also poor and non-white, a condition referred to as high concentration of minority poverty.

WHO BENEFITS MOST FROM NEGLECT?

When we think about cities this way, it's usually apparent that policies and actions benefit the places where those with money and/or power live, at the expense of the places where everyone else lives. Suburbanization is the classic example of this, along with the related disinvestment in the city and paired investment in the suburbs and exurbs. We might expect neglect to follow this same pattern, but remember: neglect and its effects are largely unintentional. It's more the absence of intention than intention itself. So it might follow the opposite pattern, providing least benefit to the wealthiest and most powerful areas of the generic city. To see this, we need to consider

---

* This source, like all Census data, actually uses the term "Hispanic," which includes anyone who speaks Spanish as their native language, like people from Spain, rather than "Latina/o," which includes anyone from Latin America. I choose to use "Latina/o" consistently throughout this book. In figures like this one, the distinction is unlikely to make much difference to the number.

how neglect affects different parts of a generic city, starting at its heart, in downtown.

DOWNTOWN/CENTRAL BUSINESS DISTRICT

Figure 14: Parts of the city: Downtown/Central Business District

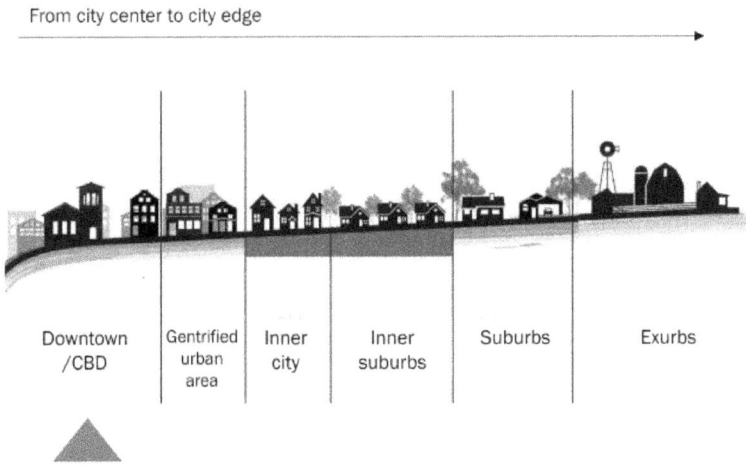

From city center to city edge

| Downtown /CBD | Gentrified urban area | Inner city | Inner suburbs | Suburbs | Exurbs |

In general, neglect is worse in the older areas of the city, and generally, downtown is among the oldest parts of the city. Thus we'd expect neglect to be most severe here, and any benefits from it to be strongest here. However, downtown areas are frequent targets of revitalization efforts. The downtown of a city is often seen as important to the image of the city as a whole in a way that residential neighborhoods are not.

In addition, property values and development pressure in downtown tend to be higher relative to urban residential neighborhoods, meaning that abandoned buildings and vacant land are less common there. Less vacant land, along with denser development (i.e., more ground is covered by buildings or pavement and less by green space), means less opportunity for wild vegetation and loose space. Worth noting is that homeless people often live or spend time in loose spaces, so if your downtown has a lot of homeless folks, there may be loose space you aren't aware of nearby (and a loose space we aren't aware of is a great place for a homeless camp, because no one bothers you if they don't see the space where you live).

In sum: **failing infrastructure is the most likely effect of neglect to be important downtown.** The impact from failing infrastructure is mostly negative, but chances are also good that investment will be made to fix or rebuild this infrastructure because of the higher profile of downtown. A different way of interpreting this same conclusion is that if failing infrastructure is a visible problem within the downtown of a city, neglect is likely to be severe elsewhere in that same metro area.

INNER CITY

Figure 15: Parts of the city: Inner city

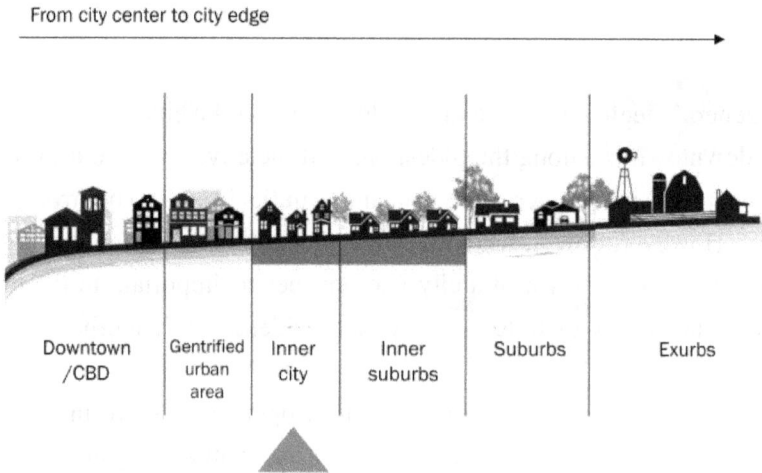

From city center to city edge

| Downtown /CBD | Gentrified urban area | Inner city | Inner suburbs | Suburbs | Exurbs |

Neglect is likely to be most severe in the inner city. Nearly every effect in Table 6 is logically most severe in the inner city. At the same time, inner city neighborhoods are among the oldest in the city, and the least likely to be a priority for limited revitalization funding. These neighborhoods are roughly equivalent to the Old Rentals neighborhood type identified in "Learning the Language," in my previous book, *Immigrant Pastoral*.[197]

The effects of neglect, both negative and positive, likely will be strongest in inner-city neighborhoods. We might also expect that the impact on residents' lives will be greatest here as well, because of other challenging conditions endemic to inner city neighborhoods. The impact of vacant land, for example, may be more negative on inner-city residents because residents have fewer resources to counteract the negative impact and are therefore less resilient to it. However, the prevalence of multiple challenging conditions in the inner city may mean that the positive effects of neglect have an impact on residents' lives that is more vital or important.

An example of this: because it is profoundly stressful to live in an impoverished, high-crime inner city neighborhood, the stress reduction of daily exposure to wild vegetation may matter more to the highly stressed residents of that neighborhood. This could be because those residents are more stressed to begin with, because they have fewer other resources to counteract that stress with, because they have less access to other green space, or some combination of these.

GENTRIFIED URBAN AREAS

Figure 16: Parts of the city: Gentrified urban area

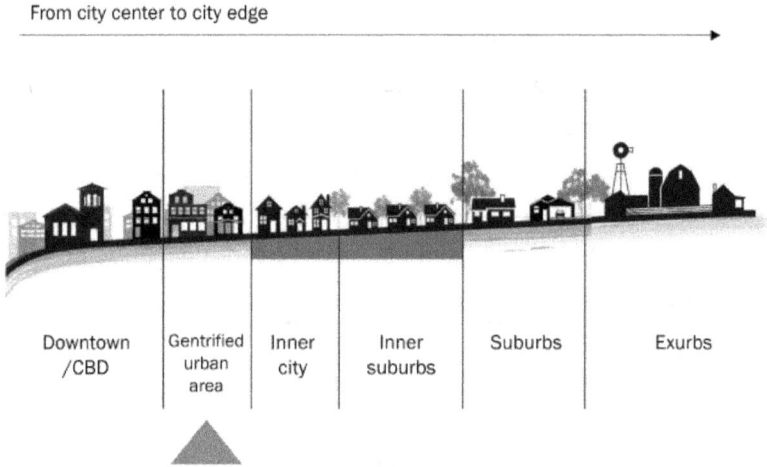

Gentrified urban areas tend to be inner-city neighborhoods that fortune has favored, so they share many of the physical and historical conditions of the inner city, with one critical difference: money and prestige. A gentrified urban area might be a historic district, or a hip loft area, or an area that's been adopted by the local gay community. Less often, gentrified areas are the product of successful top-down revitalization efforts, but these often aren't effective in the absence of grass-roots interest in the neighborhood. Gentrification is great or evil depending on your point of view. For everyone mourning the loss of authenticity or soaring rents, someone else is grateful that the old family home is no longer on a street of crackhouses. To me, gentrification seems to be good up to a point, then tips into bad beyond that, a victim of its own success. It's a fine line between investing in a destitute neighborhood and promoting gentrification, not always good or always bad.

Regardless of the ethics of gentrification, its impact on urban neighborhoods is familiar: renovated buildings, high-end infill construction (i.e., new buildings on vacant land), and higher property values and rents. All of this is indicative of new investment in the old neighborhood, which essentially counteracts neglect. Everything in the neighborhood isn't private, though, which means that the public components of the neighborhood remain vulnerable to the age and decrepitude of the inner city—failing infrastructure in particular, but also wild vegetation and loose space on parcels that aren't in private hands, such as transportation corridors.

Gentrification also brings new people into a neighborhood, generally by pushing out the previous residents (and therein lies the biggest indictment against gentrification, because where will Granny live now, and what's the old neighborhood without her?). The new people are wealthier. Perhaps saying the same thing, they are the kind of people who move in and gentrify an urban neighborhood. These are people who get listened to when they complain about failing water pipes or electric lines, and they are also people who have the time and resources and confidence in the system to make those complaints.

The shrinking city sees a gentrified neighborhood as a success story—people moving in, not out; tax base expanding, not shrinking; investment increasing, not falling. So the city may be eager to do what it can to keep the magic going. That may include fixing those combined sewers or at least mowing the lawn in the park. Finally, gentrified neighborhoods are likely to have strong, active neighborhood organizations of various kinds, and fighting effects of neglect are likely to be a high priority of these groups.

All of this can be neatly summarized: the conclusions about neglect in inner city neighborhoods don't apply if that neighborhood is gentrified. As the neighborhood becomes more gentrified, the effects in Table 6 will become less present within it, and so their effects on residents will also become less and less. Notice that this runs counter to the prevailing assumption made by both opponents and advocates of gentrification. Both sides tend to see gentrified areas as winners within their cities. You may hate gentrification and say, "The Old

North Side gets everything, and isn't that terrible?" or you may love it and say, "The Old North Side gets everything, and isn't that great?" but you both think the Old North Side gets everything. In terms of benefits of neglect, the Old North Side and its ilk aren't getting everything: they are getting less and less the more gentrified they become. Neglect, of course, has plenty of negative impacts on residents, and those, too, become less and less as a neighborhood becomes more gentrified.

INNER SUBURBS

Figure 17: Parts of the city: Inner suburbs

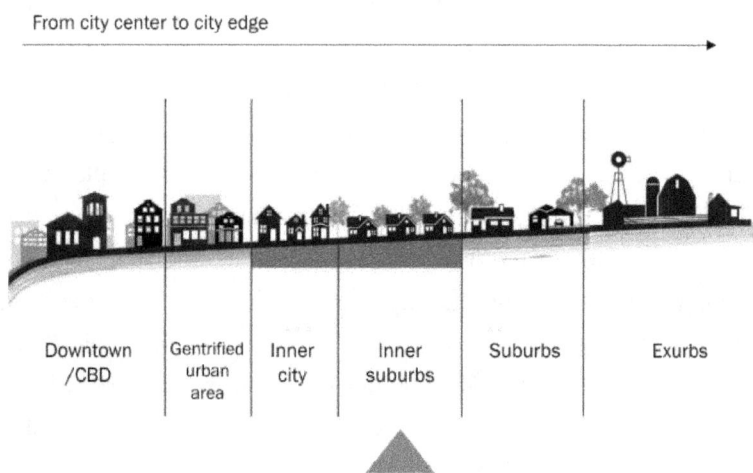

From city center to city edge

Downtown /CBD | Gentrified urban area | Inner city | Inner suburbs | Suburbs | Exurbs

"Inner suburbs" is a catchall term for neighborhoods between the inner city and the suburbs proper, as used here. An inner suburb is still within the city limits, but is newer and more residential in character than the inner city. Inner suburbs typically have less dense patterns of development, meaning that lots are larger and contain more green space. Housing units are often larger as well. Inner suburbs often include the neighborhood types Company Housing and Modern Tracts, as described in my previous book, *Immigrant Pastoral*.[198]

Inner suburbs are midway between the inner city and the suburbs in terms of socioeconomic status as well. They may be working class or middle class, but are not as affluent as suburbs outside the city limits. By definition, inner suburbs were developed later than the inner city, and therefore have infrastructure and building stock that is not as old. These structures will logically be in better shape than those of the inner city, although they may still not be in great shape, especially for housing originally constructed with cheaper materials and methods.

However, inner suburbs are part of the city in a jurisdictional sense, meaning that in a shrinking city, there is little money in the municipal coffers for upkeep of anything or investment in anything in the inner suburbs. This is especially true where neglect is advanced in the older parts of the city, because that limited municipal funding is in demand to counteract neglect there. **Neglect in the inner suburbs may be manifest less in crumbling infrastructure and buildings or vacant land, and more through a lack of investment or upkeep of anything that is the responsibility of the municipality.** This may pull standards of maintenance downward on privately owned land and public land that isn't maintained by the city. Wild vegetation and loose space are more likely to be seen in the inner suburbs because of this dynamic.

SUBURBS

Figure 18: Parts of the city: Suburbs

From city center to city edge

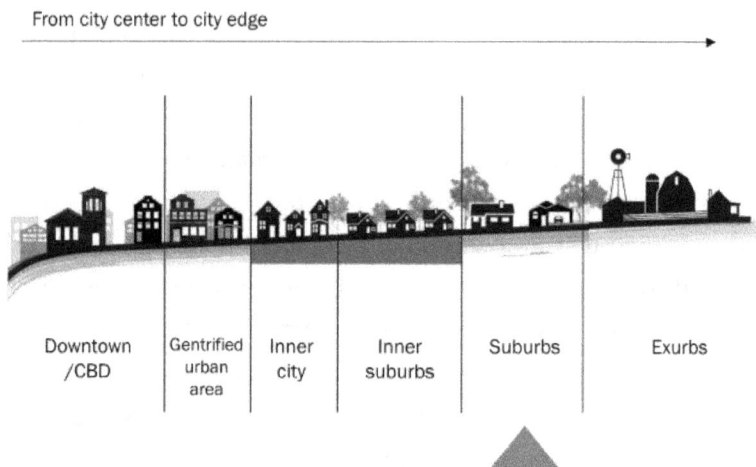

| Downtown /CBD | Gentrified urban area | Inner city | Inner suburbs | Suburbs | Exurbs |

Things get more complicated as we move outward to the suburbs in our assessment of the impacts of neglect. Why? Because the big story of the suburbs is people moving there to escape the problems of the city. One of those problems is neglect.

Suburbs are both part of the city and not part of it. They are economically and culturally part of the larger metro area, meaning that people who live in the suburbs work within the city and depend on the city for cultural and social amenities. The neighborhood type Modular Housing, described in my previous book, *Immigrant Pastoral*, is most likely to be found in suburbs.[199]

Yet suburbs are separate municipalities, so the financial problems of the city are not those of the suburb. This, too, is a large part of the appeal of suburban living, even if many suburban dwellers don't realize it. "Better schools" is a classic reason for moving to the suburbs; the schools are better often because they are better funded, and also because their facilities are in far better shape and are much newer.

The schools are also better (or perhaps "better") because the students who attend them are almost universally from more affluent families in less challenging neighborhoods, and their parents are usually able to invest more in their children's education. If a lot of people move to a suburb because of the schools, it also means that a lot of people sending their kids to the schools see education as a priority, which has an effect, too.*

Nonetheless, suburbs remain economically tied to their city. If suburban denizens commute into the city for work, they need jobs to be available in the city—not just any jobs, but jobs that pay enough to finance a life in the suburbs. The attraction and retention of employers is partly due to the reputation of the city as a whole. Is it an address that speaks well of the company? Will desirable future employees want to move there?

Suburbs, though, often have their own challenges where municipal funds are concerned. The classic problem is about taxes and land use. Who moves to suburbs is intimately entangled with those two rather dull-sounding items. Two of the big attractions of suburbs, aside from those better schools, are lower taxes and a lifestyle based on uniformly residential development of a certain socioeconomic level. That's a clunky way of saying that you move to the suburbs because you want to live (or you want your children to live) in a comfortable, safe, leafy world that is populated by people just like you.

THE IMAGINARY SUBURB

When I say "suburb," what comes to mind? I picture houses, streets and streets of houses, most of them new or new-ish, most of them looking the same. Those streets I envision are made for cars, at a scale

---

* We call this self-selection, meaning that the only people involved in the phenomenon being studied are those who have chosen to put themselves in that group for some shared reason, in this case valuing education for their kids.

that needs to be traversed by an automobile. Maybe you see back-yards and charcoal grills and kids on bikes and moms in yoga pants at BigBox. Around that BigBox, there's probably other big boxes, some strip malls, fast food, and so on. Your imaginary suburb doesn't include many places to work, other than those big boxes and strip malls. If you live in one of those imaginary houses on those imaginary streets, you don't walk to the store. There aren't stores you can walk to, because BigBox is miles away and there's no sidewalks and the streets aren't laid out for you to go directly from your house to BigBox, anyway.

This world we picture, the imaginary suburb, is a place without much to tax. All those houses? That's property taxes, and low property taxes are what drew people to the suburbs, so they certainly will not support increases. You can tax the big boxes and strip malls, but there really aren't that many of them, and—surprise!—part of what creates that iconic suburb we're imagining is carefully controlling and restricting where those retail strips can be built. That's why you can't walk to the store—because there's only a few areas where the stores can be built, and that's not near your house.

What really drives tax base is industry and bigger employers, and suburbs have very little of that, by design. A successful suburb is built out with houses, and you can't raise taxes on those houses, so...who pays the taxes?

INFRASTRUCTURE ISN'T FREE

The other part to this is our old friend infrastructure, but not at the end of its lifespan this time. All those new or new-ish houses in the suburbs need roads and sidewalks (maybe) and storm sewers (maybe) and water lines and gas lines and streetlights. Who pays for those roads and water and sewer? Usually, the suburb does—the municipality of the suburb.

So every new subdivision creates more houses, that you can't tax much, filled with people who moved there for low taxes and won't support increases, served by infrastructure that the municipality had to pay for. This is a Catch-22. **It's why the typical suburb is an affluent community with no public money for anything.**

It's simplistic to say " cities are poor and neglected, suburbs are rich and well-maintained." In terms of public funding, suburbs are often quite limited. The big difference is that everything is so much newer, and infrastructure and buildings have long lifespans. The feedback loop by which lower standards of maintenance beget even lower standards of maintenance has not begun. In fact, there's likely to be more of an upward pressure on maintenance standards as status symbol, the urgency of keeping up with the Joneses. Vacant land in the suburbs tends to be land awaiting initial development, either tied up in construction and planning approvals or, in some cases, in land speculation.

CITY PARKS, SUBURBAN PLAYING FIELDS

One result of the suburban tax problem is that suburbs often have less public land than urban areas, especially when you subtract school properties from the equation. Suburbs are often parks-poor.

Contrast that with the grand parks systems many shrinking cities have from their earlier eras of wealth. These cities benefit still from having been developed in eras when grand parks and public squares were fashionable, buildable, and seen as worthwhile investments to raise the status of the city, among other social goals (not all of them laudable by contemporary standards).[200] Built from the mid-19th century into the 20th century, these parks emulated the great estates of Britain, with rolling hills, picturesque views framed with artfully placed woods, and monumental stone structures. Central Park is probably the best known of these grand American urban parks, so it's fitting that we describe this type of park as Olmstedian, after Frederick Law Olmsted,[201] one of the designers of Central Park.

Olmstedian parks are not only large, but were often planned as systems, linked with scenic boulevards or parkways or waterways. Boston's Emerald Necklace*—again, by Olmsted—is the perfect example of this, but other places had this kind of system built, too. Buffalo, Louisville, and Indianapolis[202] are a few examples.

The handful of soccer fields and playgrounds of your average suburb cannot compare with this inheritance. Yet those soccer fields and playgrounds are all you're likely to get as a suburban parks user. The economic workings of the real estate industry that developed suburbs did not value, promote, or reward the same kind of grand public spaces that our cities have. Successful suburbs become built out with buildings and development that aren't parks. All the available land is rapidly covered with subdivisions, leaving no room for additional recreational land uses by the time anyone realizes they forgot to include any.

This is largely about economics, but also has an attitudinal component, in that families moved to the suburbs to have their own private parks—their backyards—and thus had no need of public space beyond that. A major part of the attraction to suburbs was (and is) protection from having to deal with anyone who wasn't a lot like you, and truly public spaces carry a substantial perceived risk of that kind of interaction. Thus they weren't valued or built.

What public space does exist in suburbs is often technically quasi-public—spaces that seem to be the same as the public spaces, like parks or plazas, that we're familiar with in cities, but that aren't legally or practically open to everyone. Quasi-public suburban land includes park-like play areas or natural areas within subdivisions, which

---

* A system of urban parks. More about the Emerald Necklace here: "Welcome to the Emerald Necklace," Emerald Necklace Conservancy, 2021, *https://www.emeraldnecklace.org/park-overview/.*

Figure 19: Signs of neglect in an Olmstedian park in a shrinking city. This is Elmwood Park in Syracuse, New York, built in 1927.

Figure 20: The low-maintenance landscape of a typical suburban park, built in the 2000s. Are there signs of neglect in this landscape? Where would they be visible, beyond the mowing of the lawn?

actually belong to the subdivision's homeowners' association and are open to residents only. There's also plazas and squares associated with shopping malls or office parks—they look public, they can feel public, but they are private property. As such, they are subject to rules the owners make about who can use them and who can't.

SUBURBAN NEGLECT IS LESS VISIBLE

It's a paradox: people move to the suburbs from the city thinking they'll have a more bucolic lifestyle, then find that there's nowhere to spend time outside beyond their own backyard. In terms of neglect, however, it can work out fairly well. Suburbs tend to have less public land and public facilities—again, excepting schools—so there's less to keep up with their smaller public coffers. Neglect in suburbs is not just less visible, but it has less potential to be visible, because there's not a lot of space that isn't in private ownership.

You can of course have maintenance standards fall on private land in response to neglect of public and quasi-public land, but many suburbs have so little public land that it doesn't make much of an impact regardless of its maintenance standards. This may be a threshold kind of situation, in which there needs to be a certain amount of public land or it needs to be visible to a certain extent before that dynamic can matter.

Secondary to much of this is the visibility of neglect in an urban park ca. 1900 compared to a suburban park ca. 1980. Grand old urban parks tend to have a lot of impressive sitework, like stone staircases and pavilions, and often their original landscapes had labor-intensive plantings to go with those. In marked contrast, a typical suburban park is a collection of playing fields, a parking lot, maybe a play area, and perhaps a walking path around the outside. What's to maintain here? There's fencing, there's a handful of small utilitarian buildings, and there's asphalt. This requires a lot less maintenance than the big city parks do, plus everything is many decades newer, plus it's all lower-profile than the grand stone structures of that city park. There's less to neglect; it's had much less time to be neglected; and what's able to be neglected is less visible overall.

Mostly Somewhere Else

In summary: **neglect in the suburbs is primarily an indirect influence, in the impact it has on the fortunes of the city as a whole.** This is particularly influential via the city's national reputation, the economic health of the metro area, and the quality of urban resources (like museums or recreational facilities) available to suburban residents. The common limitations of public funds and public land within suburbs may also limit the extent to which neglect can vary in suburbs—meaning that you might not be able to detect any difference between a suburb with a lot of neglect and one with none.

If you live in a suburb, the negative and positive effects of neglect are largely things that happen to other people. You avoid the problems, but you also don't get the benefits. However, some of the benefits operate at a larger geographic basis than that of suburb or inner city. These benefits, such as carbon sequestration, resilience of wildlife to climate disruptions, or improved regional air quality, can do just as much good for suburban dwellers as anyone else. We might call these **common goods**, as a shorthand.

Because of these common goods, neglect probably benefits suburban residents overall. It's disappointing and a little surprising to find that, just like in so many other facets of life, the suburbs win, but this difference is far less stark and unyielding than the typical suburbs vs. city competition. Neglect's effects are more subjective and perhaps more variable from place to place, suburb to suburb. There seems to be less of the suburbs gaining directly from the city's loss, but rather that city residents are subject to some negative effects that don't affect suburban residents. **Everyone, regardless of where they live, realizes some gains.**

EXURBS

Figure 21: Parts of the city: Exurbs

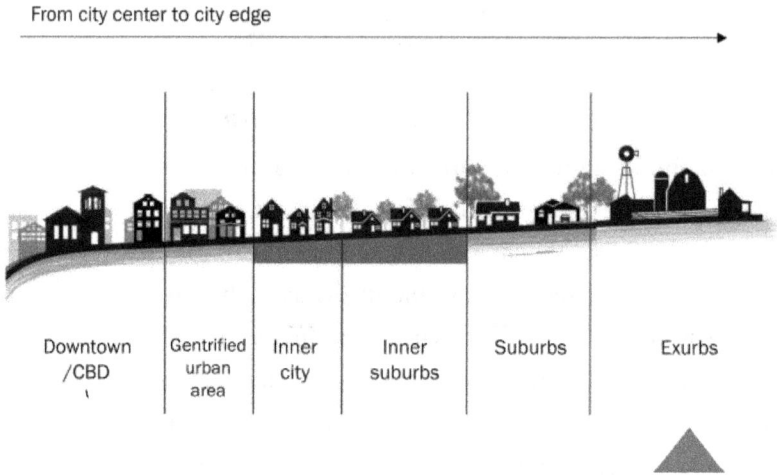

Exurbs lie beyond suburbs and are primarily rural in character, but still have many residents who commute into the city for work. Exurbs have a mix of large homes on multi-acre parcels of land, including so-called hobby farms, and the traditional farmhouses and more modest dwellings. Residents' socioeconomic status reflects that mix, with a considerable number of residents who are quite affluent and a considerable number of modest income. Exurbs can be very protective of their rural landscapes and way of life, using development controls and a deliberate lack of infrastructure (like municipal water or sewer) to discourage development.

What's neglect got to do with exurbs? Not much. You move to the exurbs (or stay there, if you're a genuine country person) to live out your dream of a rural lifestyle and leave the city behind. **One of the city things you leave behind is neglect in its entirety, loose space and everyday nature and all.**

The effects listed in Table 6 are not at all present in exurbs—and yet, in a way, all these effects show up in exurbs, too. Wild vegetation, loose space, and vacant land are all more or less present in rural areas, in somewhat different manifestations. It's not the least bit unexpected to have wild-looking vegetation in rural area, nor undeveloped (aka vacant) land. Loose space looks somewhat different and is often privately owned, but the same types of transgressive activities happen at old quarries and gravel pits, along railroad corridors, in river bottoms, and sometimes just along fencerows or creeks. The essential idea is the same: here is a place you can escape the rules of society, where you can get away with things.

RURAL BLIGHT AND INEQUALITY

Failing infrastructure and abandoned buildings speak to the issue of rural blight, which is indeed a phenomenon.[203] There are plenty of crumbling buildings in rural areas, and crumbling roads, if no other infrastructure. The amount of infrastructure failing or otherwise in many rural areas is pretty limited—no municipal water or sewer, no storm drainage facilities, essentially just roads and electric lines and perhaps gas lines. There are larger flood control systems that are of profound interest to the rural areas near them, and some of them are indeed some of that failing US infrastructure, but that's not really the phenomenon we're dealing with here.

The question at hand is about exurbs, not just any rural area, and I question whether a particular town/township can both be home to the affluence that defines exurbs and rural blight of this kind. **We are a country beset by yawning inequality, and decay next to affluence is a clear physical manifestation of inequality.** However, I suspect that rising property values and some stimulation of local businesses tends to make exurbs not the rural areas with the most blight. I further suspect that potential exurbanites, being people with plenty of income and therefore plenty of choices, tend to select pretty rural towns for their hobby farms, and therefore, the more blighted towns don't become exurbs. Once the exurbanites move in, they are also likely to make the town even prettier, by pushing for beautification or even buying up vacant properties themselves. In cities, the answer to blight is essentially held to be attracting more people with money (or less commonly but more happily, getting more money into the hands of the people who already live there). Exurbs are exactly that: places that have attracted more people with money.

That said, the same points made about suburbs and neglect hold for exurbs as well. Because they are satellites of their cities, exurbs are affected by the overall city's reputation, prosperity (or lack thereof), and resources. Exurbanites benefit from neglect's common goods while dodging neglect's local costs, just like suburbs do. Exurbs don't have suburbs' reputation for financial limitations regarding public funds and public facilities, perhaps because exurbs are less well studied. The bottom line, therefore: **exurbs share the common goods of urban neglect, but dodge most of the costs. Neglect is probably a net gain for the exurb.** An exurb's relationship with urban neglect is less substantial, however. In this case, farther away is just farther away.

A Universal Cost

A catch to the conclusion that suburbs and exurbs primarily benefit from urban neglect: If we let poor urban areas take all the hits from neglect, we'll all end up paying more total costs overall. Poor urban areas are characterized by a number of fragile systems. One system failing due to neglect can push several others over the edge.

When everything is stressed, everything has less capacity to carry on when one thing fails. A pothole develops, then gets bigger and bigger because it's not fixed. Traffic diverts around it, which adds to congestion on already inadequate nearby roads, and puts more wear on their surfaces, which encourages more potholes to develop on these other roads. A car swerves to miss this monster pothole, and hits a utility pole. One of the fragile lines on the utility pole snaps, and the neighborhood goes dark.

Fragile systems are just barely adequate. They need the support of perfect functioning in everything around them, to prop them up. When something doesn't work perfectly, those fragile systems can fray, stop being barely adequate, and fail.

Thus, the total cost is more if neglect is allowed to pile up where other systems are fragile and resources to cope are few. This is pretty similar to the cumulative costs of deferred maintenance. Nonetheless, as a country we do a great job of denying the reality of this kind of idea. We do it exceptionally well regarding health care, where we continue to be seduced by the fallacy that the healthy can get away with paying nothing toward the health costs of the sick (in denial of the essential premise of health insurance), or the similar fallacy that the rich can contribute nothing toward health care for the poor, when that simply forces the poor into higher cost emergency care and raises rates for all of us. There is no free lunch. **You pay now or you pay later, but the bill always comes due.**

NEGLECT BY REGION

Speaking of bills coming due, let's talk about neglect's impacts by region, an inequality of a different sort. On the whole, we are talking and worrying a lot about political divisions and that means mostly talking about regions. Political divisions in this country are often depicted as being along geographic lines, which more or less delineate regions: urban vs. rural vs. suburban, coastal vs. interior, the East (which means Northeast, not South Carolina) and California vs everywhere else. The rediscovery of the white working class has also been a rediscovery of the Rust Belt, the South, the Intermountain West, and of small towns and rural areas across the country. Familiar as this picture is, it's an oversimplification. There are blue households in red neighborhoods and red towns in blue states. There are even a few apolitical people left out there who care more about their own lives and affairs than anyone's ideology. Nonetheless, we find ourselves surrounded by conversation about Red America and Blue America, and a lot of that views the country as regions. So what about neglect, viewed through this lens of regions? Two regions of the United States stand out: the Midwest and the Southwest.

MIDWEST: NEGLECT'S DARLING

Shrinking cities characterize the Rust Belt, and the Northeast and Southeast, to a lesser extent. This isn't uniform—there are growing cities in the Midwest and shrinking cities elsewhere—but that's the trend. In general, this country was developed from east to west, with some hopscotching to California and contributions by the Spanish in the Southwest and Florida ahead of the Anglo-American frontier. It follows that infrastructure and building stock are generally older in the east than the west. Accordingly, failing infrastructure and, to an extent, abandoned buildings* may be more of a problem in the east. The climate of the United States is hugely varied, from hot to cold and wet to dry, and both temperature extremes and moisture encourage the decay of structures. Thus, the arid parts of the country—essentially the inland West and Great Plains—are better for preserving structures of all kinds and may see less infrastructure and building decay. The Midwest, with its frigid winters, blazing summers, and plentiful precipitation, may again be neglect's darling in this respect.

---

* An important note to this is that construction from before the mid-20th century was often done with techniques and materials designed to last far longer than construction done more recently. So newer buildings may indeed succumb to decay at a younger age.

THE SOUTHWEST IS DIFFERENT

Figure 22: Sparse vegetation in arid New Mexico.

Climate also matters in terms of wild vegetation. The ideas of wild vegetation we've discussed so far are predicated on some climatic conditions, chiefly precipitation. Weedy vegetation needs it, or rather, any vegetation needs it. One of the ways plants adapt to arid conditions is to spread out, creating the sparse cover we see in the Southwest. You need water for dense vegetation. Where there's not enough precipitation to allow that, you only get dense vegetation where someone is irrigating. That makes all dense vegetation in arid conditions intentional, because someone is keeping the irrigation going. So the process of vacant land being colonized by weedy species and going through succession into woodland does not apply to the drier parts of the country. Logically, there's not a stark division between "wet enough to be weedy" and "dry," but rather a gradation as one moves west, paralleling the reduction in average annual precipitation.

It's surprisingly rare to find a nature-health study that acknowledges the role of climate in vegetation's variation by region. The bulk of these studies were done in cool temperate climates like the northeastern quarter of North America and northwestern Europe, places like Michigan and the Netherlands, mostly because it's easiest to conduct a study where you live, all things being equal, and the majority of researchers in this area have lived in these climates.*

It's easy to be lulled into thinking that the findings of these studies apply not just to people (and mostly educated, mostly white people at universities at that) in these temperate climates, but everyone, everywhere, all the time. It's easy to be lulled into that, because that's the unstated world view of the research—its paradigm. Because it's unstated, it's perhaps more influential, because you, the reader, do not think to question the viewpoint of an article in the same way that you might question its individual statements. You might not even notice the viewpoint, just absorb it uncritically. This "everyone, everywhere, all the time" viewpoint comes from psychology, which is the original home discipline of nature-health research. Not everyone who does nature-health research is a psychologist—I've done some[204] and I'm certainly not. But it started there, particularly with the work of a few very influential scholars about forty years ago.

This paradigm is still present in the way that nature-health research tends to place the benefits—the psychological or other human behavior—in the foreground, and place the nature—the vegetation or "green space"—in the background. If the first studies had been done by, say, horticulturalists or botanists, these priorities would surely be reversed, and we'd be talking about mesic prairie grass and forb communities rather than "green space." That same botanist's study might speak of "wellness" rather than Stress Reduction or Attention Restoration, too, being vaguer about what's in the background. None

---

* In an informal tally, I found that out of thirty studies listed in reviews of nature-health research, only seven were set outside the damp, temperate, four-season climates of eastern North America, Britain, and northern Europe.

of this is to say that nature-health research is bad or useless—far from it!—but that the paradigm of the authors matters.

Leaving aside this lesson about being critical consumers of information, the question remains: is neglect a shaper of cities in arid regions like the American Southwest. **Does it play in Phoenix?** Wild vegetation is one of six effects listed in Table 6, and wild vegetation may be irrelevant or at least different in arid cities. Wild vegetation is also important in understanding the impact of loose space and vacant land. If there's not enough precipitation to support such vegetation, do the same rules apply?

In Phoenix and similar locales, what marks a plot as cared for is likely the presence of green, non-native vegetation—essentially if someone cares for it, it doesn't look like desert, or it looks like an unnaturally lush and dense version of the desert. Land that's uncared for isn't irrigated, so it's brown and sparsely vegetated.

This reverses the dynamic in wetter regions where the studies about landscape perception were done. It might be just as clear what's cared for and what's not, but plenty of land that is indeed in productive use of some sort, i.e., cared for by someone, likely is not irrigated sufficiently to produce lush greenery, because irrigation is expensive and not necessary for, say, a lumberyard. Part of the dynamic of vacant land and loose space is the deviation from the norm, that this land does not conform with our expectations. In arid cities, it may really be more the expensive greenery that doesn't conform with expectations. The difference between forgotten land and land that is in current utilitarian use may be undetectable at a glance. This upends the whole dynamic of vacant land.

Does loose space exist in Phoenix? Surely it does. In this case, people are people, and the same release valve from societal pressure is as in play there as anywhere in the green East. Because the desire for a place to do transgressive things is the same, I'm sure places to do them exist. One practical consideration is that tall dense vegetation, like large shrubs or trees, provides privacy for those transgressive behaviors. Your loose space is looser because no one can see you through the trees. In arid climates, that screening vegetation is absent, so the privacy is, too. I suspect it takes a bigger space to get the same degree of privacy and lack of inhibition, the same degree of looseness, if you will.

In summary: **when we look at neglect by region, the Southwest is different.** Neglect may still be in play in the cities there, but it's different enough to deserve a second look. I suspect that as one travels from Phoenix to wetter and older cities, neglect becomes more and more the phenomenon we've discussed generally, that there's no more of a hard line than there is in rainfall totals. It's also worth reminding ourselves that precipitation patterns are more complex than simply, "west–dry, east–wet." Mountain ranges and the Pacific come into play, and parts of the West Coast are wet, indeed.

Inequality is, as I said, a massive problem. We are very good at not seeing it, partly because we are used to it, partly because those of us with comfortable means exercise the privilege of not seeing inequality, and partly because we as Americans are very good at telling ourselves that there is no inequality in the United States. Unlike many problems, though, inequality is really about numbers. It's easy to count and calculate and quantify who makes how much money and who doesn't, and who lives where and who doesn't. It's harder (but not impossible!) to deny such objective-seeming data.

As a massive nationwide condition, inequality both pushes and pulls at neglect. As we've seen, inequality makes some aspects of neglect worse, while simultaneously making the benefits of neglect more worthwhile or more beneficial. The complexity of this interaction means that when it comes to neglect and the city, we need to take inequality into account, and avoid the easy habit of not seeing what's all around us.

CHAPTER 12

PUBLIC HEALTH

The Hidden Bottom Line

Public health is the hidden bottom line in much of what we've discussed about neglect and the city. Designers often don't pay attention to anything said about public health, but they should. For that matter, all us humans should pay attention to public health. If you're breathing, this matters to you.

But it's not just mortality that makes public health our business. It's also the common link in questions arising from the previous sections of this book. Questions that may have popped into your head. Such as: will mosquitoes and ticks end up killing me? Or: will people get sick from this system falling apart? Or: will crime rates rise?

All of these are public health questions. If you care about questions like these, you care about public health.

Public Health and Urban Environments

But weren't we talking about urban environments? What does public health have to do with it? Quite a lot, but we do a good job of acting like it doesn't. That's changing, but not fast enough.

Design people and public health people have a lot of overlap in outcomes we're interested in, and outcomes we want to see. We may care about those outcomes for different reasons or approach them from different directions. What matters in the real world and in real world applications is outcomes: what actions are taken, and what their effects are. The scene is set for worthwhile collaboration.

WALKABILITY

Examples make this clearer. Take walkability. A walkable neighborhood is one that pedestrians can navigate on foot safely and comfortably, and that is appealing enough to walk in that people will do it, even when they have the choice to drive. Walkability is comprised of a host of smaller elements: sidewalks or walking paths, crosswalks, lighting. Is there enough shelter from the elements that a person doesn't freeze or bake while she walks? Are snow and ice reliably cleared from the pedestrian's path? A neighborhood that has these elements, plus desirable destinations that are within walking distance and a perception of being safe enough to walk in, is walkable. A neighborhood lacking these elements is not walkable, a place where you travel by car if you can. We have a very large number of those neighborhoods

Lots of stakeholders love walkability (although whether they love it enough to pay for it is a separate matter). Walkable neighborhoods are desirable to many homebuyers, and certain kinds of businesses as well. Walkability is a real Creative Class[205] draw, to use the language of a few years ago: the kind of characteristic that makes a place appealing to professional class residents and the firms that employ them, people with a lot of disposable income and a lot of choice in where they live. Anyone interested in the economic health of a neighborhood, such as municipal government or real estate development interests, might champion walkability.

Designers like walkability in large part because we like lively, vibrant streets full of people rather than sterile car-only landscapes. Walkable landscapes tend to be more aesthetically pleasing, compared to those designed only for cars. Walkability is also of keen interest to public health folks because walking is really great exercise:

cheap, readily worked into one's daily life, available without special equipment. All you need to be able to walk is the ability to do it and a place where you can do it safely.

Walkable neighborhoods not only provide that place, but also incentivize walking by allowing people to get around without driving. Walking becomes a utilitarian way to go about your business, rather than a workout to tack on the end of a busy day. This means you're more likely to do it, and the exercise you benefit from is the exercise you do.

So we have a variety of stakeholders all in favor of walkability, each for different reasons. But: the to-do list of physical changes to the environment you must make to make the neighborhood walkable is **the same no matter which stakeholder does it**. It's still sidewalks, crosswalks, and lighting. Shared outcomes. Everybody wins.

STREET TREES

Street trees are another good example. What do you get from canopy trees planted along a city street? If you're a designer, you get a leafy softening element that enlivens the hard-edged building facades, and makes the sidewalk a more comfortable, human-scaled space. If you're a climate activist, you get a reduced temperature around that tree on the hottest days, which lessens the heat island effect of that city. You also get carbon stored in the tree's structure itself, which is less carbon clogging up our atmosphere. If you're a public health advocate, you get cleaner air, which is a direct health benefit for residents, as well as greater appeal for walking as exercise, and a little less risk for excessive heat events, through that reduction in temperature. Again, it's different objectives, but the same outcome: install street trees. Everybody wins. We're natural allies.

Public health is also the bottom line of many of the opportunities that neglect provides to make things better in our cities. Recreation, fitness, climate action, cleaner air and water: it ties together.

NEGLECT'S IMPACT ON HEALTH

Let's look again at that table of effects of neglect from the chapter on inequality. Here it is, for your convenience:

Table 6: Effects of neglect by neighborhood, again

Effect of neglect	*Variable by neighborhood?*	*Where most severe*	*Effects positive or negative*
Failing infrastructure	Yes, depending on system	Central city Floodplains	Mostly negative. Some benefits
Abandoned buildings	Yes	Inner city Poor neighborhoods Redlined neighborhoods (these are often same places)	Negative
Vacant land	Yes	Inner city Poor neighborhoods Redlined neighborhoods Along watercourses and railroads (industry)	Mixed
"Wild" vegetation	Yes/no (depends on impact of vegetation)	Inner city Poor neighborhoods Redlined neighborhoods Along watercourses and railroads (industry)	Mixed
Wildlife	Yes	Inner city Poor neighborhoods Redlined neighborhoods Along watercourses and railroads (industry) Affluent neighborhoods Suburbs	Mixed
Loose space	Yes	Inner city Poor neighborhoods Redlined neighborhoods Along watercourses and railroads (industry) Along transportation corridors (road)	Mixed

▶ *What do these effects of neglect mean for public health?*

INFRASTRUCTURE FAILURE AND HEALTH

In the post–Flint water crisis era, it's almost too obvious to point out that failing infrastructure has massive implications for public health. Yet it needs to be said. We bicker and argue and delay investment in infrastructure, and all the while, the water mains break and the bridges crack and the sewage overflows into the river. Maybe you'll be lucky and it won't happen to you, but it will happen to someone. It keeps happening to someone, then someone else, and it's going to keep happening to more someones until we finally fix things.

The effects on public health from failing infrastructure are all serious as a heart attack (although heart attacks are not one of them). Dirty drinking water is a very serious problem. Heatstroke and hypothermia are very serious problems. Traffic accidents are serious. Bridges and dams at risk of collapse are about as serious as anything I can name. This is life and death stuff. That we don't take it seriously is difficult to comprehend, except that it's infrastructure. It's boring. It's the background, one we don't even see, except when it fails.

Table 7: Examples of public health impacts from failing infrastructure

Necessary medications unable to be refrigerated during power outage
Gastrointestinal illness from contaminated water containing E. coli.
Increased asthma next to highways with frequent traffic jams
Mosquito-borne disease due to dysfunctional stormwater drainage
Traffic accident injuries due to potholes
More sedentary lifestyles due to lack of safe pedestrian routes
Stress-related disorders in commuters with daily exposure to traffic

This is a scary list, and yet, it is so dull. This is the evil superpower of health consequences of failing infrastructure—it's like a killer that's just too dull for anyone to investigate. It's hard, therefore, to see it as a threat, even when it is.

The other half of that is that these are public health consequences we're talking about, not personal health consequences. If it happens to you, it's all personal, but what I mean is this: it's about large numbers of people affected. And they are real deaths or real harms happening, not theoretical ones or some urban myth story that might have happened once to someone somewhere, but is extremely unlikely to ever happen again. Heatstroke deaths really happen. They happen every summer. In 2017, 107 Americans died heat-related deaths.[206] In 2018, at least 172 people died in a series of heat waves across the northern hemisphere.[207] A certain number of people who are alive right now will die next summer due to heatstroke. If there is a blackout during a heat wave next summer, that number of deaths due to heatstroke will be higher, since air conditioning, fans, refrigerators and other ways to cool down won't work. This is a guarantee.

SNAKES AND CHEESEBURGERS

We seem to be wired to fear unlikely harm from everyday actions or objects that we see as benign. I say this because a fair number of urban myths fit this template, like the deadly overheated water in the cup in the microwave that will splash into your face as soon as you touch it. Or the classic deep-fried rat one, in your bucket of fast-food chicken. Or any kind of reptile surfacing in any kind of plumbing fixture. This idea, that there are killers lurking in our homes and everyday lives without our knowledge, is a potent one. But these are urban myths because they are, indeed, myths. The likelihood of harm is very, very slim, if there's any likelihood at all.

Yet we have trouble getting worked up about—fearing—the harms listed in Table 7, even though these are real, guaranteed harms that regularly happen to large numbers of people every year. Why?

Psychologists tell us that we, as humans, are not really designed to fear threats that build over the long term, even if they are mass killers. **This is the "snake vs. cheeseburger" problem.** Lots of people,

242 • DESIGN BY DEFICIT

probably including some of the readers of this paragraph, are afraid of snakes. For some, this fear rises to the level of phobia, but lots of the rest of us are uncomfortable around them, enough so that if there's a snake in the room, you're looking at it.

In contrast, probably no one reading this paragraph is afraid of cheeseburgers. You may not like them; you may eschew eating them because you avoid meat or beef or any animal product. You may not eat them because you avoid the dairy in the cheese or the gluten in the bun. But avoidance and dietary preferences are not the same as fear. If there's a burger in the room, you can be wholly indifferent toward it, and it's not likely you know into anyone with a full-blown cheeseburger phobia. Who's afraid of the big bad cheeseburger?

Yet consider: about five people die from snakebites in the United States each year.[208] Five, in a country of nearly 329 million. For reference, your odds of being struck by lightning in any given year are 1 in 1,222,000.[209] Heart disease, on the other hand, is the #1 killer in the United States,[210] the cause of a shocking one in four deaths here each year.[211] The path to heart disease is surely paved with foods like cheeseburgers, as well as the path to three of the other top ten causes of death in the United States: diseases of obesity, like diabetes (#7), and those associated with obesity and poor diet, like some cancers (#2, when lumped altogether).* Clearly, the cheeseburger and its ilk are the greater threat to you by far, whereas the snake is inconsequential, at best.

Still, we fear the snake and not the burger. We're told that we're wired this way as a result of our evolution, because immediate threats in the natural environment (like snakes) were more relevant to our

---

* The other obesity-related top cause is stroke (#5); see "Adult Obesity Causes & Consequences," Division of Nutrition, Physical Activity, and Obesity, National Center for Chronic Disease Prevention and Health Promotion, Centers for Disease Control and Prevention, March 22, 2021, *https://www.cdc.gov/obesity/adult/causes. html*.

distant ancestors than low-term, slow-building threats (like heart disease). Obviously, processed foods were not a part of that evolutionary past at all, and even if early humans had eaten nothing but French fries, their dangerous and disease-ridden lives would have been ended by something else before the fries caught up with their hearts. The early human who feared the snake stayed alive to reproduce and end up in your genetic stock; her sister who pondered the potential long-term harms of dietary choices while stepping on the snake did not.

Failing infrastructure is the cheeseburger, not the snake. We can't pay attention to it long enough to learn to fear it. Unfortunately, it remains just as deadly to us, even if we never learn to fear it.

ABANDONED BUILDINGS AND HEALTH

There's another tension between what we fear and what really endangers us in the public health implications of abandoned buildings. Imagine you're passing the building in Figure 23. Does it scare you? How about if you're alone, and on foot? How about if it's night?

Figure 23: Spooky-looking house, no?

Take a moment, and interrogate that fear: what exactly are you frightened of? We won't admit it, but in the back of your mind is that it looks like a haunted house, and a thousand ghost stories and horror movies spring to mind. Beyond the supernatural, we might fear bad people of one sort or another—criminals, rapists, murderers—will stream forth from the vacant windows and sagging doors. I spend a lot of time in the outdoors, and there are a few vacant buildings I regularly pass on trails, always with a bit of trepidation. Illogically, I worry about aggressive animals jumping out from the various nooks and crannies—the rabid raccoon, the very unlikely bear, the impossible mountain lion. Is this likely? Of course not.

What's actually dangerous about abandoned buildings?

If you go into them, the risk of being injured by something falling on you or you falling through the floor is pretty decent, but you're whistling by on the street, not going inside. Yes, there could be hostile animals or people living there, but the odds of them rushing out at you as you pass are very slim. The big danger to public health from abandoned buildings is environmental: the contaminants released into the soil and groundwater as the building decays and collapses. Lead is a biggie here, and lead in urban soils is indeed worrisome. It's the most common contaminant in urban soils, with 4.5 to 5.5 million tons of lead remaining in soil or dust nationwide. That soil + dust detrimentally affects an estimated 5.9 to 11.7 million American children.[212] Lead in urban soils is in large part due to the lead that was present in gasoline until the 1990s, but it's also due to lead paint in buildings (also outlawed in 1976).[213] Asbestos (heavily regulated—not outlawed—starting in 1973) is another concern.

To state the obvious: **these materials don't magically vanish once they are outlawed.** They remain in existing buildings until someone cleans them up or until the building crumbles, one or the other. If the building crumbles with the toxic materials still in it, the toxic materials crumble, too. Buildings and their immediate surroundings can also contain a number of substances that aren't outlawed, but require care to not be a danger, such as petrochemicals. **These hazardous substances, too, go wild as the building decays.**

There's a kernel of truth in the fear of varmints from abandoned buildings, because they can provide good habitat for various beasties you do not want to come into contact with. Rats, for one. Mice, obviously. Bats and raccoons and skunks, all of which are notable rabies carriers. Some experts link serious mouse infestations in abandoned buildings to the higher rates of childhood asthma in poorer urban neighborhoods, tying it to a demonstrated association between exposure to mouse droppings and asthma.[214]

The greater threat, though, is those old infectious diseases, in that some of them may be carried by critters and insects living in the abandoned house (and its overgrown yard). Are there more ticks because there's an abandoned house? Probably not, but the tall grass in the yard is good habitat, and the whole place is ideal for mice, which are a crucial link in the lifecycle of deer ticks.

Overall, though, this isn't a particularly terrifying portrait. It doesn't match the creepy feeling you have walking by at night. **No one dresses as failing infrastructure for Halloween, yet it's the bigger threat to public health by far.**

Vacant Land and Health

Vacant land's threat to public health is exactly that we've just touched on: infectious disease via the critters living therein. Mosquitoes and ticks, and all their unpleasant diseases, find a good home here. Although...what mosquitoes really need is standing water without a ton of pressure from predators, in which to breed and mature. They may like to hang out in the tall grass or shrubbery of the vacant lot, but to exist in the first place, the water is necessary. So it's less the overgrown lot and more the old tires within it.

Can you have a vacant lot without tires or similar artifacts in which to breed mosquitoes? Of course you can. Vacant lots, especially bigger ones, also can be home to a variety of species that prey on mosquitoes, like bats and frogs. For truly impressive mosquito hordes, you need an imbalance in the predator-prey relationship, meaning lots of mosquitoes, not many predators (unless you're in Alaska—then all bets are off). In a way, the wilder the vacant land is, the less threat from infectious disease via mosquitoes it may be, because the wilder lot also harbors enough predators to keep a lid on the mosquitoes.

Emerging research suggests that there may be a similar dynamic in play with ticks. Much of what you hear about ticks, or more specifically, tick-borne diseases and how to avoid them, focuses on taking precautions when you are in wooded areas or those with tall grass, or on avoiding these areas altogether. The implication is that every woods or meadow is equally teeming with ticks, and our only defense lies in our behavior (including just staying out of these areas).

To a tick, though, woods are not simply woods, nor are all meadows the same. They are intricate environments with some aspects that are great for tick life and others that aren't. Ticks lie at the bottom of the food chain, and thus one of those "not so great" aspects is the presence of predators. Research being conducted currently, taken as a whole, seems to suggest that tick troubles are worst in places that are a little wild, but not too wild. Just like mosquitoes, the worst problems with ticks happen where there's tick habitat, yet not enough predators to keep the ticks under wraps.

Because the presence of ticks is more subtle than that of mosquitoes (i.e., they don't buzz around you in a cloud), it's not nearly as obvious what places are ticky and what places aren't. Lyme disease and the host of very rare but very scary other tick-borne diseases are far more serious than a few mosquito bites,* so the stakes are higher.

---

* Although mosquitoes can carry a few very, very rare but pretty scary diseases, too.

But the bottom line at present is that there may be some value in the tick suppression of predators made at home by wild vacant land.

WILD VEGETATION AND HEALTH

This leads us to wild vegetation and public health. Health is often used to justify removal of wild vegetation through some pretty dubious claims. These claims play to what we fear about wild vegetation, but they don't really address actual public health threats from it.

WEED ORDINANCES

Wild urban vegetation is usually addressed by weed ordinances, rules made by the city or town. These typically forbid vegetation over a certain height, such as 6", with exceptions made for plants like flowers and ornamental grasses, and for larger woody plants like trees and shrubs. Weed ordinances are usually weakly written in the way that they define "weeds" and in how they attempt to differentiate between what vegetation is OK to let grow beyond that magic 6" height and what must be mowed. Some name specific plants, like goldenrod or milkweed, as example weeds that must be mowed, but common names of plants are vague in terms of exactly what species they refer to. Latin names, in this case *Solidago* and *Asclepias*, often include related species that are sold as garden plants. It's slippery. When we consider wildflower gardens designed to attract butterflies or to showcase native plants, the line becomes fuzzy indeed.

The intent of weed ordinances is to make property owners mow the lawn. Why do we want that? Mowing the lawn is part of keeping a property up, and so it plays into the aesthetic of care, as we've talked about. We believe good citizens mow the lawn, so we think that having neighbors who mow means we are among people who hold up their end and meet their responsibilities. They think the same of us and our lawns. We mow the lawn because we have a strong strain of cultural heritage from Britain, and that lawn is our little pastoral estate. Some of us mow because we want to use the lawn as a space for our kids to play or our pets to roam, or even for ourselves to relax and enjoy some fresh air.

If you ask people why they mow, it's unlikely you'll hear any of this. People might tell you it's because the lawn is pretty or it looks nice mowed. You'll surely hear something about health: that an un-mowed lawn is a health hazard. This is the foundation of weed ordinances. For the most part, it's tough to enact and enforce municipal ordinances that are merely about looks. They exist, but they often have some camouflage of economics or health. Paint your house, because it will keep property values up. Mow the lawn, because tall grass is a danger to health. Again, the stakes are so much higher with health concerns that it's easy to make a compelling argument, and to win it.*

But is it true?

Vermin in the Grass

Sort of, but not like you'd think. If you challenge the logic of weed ordinances, you'll hear that tall grass provides a home for vermin, a pejorative term if ever there was one. Naturally, no one wants vermin around. What's "vermin"? My mind goes to rats immediately; mice are probably fair game. A link between mice and rats and disease in humans is easy to make (see: bubonic plague, hantavirus, tularemia). But...the thing about rats and mice is that where we go, they go, too.

---

* The American lawn is a pretty complex cultural artifact and pretty influential eco-logical player, yet we have to make an effort to even see it, because it's so pervasive. More about this in Chapter 3, "Learning the Language," in S. Dieterlen, *Immigrant Pastoral: Midwestern Landscapes and Mexican-American Neighborhoods* (London, UK: Routledge, 2015).

At least that's true of the rats and mice that live close to us, in and around our buildings.

Think about this: there are 78 species of mice and rats in the United States and Canada, all within the family Muridae. Of these, three introduced species are the notorious pests we can't keep out of our homes and buildings: the Norway rat (Rattus norvegicus), the black rat (Rattus rattus), and the house mouse (Mus musculus).[215] We Americans of European descent are old, old friends with these three species, because they came with us from Europe, where we lived closely with large numbers of them, notably in the crowded, dirty cities that gave rise to a number of the most deadly diseases the world has ever known.*

Cut to the New World and the present day, and our old pals are still around, despite all the traps and poisons. But they aren't the only rats and mice around. Those other 75 species of native rats and mice that were here before the Europeans mostly live outside, like they have always done. Without question, tall grass is a better habitat for various creatures, i.e., "vermin," than a manicured lawn (particularly since to be manicured, that lawn is soaked in herbicides and pesticides and fertilizers, none of which are great for wildlife), but quite a few of those creatures are not particularly interested in moving in with you. The three that have adapted over centuries to living in our buildings? They're delighted to be your roommates. They like living in buildings.† They can thrive in buildings, to a disgusting degree, with or without tall grass outside. See the disconnect?

---

* The shocking death toll of these diseases, including smallpox, influenza, measles, typhus, and plague, played a major role in European conquest of much of the rest of the world, especially the Americas. J. Diamond, *Guns, Germs, and Steel: The Fates of Human Societies* (New York, NY: W.W. Norton, 1999), provides an in-depth look at this.

† Although Norway rats and house mice are also common in cultivated fields— but not undisturbed natural areas. Still human-dominated environments, just outside.

These aren't hard and fast divisions. Having ideal mouse habitat next to your home, particularly within a few feet of the foundation, will indeed increase the chances of having mice in the home, especially during the winter, because a number of mouse species are happy to move indoors with you for the cold season. **I challenge you to find a building with a truly horrifying level of mouse or rat infestation and eliminate that infestation simply by removing the vegetation around the building.** It won't work, because big infestations are more about the building than the tall or short grass. They are, in fact, coming from inside the house.

ACTUAL HAZARDS

So much for the "vermin" argument. Except...tall grass really is a health hazard, in the ways that we've discussed about all wild vegetation. The mouse that matters is not your roommate the house mouse, but rather the white-footed mouse, because it's the Lyme disease reservoir that's going to infect all the deer ticks enjoying that tall grass. Those **ticks** are a problem, if you're in an area with deer ticks and Lyme. **Mosquitoes** like tall grass, if you've got mosquitoes around, because remember, they need standing water to breed. They don't spontaneously arise from tall grass, although it can seem like it. **Pollen** is a genuine health hazard for the many people who suffer from allergies and asthma, but tree pollen is a potent allergen, too—you don't eliminate allergies by eliminating tall grass. There's no rule that says you only react with allergies to pollen from renegade wild species and not to expensive cultivated ones, but grass pollen is indeed a common allergen. **Mold spores** are a really common allergen, too, and tall grass can create a good place for molds, since the taller grass shades the ground. But mold grows a lot of places—in fact, it's pretty

---

Black rats also like ships—they are those rats.

much endemic to the outdoors in our damper, warmer places and seasons, which is what makes mold allergies such a misery.

It's not clear cut, in short. Recall all the health benefits of wild vegetation, and realize those are relevant here, too. There's no discussion of this in weed ordinances, just the vermin. **It's tough to argue that the health costs of pollen and more field mice outweigh the health benefits of cleaner water and less carbon in the atmosphere.**

LOOSE SPACE AND HEALTH

Take away the failing infrastructure, abandoned buildings, vacant land, and wild vegetation from loose space, and what remains in terms of public health? The behavior of humans in those loose spaces. You'll recall that the transgressive behaviors attracted by loose space range from the playful to the criminal. This behavior is a very mixed bag, so you can't speak about its effect on public health in a single broad generalization.

GARDENS AND RECREATION

On the one hand, there's what we might call guerrilla community gardens, or community gardens on land to which you have no legal right. This is a common loose space behavior, and it certainly has benefits for the gardeners and victimizes no one. Is this a public health benefit? Sure—gardening encourages the consumption of produce, it's good exercise, it gets the gardener out in nature and away from the screens and stresses of daily life, and it arguably builds community ties.

In a similar vein, recreational behaviors in loose spaces—things like kids playing, unauthorized mountain biking or hiking, and dog walking—have health benefits. These behaviors are more or less equivalent to those in parks, so the benefit is similar to that of parks: exercise, exposure to nature, escape from the stresses of daily life, perhaps some community tie strengthening. Loose space is probably wilder than a park, although that depends on the park, so the risks we've covered from wild vegetation and so on apply here. But on the whole, recreational uses are probably a win from a public health standpoint.

HOMELESSNESS IN LOOSE SPACE

These light, bright, fun behaviors are certainly not everything people do in loose space. The big bogeyman lurking in this conversation is crime, but before we get to crime, let's spend a moment with the homeless. **Use by homeless people is one of the common behaviors seen in loose spaces, or rather, it's usually not seen, and that's why it's so common.** A loose space is a great place for a homeless camp, or to find the privacy for a nap or personal care, or just to hang out without being bothered. A loose space can be a good place to stash a few belongings in the hope that no one will find them before you come back to retrieve them. That homelessness exists at this kind of scale is such a breakdown of society's care of the health of its members, that it's difficult to say there's any kind of public health benefit to this use of loose space. I suppose, if we accept as a given that homelessness is a necessary evil (which I do not) and that we as a country cannot even manage the most rudimentary shelter for these individuals (and I don't buy that, either), a loose space is perhaps a better place in which to spend time as a homeless person than many other spaces. If s/he feels safe enough in a particular loose space to let his/her guard down, a homeless person could get all the same benefits from time spent with nature that anyone else would, including some badly needed health benefits and stress reduction (more about PTSD and natural urban environments just below).

▶ *Are there victims in the use of loose space by homeless people?*

PUBLIC HEALTH • 253

Obviously, those most victimized by homelessness are homeless people, but there may be negative impacts on other residents, if they also use the loose space or if they realize the homeless people are there. The big potential negative for other residents is one of perception, that other residents may see a loose space as dangerous because it is frequented by homeless people. This could feed into the dynamic of loose wild spaces as scary and property-value-lowering, but is it a public health concern?

The questions this raises about homelessness, whether it's inevitable, how to best accommodate homeless people and balance their needs against those of other residents, are important. Because they are important questions, they deserve a much more comprehensive discussion than I can give them here. They deserve their own book. But it's important to acknowledge that this is a common use of loose space, because we become very good at not seeing homelessness.

CRIME, OF COURSE

And so, to crime. Crime is the obvious behavior that comes to mind when we talk about loose space, and crime is very obviously a detriment to public health. Violence, including gun violence, is being thought of more and more like a disease, which puts it squarely in the realm of public health.

While "crime" in loose spaces includes more than just violence, it's the violence we tend to worry most about. The definitions get a bit fuzzy here, and don't entirely overlap. Violence most concerns public health. Our discussions of loose space and behavior focus on crime, some of which is violent and some of which isn't. Perhaps most important is that we're all most concerned with the overlap of these two definitions: violent crime.

Some non-violent crimes can have public health implications as well. Consider contamination from illegal dumping. Consider the problem of discarded syringes and needles from drug use. There's not much good here.

Amid this comprehensive bleakness, there are a few points to emphasize. First, if we observe the letter of the law, most if not all behaviors in loose spaces are illegal or criminal. The most delightful child playing is trespassing. That community garden is a liability problem for the landowner, whoever that may be. So talking about crime vs. other loose space behaviors is a matter of degree and ambiguity.

Second, recall the relationship between visible neglect and the perception or fear of crime, and how that is distinct from actual incidents of crime. That applies to loose spaces' impact, too. In terms of public health, the actual incidents of crime are the main concern, but if we believe that loose spaces can have public health benefits, those benefits can be negated by this fear of crime. **If you see the loose space as a frightening hotbed of crime, you won't recreate or play there, and you certainly won't be growing tomatoes there.**

Once again, this barrier to benefits is about fear, not actual threat. You could be happily walking your dog through the vacant lot and be in great danger, but if you aren't aware of that danger, you continue being happy to walk the dog. It's the fear that's the barrier.

Of course, they can be connected—you may have very good reason to fear crime in that loose space, because there's a murder there every week. But you can have the fear without the danger. The way to measure this in cold hard facts is through heart rate, an indicator of stress response, which has been shown to decrease when local residents walked by a visibly cared-for and cleaned up "green" lot compared to a standard overgrown and trash-strewn vacant lot.[216] In terms of health, this stress response to scary vacant lots and stress relief from cared-for ones can pay off in a lot of ways. This is true even if it's the care or the relief from threat that matters and not the greenery at all.

PTSD in the Inner City

According to Dr. Margaret K. Formica, an epidemiologist with SUNY Upstate Medical University and the States for Gun Safety Regional Gun Violence Research Consortium,[217] violence and post-traumatic stress as a self-perpetuating cycle is an accepted view among those who study violence in urban neighborhoods or those who do hands-on work to prevent it.[218] More research relevant to this link has studied veterans or refugees who've been diagnosed with PTSD as a result of their wartime experiences,[219] but as always, research follows funding, and it's much easier to find funding to study these groups. It's also much easier to know who to study if people have received an official diagnosis of post-traumatic stress disorder, rather than having the symptoms of post-traumatic stress, but no diagnosis. Those vets and refugees are more likely to have that diagnosis, and to have them recorded in single databases, like at the VA, while ordinary people in the neighborhood aren't.

Nonetheless, the view that poor inner-city neighborhoods are full of traumatized people is a common one among those in the know. At least some of that trauma seems very likely to be due to the environment of the neighborhood itself, including very difficult life conditions and witnessing violence, even in the absence of violence in one's own personal life.[220] For crime based in neighborhoods, such as gang violence, each incident does not just affect the victim. It affects his or her friends, family, neighbors—the victim's entire social network and circle of acquaintances.

If you live in a high-crime neighborhood, you therefore are affected by many incidences of violence in this way. It's the same people over and over. Add to this the aggression typical of PTSD, and you have a very violent, very traumatic environment. And it's not post-, but ongoing. This dire situation leads some researchers to conclude that rates of PTSD, mostly undiagnosed (reflecting lack of access to health care), are likely far higher among regular people in our high-crime inner city neighborhoods than they are among veterans. Let that sink in a moment.

This looks like a chicken-egg relationship, in which violent surroundings traumatize people, who are then more likely to be violent themselves, making their surroundings more violent and traumatizing others. The few studies that have looked at this relationship support that, too,[221] also noting that reducing PTS symptoms via medication reduces aggressive behavior in those patients as well.

So what if we had a way to make those surroundings, those neighborhoods, just a little more supportive of mental health and managing post-traumatic stress in particular? We do, of course. Exposure to nature can't end gun violence, but it is demonstrably effective at lessening PTSD[222] and lowering crime rates. With the ongoing and comprehensive life-and-death stress of living in a high-crime urban neighborhood,[223] it's an open question whether the "freedom from vigilance" requirement for nature-health benefits can happen, i.e., whether enough residents can get enough respite from stressors and PTS symptoms like hypervigilance to receive any mental health-nature benefit. Nonetheless, since the stakes are literally life and death, an intervention as cheap and benign as trees and vegetation is well worth trying, even for a small improvement.[224]

In summary, the transgressive behaviors that loose space attracts are a mixed bag for public health. Crime, particularly violent crime, can be such a strong negative that it outweighs a considerable amount of benefit. Some of the non-violent criminal behavior is related to illegal drugs, and drugs like opioids and meth are a massive public health crisis, so any behavior that supports drug trade comes at a very high cost.

However, we need to keep loose spaces and wild urban spaces in perspective amid the huge public health issues of violent crime and illegal drugs. We do not have an epidemic of gun violence, of sexual assault, of domestic violence, or of opioid use because we have the odd vacant lot in our cities. Loose spaces may play a small part in the criminal life of a neighborhood, but these crises would rage on without them. It's important to weigh the public health benefits of loose spaces against this possibility of harm, with this perspective in mind. The benefits directly related to transgressive behaviors may be unimpressive, but remember, you likely get the benefits of wild vegetation with that loose space. The climate change mitigation and adaptation benefit of loose space covered in wild vegetation is a public health benefit that can't be ignored and must also be weighed in that balance. Climate change, too, is a public health issue, and is becoming the crisis to end all crises.

CLIMATE CHANGE AND PUBLIC HEALTH

Public health measures are, like infrastructure, dull but necessary. They both operate on a long timeline, and although the average person depends on them to keep life and limb whole, that average person is able to operate in near-total ignorance of them. Thus, like infrastructure, public health looks like a great place to cut costs if you profit from making a big splash now at the expense of future prosperity. A long timeline means you can cut and cut, without the cost of your irresponsibility becoming visible for some time, long after you are out of office, perhaps after your lifetime. Someone will pay, but it won't be you. Epidemics, though, do not care about politics, and pollution does not pay attention to political speeches. Someone's going to pay, sooner or later.

While we wait to find out who pays, how much, and when, the climate continues to go to hell. Climate change is turning up the heat, so to speak, on all these other public health shortfalls. Heat, alone, kills people. The more frequent, more severe storms of all kinds are killing people now and will kill more in the future, as will additional, more severe wildfires. Storms don't only kill people outright, but create conditions that kill us more slowly (such as disease outbreaks from floodwaters or mold) and disable the systems we depend on to keep us healthy long term (like water and sewage treatment).

A warmer world, and for many of us, a wetter world, is a dream come true for a number of unpleasant diseases, some of which have been restricted to the tropics by the vanishing cold winters of more temperate climates. In the many regions of the world that are becoming drier due to climate change, the availability of enough safe drinking water will have profound public health consequences. As with many topics in this book, these climate change-public health concerns are of greater concern for those who are already at a disadvantage due to lower income or societal bias. This compounds the consequence of every climate change-health concern.[225]

APPLICATIONS TO THE CITY

What to do about this apocalyptic vision? **The best thing to do is get to work.** Where the connection between public health and the urban environment really shines is in applications, or what you're going to do with all of the information we've talked about, and how you're going to use it to make the neglected city a better place for all residents. A healthier place is a better place, by any standard. Several of the topics we've covered converge at their sharp ends in health.

We care enough to act when "it", whatever it is, affects our health. It's serious, once it affects our health. So, potholes are a problem, but once they become severe enough to endanger drivers, we act. Aging drinking water systems are a problem, but once the water coming out of the tap is no longer safe to drink, we act. The overburdened electrical grid is a problem, but once power outages affect hospitals and nursing homes, we act. Or so you'd think, but we've got examples aplenty that indicate that we act, but we act mostly when it's us, or people close to us who are in danger. Other people? Not so much, and here's the connection to inequality, back again. Climate change, infectious disease, failing bridges—all of these topics are most urgent where they endanger health, and the most urgent of urgent where they endanger YOUR health.

The "public" in public health points at the truth here: we're all in this together. You can't actually fix climate change or the electrical grid or infectious disease for you and me, but not all those other people. Or rather, you can—you can employ a number of stopgap measures to protect just yourself and people close to you, build a wall around yourself with wealth and privilege—but it doesn't really work and it doesn't make much sense. We need all those other people to have a functioning economy, if not a worthwhile society. Life as we know it depends on things like electricity and potable water being a given, and when those things become privileges rather than givens, life as we know it no longer works.

This chapter opened with the observation that public health and environmental design often converge in the outcomes we want. When you apply your learning about neglect to improving your city, you begin to deal in outcomes. You find that very often, your design scheme is also a public health scheme, and vice versa. A trail is a recreational amenity and a wildlife corridor and a way to repurpose vacant land, but it's also a free fitness resource and a setting for high-quality exposure to nature and a giant air and water filter. One trail, all these benefits. Transit-oriented development* can revitalize moribund neighborhoods, produce vibrant streets and public spaces, and attract the creative class, but it also cuts down on one of the largest greenhouse gas emitters (transportation) and makes it easier to walk or bike for fitness in your neighborhood. Everybody wins. One of the best places to connect urban environments and public health is in the applications. Conveniently, that's also the next chapter.

---

* Simply put, homes and businesses designed to be conveniently and comprehensively served by mass transit rather than private cars. More detail about this at the website of the Transit Oriented Development Institute, US High Speed Rail Association, *http://www.tod.org/home.html*.

CHAPTER 13

SAIL WITH THE CURRENT

Neglect is the unseen hand shaping our cities. What matters about that is what we do with that knowledge.

▶ *What does this exploration of neglect mean for making our cities more livable and sustainable?*

That kind of question often opens a process that results in a master plan, a many-page report in a binder. It represents months of work, sums it up neatly, and then—sits on a shelf. Master plans can guide actions, but they tend to be too big to accomplish in their entirety: it's right there in the name, "master plan."

For shrinking cities shaped by their continuing lack of investment, it's unbearably ironic to propose a grand master plan. Quite obviously, there's no money for that. **If there was money to implement that kind of plan, there would not have been decades of neglect shaping the city in the first place.**

What's needed is a light touch and a keen eye. We've seen that neglect is already shaping the city—the task is not to undo everything that's been done, or implement sweeping changes to fix it all. The task instead is how to channel the changes already happening, the shaping from neglect that is underway today. Even in the most destitute of cities, projects do get implemented. They may be small, but they do happen. The task is also, therefore, to guide these small-enough-to-happen efforts in service of a larger goal.

Perhaps most important is to learn to work with the energy of neglect as a shaper rather than fighting against it, thus allowing the small investments that can happen to produce maximum impact, rather than just whistling into the wind. That's important enough to say it again: **the big takeaway from studying urban neglect may be awareness of neglect as a force you can use to do what needs to be done and to make the most of what resources remain in the shrinking city, rather than fighting the current.**

LAND BANKS, BUT NOT ALL THE TIME

Where neglect is a problem, there is typically a surfeit of vacant land, as well as a low standard of maintenance of non-vacant land. You'll remember that vacant land is one of the big effects of neglect, and wild vegetation, urban wildlife, and loose space often occur within those same vacant parcels. The other big effects of neglect, failing infrastructure and abandoned buildings, are frequently adjacent to vacant land—because neglect piles up—or even within the vacant parcel itself. So handling vacant land is key. Accordingly, this chapter primarily focuses on vacant land and urban wilds (often the same thing), with some points about infrastructure and wild vegetation, too.

Land banks can be a great help in this effort. The land bank model, at heart, is to acquire problem properties, remove whatever barriers have kept them from being appealing to buyers, and transfer ownership of the property to new owners. Properties acquired by land banks are usually vacant, abandoned, or tax-delinquent. These properties are most often single-family homes or vacant lots, but other types of properties and land uses can also be involved. Land banks are usually government organizations or not-for-profits. They thrive in cities with an abundance of vacant and abandoned properties, where property values have become very low, and where there are large numbers of properties with legal complications, like title problems or difficult processes for buying tax-delinquent properties.[226]

Land banks are a fairly recent innovation that has been very successful in a number of shrinking cities. They have a lot to recommend them, but like every good idea, land banks are not a panacea. Some people criticize the land bank concept at its root, for once again profiting those outside downtrodden neighborhoods by selling yet another asset from the downtrodden neighborhood.[227] Even the biggest supporters of land banks readily concede that they can't do it all. Not every property is easily redeemed. Even with a straightforward title, a good clean-up, and a rock-bottom price, some parcels just aren't appealing. This is especially true when there is a large catalog of other redeemed properties available at equally low prices—which tends to be the case where there's a land bank. Properties with unusually unappealing locations or neighboring disamenities may not find new owners, as well as properties with serious contamination (although some land banks specialize in brownfields). It's hard to overcome substantial population decline with even the most dynamic and well-run land bank, and this is exactly the situation in the shrinking city. To find new owners, you need to have potential new owners, which can be tough with fewer people.

THE QUESTIONS THAT MATTER

If you can't redevelop it, what do you do with the extra land? How about doing nothing—allowing neglect to turn extra land wild? Wild parcels can serve a variety of functions for the greater good. Climate change mitigation alone could be reason enough to reevaluate urban wilds. That notion raises a few questions:

▶ *How can cities best incorporate urban wilds, with their tensions and ambiguity?*

▶ *How can they maximize the benefits and minimize the costs of urban wilds?*

▶ *Can this make the city more just and livable for its most vulnerable residents, rather than exacerbating our already unsustainably unequal society?*

Vacant and unmaintained land tends to be concentrated in the same challenged neighborhoods that have borne the burdens associated with redlining, urban renewal, disamenities, and environmental injustices. **By their nature, therefore, urban wilds are positioned to most benefit these neighborhoods—to situate as the greatest winners those who have too often been the biggest losers in any zero-sum decision. The question is how to reshape wilds as an asset instead of a detriment.**

All the foregoing factors laid out in this book must be balanced. Weigh them against each other, in the context of this city, this region, this neighborhood. What's most important? What stands to produce the greatest gain? What is the deepest need or division to be remedied?

Key point: this is about balance, and how to tip it toward the positive. Neglect is ambiguous, viewed as a whole. It has good aspects and bad aspects, and it's no one's idea of an ideal situation.

Yet it's the situation in which we find ourselves. If you wait for the ideal situation to materialize, you'll never change anything at all. If you can work with the situation as it is, you have the opportunity to improve the status quo. Make peace with a lack of perfection, and with the idea that change and improvement will be incremental. The goal is to make the impacts more good than bad, and to blunt the bad impacts enough that they are a manageable cost for what's gained.

Is neglect good or bad on balance? This is one of the most interesting aspects of neglect—that there are benefits from letting everything run to ruin. If we fixed everything, what would be lost? What's the benefit of neglect and what's the cost? Who gets the benefits and who pays the costs?

Consider geography and landscape scale. It doesn't just matter who wins and who loses, but where the winners and losers are. A large swath of wild land in the city center could counter air pollution from an adjacent gridlocked highway and lower the temperature of the city's heat island, benefiting those residents one half mile away. They win. Meanwhile, residents immediately adjacent to the wild land will suffer the property value depression and the increased crime rates. They lose, and whether you're a winner or a loser depends on where you live.

Children walking to urban schools may bear the brunt of increased crime rates, increased fear of crime, and increased pollen, but people working in professional offices in downtown high rises may benefit from the exposure to nature of green views. **These competing benefits and costs have a spatial dimension that is key to determining who will benefit, who will pay, and what balance between those pluses and minuses is appropriate.** It's about space, as it so often is. We do a really good job of ignoring that.

WILDS THAT HELP

Neglect tends to pile up, with the same locations in the city bearing multiple effects at once. It's natural, therefore, that urban wilds will occur in these same locations as well. **The genius is to determine how to shape the wilds so that they help more than hurt**, especially since they are neighbors to the same people so often hurt most by other urban issues and imperfect past solutions. This is where a spatial approach reveals relationships you might otherwise have missed. Think back (or look back to Chapter 11—Inequality) at that table about what types of neighborhoods within the city we expect to exhibit various effects of neglect. Then think back (or look back to Chapter 11) about who typically lives in these types of neighborhoods. If you want to help the people in those neighborhoods, urban wilds are ideally positioned to do it—without any expense or effort. Wilds are already there. It's about how to use them and make them work for us to do what we know needs to be done, rather than serving to multiply other ills.

The cruel arithmetic of environmental racism is that disamenities—bad things, simply put—tend to be sited or show up or cluster where the resistance is least. The resistance tends to be least where there are already other bad things. So the bad stuff clusters and piles up.

This works through several mechanisms, among them analysis of property values and naked prejudice. The freeway was built through the redlined neighborhoods, which were redlined because they were Black or immigrant or poor or all three. All those "others," those people with limited options, lived in those neighborhoods that became redlined because they were shut out or priced out or driven out of other neighborhoods. Once the freeway is in, more troubles mount: cut-off streets become more attractive for crime due to the absence of through-traffic and its casual surveillance. Air quality suffers from the traffic; the noise of traffic harasses day and night. Deteriorating quality of life pushes more people to leave the neighborhood, if they possibly can, and makes it more and more a place where no one lives except those with no other choice. That concentrates poverty, and that concentrates all the social ills that attend poverty, and makes it all worse, because it's everyone, all the time. The poorer the neighborhood, the fewer resources there are to mitigate all these burdens.

When some new disamenity needs to go somewhere, this afflicted place is the "natural" fit, because who will object?

None of this is natural. **None of this is random. It's the product of a manmade system to benefit a few at the expense of everyone else.** Consequently, the same neighborhoods lose every time, and the people in them lose, too.

Neglect Is Already There

Because wild land and other manifestations of neglect are symptoms of disinvestment, they tend to be overrepresented in such neighborhoods—land like this is one of the signs that this neighborhood has lost in various ways. Cleaning up or repurposing such land is a lower priority in these neighborhoods, so it endures. **Unlike many of those other burdens borne by these neighborhoods, wild land can be redefined from burden to benefit.**

If that happens, the parcels don't move—they are still concentrated in these, the most disadvantaged of urban neighborhoods. That means that wild land is perfectly suited to address some of the problems of these areas. **It's right where it needs to be, right where it is most needed.** It's an asset waiting to be seen and shaped.

McHarg Gone Wild

There's not a one size fits all solution. Places are individual. They are individual in their histories, their relationships between different demographic groups, and their relative resilience. They are also individual in their topographic, hydrologic, and ecological characteristics.

As you think through this idea, it may sound a bit familiar, if you know the work of Ian McHarg. McHarg's work, especially as depicted in his 1969 book *Design with Nature*,[228] was tremendously influential and remains so to this day. The central idea of McHargian planning is to let ecological suitability guide land planning and design. If this doesn't sound earth-shaking to you, it's because his ideas were so influential that now, decades later, his way of planning seems like the regular way of planning, the way everyone does it. (This kind of future-invisibility is a hallmark of revolutionary ideas that are widely adopted—because they change everything afterward, you no longer understand how revolutionary they were.)

At the time, this was a disruptive notion, starkly contrasting with the accepted way of designing, planning, and developing land. McHarg advocated for deep, methodical analysis of different ecological aspects of a piece of land. This revealed areas that were more fragile or more valuable, ecologically speaking, and parts that were less valuable and more resilient to development. By adding up all of these ecological aspects and their relative merit, the portions of land that most needed protection from development and those that could best withstand development became clear.[229]

The McHargian construct of identifying the most valuable and most vulnerable land is appropriate here, with a twist:

▶ *What's the most valuable urban wild, in terms of all the benefits detailed in previous chapters?*

▶ *What's the most vulnerable neighborhood, in terms of all the costs detailed in previous chapters?*

Most especially:

▶ *How can those valuable benefits of neglect counteract or mitigate the vulnerable neighborhood's costs of neglect?*

▶ *What does it mean to view wild land as a resource instead of a problem?*

▶ *What does wild-land-as-resource look like and how does it function?*

PRIORITIZE PERCEPTION BY PEOPLE WHO NEED BENEFIT

Don't forget the social aspect, and the need for public input from whatever publics are directly affected. Sacred spaces are important here, too, because the informality and the ambiguous character of urban wilds makes them ideal for hiding the sacred landmarks and sites of various communities within the city.

It's easy to be fooled into thinking that everything that matters about land and the built environment is straight-forward, objective, and readily visible to the trained eye. We see roads, we see building types and conditions, we see drainage patterns and vegetation, and we can easily think, "what else is there?" What we can't see is cultural resonance, the spiritual, emotional, and historical meaning that places in the landscape hold for various communities. You have to belong to that community to be aware of these things, and often, we designers and planners and public officials making decisions about the future of places are not a part of the diverse communities around us.[230] Who knows what's hidden in that thicket of buckthorn? Someone does— it's just not you.

This community input from the relevant community is utterly vital to maximizing the social and health benefits of productive wilds because **people near the wilds need to be comfortable with them and see them as desirable assets for many of these benefits to accrue.** Their perception is the one that matters. We are not used to seeing the world that way, that the perception of poor non-white urban residents is the most important one.

A wild parcel can provide space for free fitness activities exactly where diabetes and heart disease rates are worst, but only if people feel comfortable and safe enough to walk or play in the wild. A wild parcel can mitigate the PTSD rampant in poor urban neighborhoods, but only if people are able to be exposed to the nearby nature in a relaxed state, without the vigilance that comes from seeing wilds as a threat and setting for threat rather than a natural area.

This effect and others like it have been noted by several researchers: that not only do people with fewer resources benefit from exposure to nature, but they have been shown to benefit **more** than the average person, in certain conditions.[231] By definition, a wild seen as yet another top-down dictate by affluent elites, yet another way the neighborhood loses, is not a productive wild but one more brick in the wall of injustice that characterizes our cities. Buy-in matters. Productive wilds can be an asset **concentrated** in the most challenged neighborhoods, something desirable that improves quality of life that those areas have and more affluent areas do not.

THE KIT OF PARTS

So how do you do it, this magical transformation of neglect from detriment to asset? Let's focus on vacant and wild land, and walk through the process. This isn't a roadmap; neither is it an example. What it is is a set of questions. **Asking the right questions is essential.** Ask these, and you're on your way.

This is not a set of instructions. It's a place from which to jump. Consider:

Suitability

How suitable is this land for redevelopment, the land bank playbook? Is it an easy sell?

Get an honest, informed assessment by those who know the local market and likely local investors or buyers of real estate. Like everyone says, location is key to this. For many land uses, visibility matters quite a bit: can anyone see this site, and where must they be to see it? Wild sites are often places that have fallen out of mind in part because they have fallen out of sight. They aren't readily visible from places where eyes that matter, in terms of decision making, are. Tied to this lack of visibility is a lack of access, meaning that it can be difficult to physically get to a site. Is there any road frontage? Is that frontage suitable for putting in a driveway? How about the larger area or multiple drives needed for fire trucks or maintenance vehicles? Wild sites are sometimes difficult to get to even on foot—is your site one of these?

What about contamination—is it likely, given the site's history and perhaps its reputation, that it has polluted soil or groundwater? That's not the end of the possibility of redevelopment, but it does make a particular site harder to move, all things being equal. It also matters what the contaminants are: some are scarier or more difficult to remove or simply more dangerous. All of this adds up to suitability for redevelopment.

Less suitable for redevelopment? Better to stay wild.

Ecology

How valuable is this land ecologically? Does it include or protect/buffer ecologically sensitive sites, such as wetlands, watercourses, or floodplains? How ecologically valuable is its vegetation as habitat?

Look closely at the ecological value of your site. Consider this systematically, e.g., assess water impacts, then habitat impacts, then air quality/greenhouse gas impacts, and so on. Think about the absolute function of the site (does it do anything?). Add in the magnitude of those functions (does it do a lot or a little of each function?) and quantify that magnitude if possible, to allow ready comparison between sites. Then add the context of those functions. Perhaps there are a lot of nearby areas that also provide that function, or perhaps this is one of the only ones. How badly needed is that particular ecological function in the area around your site? Together this comprises the ecological value of the site.

More valuable? Better wild.

Climate

How valuable is this land for climate change adaptation or mitigation? How close is it to the hottest parts of the city? Do adjacent residences have air conditioning? How close is it to areas of greatest ground-level ozone formation? What is the vegetation character—and what does that mean for carbon sequestration?

Overlapping somewhat with ecological value, but worthy of its own category, given that climate change is a real present danger to the survival of humanity. Don't just think about the obvious climate value—sequestering carbon or reducing greenhouse gas emissions. Think about adaptation, of what matters to make life possible and as good as possible for as many of us as possible in a warmer world.

Revisit climate change predictions for your region, and think about what will be needed in terms of those, in broad strokes. Wetter regions need more flood protection and stormwater management. Hotter regions (which is pretty much everywhere, because global warming) need more defense against heat island and excessive heat deaths. Coastal areas need more defense against the impacts of killer storms and sea level rise. What can your site do for the impacts your region is expected to see, and for impacts it's already seeing? Like ecological value, climate impact is best viewed as not just what your site can do, but how much it can do and how badly each function is needed.

More valuable? Better wild.

Cultural Sanctity

How significant is this land to the adjacent communities? Is it sacred or profane, notable as a landmark or as a site of past tragedies? What is its social history?

The previous questions feel quantitative, even mathematical, but this one doesn't. This is the soft, fuzzy one. That doesn't make it less important, but rather more important to pay close attention to, since there's not just a number to throw at it.

A good approach to this point is to approach your site with the attitude that you don't know everything about its cultural significance, and that no matter how unlikely it might seem to you, it may indeed be an important cultural site to someone else. Think about who that might be: what communities exist in the area? If you aren't local, ask someone who is, and look at other local resources. If you're getting paid to come in from outside and do this work, remember that your local contacts (clients, etc.) may tailor their answers to these questions to present their community to you, the outsider, in the best light (or what they see as the best light), so confirm with more objective sources whenever possible.*

It's harder to have a clear directive for significant sites. There's not a one-size-fits-all axiom about keeping them wild if there's anything culturally significant. It all depends on their nature as to whether they can be best honored or redeemed as wild sites or as built ones. What matters at this point is to give yourself the chance to do the right thing by asking the right questions and tracking down answers.

Cultural significance? It depends.

Recreation/fitness

What is the recreation or fitness need of the adjacent community? Obesity, diabetes rates? What parks or other public recreation amenities are available nearby—are they adequate and does the community feel well served by them? Does the wild site connect critical facilities, making it a potential route for walking to school or work? Does the character (topography, drainage) of the wild site make it suitable for fitness or recreation use?

This is often omitted in decisions about land use or preservation. Nonetheless, it's key to making progress on many public health benefits that we desperately need. Too often, parks or recreation land are

---

* I talk much more about this possibility and its impacts in terms of immigrant communities in surprising places, and what that means for the work of designers and planners in practice in S. Dieterlen, *Immigrant Pastoral: Midwestern Landscapes and Mexican-American Neighborhoods* (London, UK: Routledge, 2015).

the leftovers, which makes manifest the attitude that fitness and recreation aren't important, or perhaps that fitness and recreation open to the general public at no additional charge aren't important.

This is flat wrong, of course. Outdoor recreation and daily fitness matter, and they are much harder to work into your life when there's nowhere to do them. This doesn't just boil down to "park or no park?" but rather whether there's a need for the opportunity for recreation and fitness, and the suitability of your site for those. It's not all or nothing. Bike paths don't take up much space; pedestrian paths take up even less. But both these are linear by nature, meaning that if you can't connect A and B, they aren't worth anything at all. The best way to get a linear corridor is to consider it first, then fit other uses around it.

Much is made of the mis/match between neighborhood demographics and various recreational facilities, sometimes with good reason. Maybe there are basketball neighborhoods and tennis neighborhoods, or maybe these are biased assumptions that drive people in different places to take up or abandon different pastimes. It's less important than you'd think to make that kind of decision (and defend it) at this point about your site. Team sport facilities all need roughly the same characteristics: a certain amount of flat open space, probably with proximity to electrical service and some means for people to get there, probably in cars. Ideally there's access to water service, too, and some visibility from somewhere, so that it's not your little secret that there's a playing field there.

Playgrounds generally have similar requirements, but smaller spaces, and more visibility and better vehicular access. Both can be loud uses, so some places aren't ideal for them. Bike or pedestrian paths are much easier to fit in and much more forgiving about terrain and access, but aren't necessarily worthwhile in places where they don't go anywhere. You can start with the rough outline of what your site has to offer, and worry about the niceties of who wants what later, at this point. But in general:

Better fitness use = better wild.

Crime/fear

What are the crime rates and perception of danger from crime in the adjacent community? What is the perception of crime in that community by outsiders? Does the character of the wild land promote perceptions of danger or crime? What would it take to give the wild land a benign appearance from adjacent public land or routes?

This question straddles the line between readily quantifiable and slippery subjective information. Get numbers for what you can: crime stats, tree canopy coverage. But like cultural significance, key parts of this question are about what people think and do who live near the site, and if that's not you, you need to actively seek out those people and ask them.

Community organizations and institutions can be good resources for this particular point. For example, a nearby school might be a good start for finding out whether kids are afraid to walk through a wild site to school, or if lots of kids do it and see it as being safer than local roads. What we know about how people see maintenance or lack thereof with regards to safety and ownership (from back in Chapter 5—Places No One Cares About) is all generalizations and averages. It might be a bit different where you are, with the people where you are, in part because of those culturally significant sites that you can't see. Ask. Assume you don't know it all. What you do know arms you with the ability to ask good questions, and you don't get good answers if you never ask.

More crime and danger? Probably better not wild, but it depends, too.

This kit focuses on urban wilds, but the same approach could be taken to other effects of neglect, some of which tend show up in or near those same urban wilds.

Assembling the Kit

Once you've answered every question in the kit of parts, what do you do with the answers? You find a way to balance different priorities against each other and make decisions that incorporate all of them, without shortchanging any.

This complex task also requires talking across disciplines and professions, because the kit of parts doesn't fall into any one field's area of expertise. It's not just tough to talk to those who don't share our outlook and vocabulary. Interdisciplinary conversations usually run afoul of the unspoken ideas we have about whose work is more important and whose voice is more worth hearing. It can be very hard to talk to each other; it's harder when you're convinced the other guy isn't worth listening to. It's tough from the other side, too—when you're sure the other guy shouldn't bother listening to you.

It's helpful to have facts on your side when you seek to bridge this gulf. Get as many facts as possible. Quantify whatever you can, and make it as objective as you can. Evidence helps.

When it comes to decisions about what matters most out of what's possible, protect what's most valuable and what's most vulnerable. Make the most of opportunities to provide the services, functions, and amenities most needed or most lacking. If you have to choose, choose to provide more for the people with least.

These are lofty ambitions, but remember that land development and conservation don't need to be done in a day. There's time to do a little bit right away and a little more later, and the rest a lot later. The most important thing is to decide where you want to be ultimately, so that those different phases all work in service of that ultimate goal.

POSSIBLE DESTINATIONS (EXAMPLES THAT AREN'T EXAMPLES)

What does this look like, in the end?

▶ *What kind of on-the-ground physical changes happen as a result of this process?*

These aren't examples. They're just thoughts made concrete, because too much abstraction makes things so vague as to be meaningless. **Sometimes you have to imagine a possible destination in order to figure out how to get there.**

Let's take another look at public health, and pick up the loose strand from the end of that chapter. "Outcomes create shared aims," means what, exactly, in reality? Here are three examples-that-aren't-examples:

NOT-AN-EXAMPLE 1: MULTI-PURPOSE INFRASTRUCTURE IN URBAN AREAS

Urban streets are spaces that serve many purposes at once, yet improvements often treat them as single-purpose, especially when those improvements are repairs to existing systems. We fix the water main. We patch the sidewalk or street. We repair the electrical service when it fails, but rarely do we look at these repairs and updates in a coordinated and proactive way.

We're aided in this oversight by the way we don't/see infrastructure. Infrastructure, again, tends to be invisible to the general public. We take it for granted—it's omnipresent and dull. Until it stops working, at which point it becomes abruptly and painfully visible to everyone affected. We take it as our birthright as Americans that there will always be infrastructure, and that it will work perfectly in the background without any effort on our part, despite plenty of evidence to the contrary. (You remember that from Chapter 2—Invisible Infrastructure, right?)

A challenge arising from this is that we, the public, often resent spending on infrastructure. In turn, elected officials are often reluctant to invest adequately in infrastructure, because the public seems to not care about it, and cares so much more about tax rates and spending. Public support is often greater for "pretty" projects—ones that are readily visible to the average person and pleasing to most. Political will is therefore also often greater for these projects. It's a lot easier to put your name, literally or figuratively, on a project that your constituents noticed.

You can work with these bits of human nature when you tie something pretty to your needed infrastructure update. The pretty part can be small and fairly minor in terms of overall project budget and scope. Part of what the pretty portion does is make the finished project visible to the public. For example, the stylish new street lights can indicate where the electrical grid has been updated and civic broadband installed. You see the lights, not the wires, but the lights become the look of the area with the better, more reliable services. **It's a visual signature of progress.**

This works well to weave disparate efforts into one multi-purpose goal, achieved through a single construction project (sometimes called Dig Once). Not only does this help cultivate public approval, but it also gets more benefits out of the same amount of funding or project budget, because progress is made toward many goals at once, perhaps with minor adjustments here and there. This is an especially smart strategy in urban neighborhoods with a lot of worn buildings and infrastructure—the very areas where need is often greatest. Where many systems are failing at once, it's much easier to get a multi-purpose bang out of your buck, because there's so much that needs doing all in the same block or square foot.

Figure 24 shows an example of this all-for-one strategy applied to infrastructure improvements in an urban street. It depicts a community microgrid, with district heat, integrated with water and stormwater improvements, sidewalks, and lighting. Community microgrids are updates to the electrical system—aka the grid—that position electricity generation close to electricity use. Microgrids also usually include energy storage, which helps with one of their primary functions: operating as a small-scale independent system to keep the lights on when the larger grid goes down. Because of this, microgrids greatly

Figure 24: An all-for-one design for infrastructure in the urban street, and one possible logo branding the improvements

increase the resilience of an area, but they also make substantial improvements to the efficiency of the electrical system when the larger grid is operating normally.*

The figure depicts integrated installation of the community microgrid, new water service, and updated storm drainage, including underground detention for big rain events. There are new sidewalks and new streetlights. District heat, where heat produced as a byproduct of electrical generation heats all buildings served by the microgrid, might be included as well. If so, it might heat the sidewalks, melting winter ice and snow effortlessly.† The streetlights make this project

---

* For more about microgrids in service to neighborhood revitalization, see S. Dieterlen, *Neighborhood Microgrids: Replicability and Revitalization* (Syracuse, NY: Syracuse University Center of Excellence for Energy and Environmental Systems, 2016), 1–24.

† If you've never heard of heated sidewalks, this might sound unrealistic, but Holland, Michigan, has been enjoying heated sidewalks for a couple decades now. Seriously, look it up: see Ryan Grimes, "Holland's Heated

visible to the public, aided by painting the utility poles that carry the lines of the new microgrid. A simple yet distinctive logo stamped on these lights and poles could help with this visibility by giving the combined improvements a name; one idea of such a logo and name is shown in the figure.

Thus are multiple objectives achieved via a single coordinated project. The sidewalk makes it easier for pedestrians to get around safely, furthering both the public health goal of making every day exercise available to more people and the sustainability goal of providing alternatives to driving. The microgrid improves the reliability of electrical service to residences, including those of limited means (social justice and public health) and businesses (economic development), while improving resilience to disasters and energy efficiency (sustainability). Storm drainage improves transportation by minimizing street flooding (public health, but also everyone's convenience, and economic development) while moving stormwater out of the sanitary sewers (public health, again, and sustainability), and makes the street less likely to flood in large rain events (resilience). District heat provides the same social justice—public health—economic development—sustainability combo as the electricity via microgrid does. Heated sidewalks are a major walkability bonus, which satisfies public health-sustainability, but also social justice, because walkability serves those who can't afford cars as well as those who can. And no one's likely to argue with improved water lines.

The streetlights and painted poles and logos help it all go down more easily with the public, but at the same time, they help establish a perception of this neighborhood as a place where exciting and positive things are happening and where the city is investing, both of which are very encouraging to anyone looking to invest in the neighbor-

---

Sidewalks, Streets Were a Gamble That Seems to Have Paid Off," *Michigan Radio.org*, March 22, 2016, available at:*https://www.michiganradio.org/post/ hollands-heated-sidewalks-streets-were-gamble-seems-have-paid.*

hood. This is the foundation of economic revitalization. Everybody wins, which is a lot to get out of a sidewalk repair or a water main replacement.

NOT-AN-EXAMPLE 2: MAKING A MORE WALKABLE CITY OUT OF VACANT LAND

We've talked about the multiple goals satisfied by walkable environments. When you craft those walkable environments out of the abundance of vacant land characteristic of shrinking cities, you add even more stakeholders to the list of proponents.[232] Vacant land creates a host of problems. (You can refresh your memory about that with Chapter 3—Vacant Buildings, Vacant Land.) Interests who want vacant land to vanish include real estate development, economic development, and neighborhood organizations. Generally, law enforcement sees vacant land as a problem, too, and there's a case to be made, as we've seen, that vacant land is a problem for public health as well. So "less vacant land, more walkability," checks boxes for a lot of interest groups.

How do you complete this magic transformation? One strategy is to fill in vacant parcels with dense, mixed-use development at a human scale. Essentially, you fill in the blanks with walkable environments. This creates places to walk to, places to walk from, and an appealing environment in which to do that walking.

Making those walkable environments appealing matters, because success in getting people out of cars rests on making walking pleasant enough that people will do it by choice, not just necessity. So some vacant land can be repurposed as projects that make the street a more pleasant and comfortable place to walk. This includes making the street visually appealing and interesting, but also includes making it comfortable for people to be in without the shelter of cars, by providing more sheltering elements like street trees and building awnings, and fewer large windswept parking lots and wind tunnel effects from massive buildings.[233]

A key component of walkability is providing complete streets, those that serve bicyclists and pedestrians just as well or better than cars. There's a known playbook of how to do this, but the changes are stymied by the status quo of everyone driving. People with cars aren't happy with making roads less focused on cars.

The excess road capacity of shrinking cities can ease these changes, especially if improvements in the **quality** of auto infrastructure are provided in exchange for a reduction in quantity. To a driving public accustomed to crumbling roads, fewer lanes with smooth new paving and fully functioning stoplights and signals could seem like a really great deal. Adding bike amenities at the expense of excess car capacity is fairly obvious; pedestrian amenities like this could include new or larger sidewalks, traffic islands, and traffic calming measures to slow traffic.

Shrinking cities also tend to be overserved with parking—fewer cars, less need for places to park them. These excess lots are often appropriately described as underused land, if not vacant land, since a parking lot is a cheap use for extra land that carries little legal liability and holds a little promise of income (however unlikely). These lots, too, are excess car infrastructure available for walkability improvements.

A less obvious strategy for improving walkability lies in the transformation of vacant land into green space, including urban farms and urban forests. This is an important component in cities with a lot of vacant land,[234] for good reasons. It can provide a walkability bonus as well in terms of making the pedestrian environment appear more cared for and maintained, thus increasing feelings of security while walking, and also making the microclimate more comfortable for pedestrians, by mitigating heat island, serving as windbreaks and providing shade.

The best wrap up to this chapter, the final chapter, is: the ultimate part in the kit of parts is the notion that neglect is not simply bad, but rather an ambiguous, qualified negative, capable of being used for good and redeemed. The most important tool in the toolbox is your mind, and an attitude embracing possibility.

There are options in front of you.

What you've got has value.

There's a lot of potential here.

CITIES THAT WORK ARE OUR BEST HOPE: A CONCLUSION

I write this at a strange point in American history. In this moment of marked division, one sentiment we may share is that government needs to do better for the people, for more of the people. We differ, vehemently, about which people those are and what strategy government should follow, but we share that directive: do better for more of us.

We also share the pit-of-the-stomach, dead-of-night sense of scarcity, that there is less now to work with than previous generations had. We look around and see crumbling infrastructure and central cities and the fraying of our society into empowered elites and the disempowered everyone else. Where will we find the money and the will to fix anything? It's tough to believe there will really be the resources to put things back together. To fix neglect means not just the repair of recent damage, but reversing decades-long trends. It's a daunting prospect.

However, the lens I've offered here turns detriment into asset. It uses the problem to solve itself. In the absence of the resources or unity to conceive and implement big plans, this kind of more-with-less approach is what we need. **Solving problems with what we already have, particularly with the results of other problems, could be the genius of the age.** Political winds shift, as winds will do, and perhaps change is already beginning. This cloud of threat and division could be just a nightmare that evaporates at dawn. In that happy day, being strategic and efficient as we improve our cities and mend inequality will simply allow us to do even more.

In any case, we must do something. The big realities of this book—climate change, inequality, public health problems—are coming for us all, not just white America or Black America, red America or blue America. The money that's increasingly concentrated in the hands of the few at the top will save them, for a while, but not forever, and they'll be saved to live in a world that's far diminished, far less, than the one we inherited from previous generations. We need to stop this nonsense and get to work.

Is neglect ultimately good or bad? If we continue to approach it with the zero-sum mindset of us vs them, it tears us farther apart, and it's bad. If, on the other hand, we use the momentum and omnipresence of neglect to make this a more just, more sustainable country, then neglect is a force for good. It's not pre-set. It's up to us.

That work needs to focus on our cities and in making them livable—healthy, sustainable, and enjoyable homes both for people who have the means to live elsewhere and those with no other choice. **We need our cities to work, because urban living, in its greater density, is one of our best hopes for countering climate change.** We need our cities to work, because the inequality and injustice that define them are antithetical to the noble ideas of America's founding, and in the end, those ideas are the best of what binds this diverse nation together. We need our cities to work, not just the big global cities of the coasts but the small shrinking cities of the rest, because we can't leave so many people behind. If we can get it right in our cities, especially the small rusty ones, we can be a healthier, cooler, kinder, fairer nation, because if we can solve problems in the most difficult situations, we can solve them everywhere. Most of us didn't get here by design, but we can harness neglect to help us out, put things right, and take us all home.

ENDNOTES

1   For example: Editor, "Interstate System Report Calls for More Funding, Tolling, VMT Fees, and Cybersecurity." *AASHTO Journal* [online], July 12, 2018, available at: *https://aashtojournal.org/2018/12/07/interstate-system-report-calls-for-more-funding-tolling-vmt-fees-and-cybersecurity/*; Erin Durkin, "New York City Subway And Bus Services Have Entered 'Death Spiral', Experts Say," *The Guardian*, November 20, 2018, available at: *https://www.theguardian.com/us-news/2018/nov/20/new-york-city-subway-bus-death-spiral-mta-fares*; Niall McCarthy, "Report: Over 54,000 American Bridges are Structurally Deficient [Infographic]," *Forbes*, January 30, 2018, available at:

https://www.forbes.com/sites/niallmccarthy/2018/01/30/report-over-54000-american-bridges-are-structurally-deficient-infographic/#b931e8419b5c.

2   Susan Dieterlen, ""City Wild Blog," 2021, available at *https://www.deftspacelab.com/.*

3   Adrian Dingle, ""The Flint Water Crisis: What's Really Going On?" American Chemical Society, 2016, available at: *https://www.acs.org/content/acs/en/education/resources/highschool/chemmatters/past-issues/2016-2017/december-2016/flint-water-crisis.html*; Merritt Kennedy, "Lead-Laced Water in Flint: A Step-By-Step Look at the Makings of a Crisis," *NPR,* April 20, 2019, available at: *https://www.npr.org/sections/thetwo-way/2016/04/20/465545378/lead-laced-water-in-flint-a-step-by-step-look-at-the-makings-of-a-crisis.*

4   Merritt Kennedy, "Lead-Laced Water in Flint: A Step-By-Step Look at the Makings of a Crisis," *NPR,* April 20, 2019, available at: *https://www.npr.org/sections/thetwo-way/2016/04/20/465545378/lead-laced-water-in-flint-a-step-by-step-look-at-the-makings-of-a-crisis.*

5   Jacey Fortin, "Michigan Will No Longer Provide Free Bottled Water to Flint," *The New York Times*, April 8, 2018, available at: *https://www.nytimes.com/2018/04/08/us/flint-water-bottles.html,*

6   Nathalie Baptiste, "Officials Say Flint's Water Is Safe. Residents Say It's Not. Scientists Say It's Complicated." *Mother Jones*, April 16, 2018, available at: *https://www.motherjones.com/environment/2018/04/officials-say-flints-water-is-safe-residents-say-its-not-scientists-say-its-complicated/*

7   City of Flint, "Flint Water—Frequently Asked Questions," n.d., available at: *https://www.cityofflint.com/flint-water-faq/.*

8   A point entertainingly made in A. Weisman, *The World Without Us* (New York, NY: Picador, 2007).

9   H. Blanco, M. Alberti, R. Olshansky, S. Chang, S. M. Wheeler, H. Randolph and J. B. London, "Shaken, Shrinking, Hot, Impoverished and Informal: Emerging Research Agendas in Planning," *Progress in Planning* 72, no. 4 (2009): 195–250.

10   R. Fox, and M. Axel-Lute, *To Be Strong Again: Renewing the Promise in Smaller Industrial Cities* (Oakland, CA: PolicyLink, 2008).

11   Rolf Pendall, "Sprawl without Growth: The Upstate Paradox," in *Survey Series* (Washington, DC: The Brookings Institution Center on Urban and Metropolitan

Policy, 2003).

12   Office of the New York State Comptroller, "Population Trends in New York State's Cities," n.d., available at: *https://www.osc.state.ny.us/localgov/pubs/research/pop_trends.pdf*.

13   US Bureau of the Census, *American Community Survey 5-Year Estimates Detailed Tables*, Table ID: B01003 (Washington, DC: United States Bureau of the Census, 2017).

14   Syracuse-Onondaga Planning Agency, *Onondaga County Trends 2007 Summary* (Syracuse, NY: Syracuse-Onondaga Planning Agency, 2007).

15   Census Reporter, "Census Profile: Syracuse, NY Urbanized Area," n.d., available at: *https://censusreporter.org/profiles/40000US86302-syracuse-ny-urbanized-area/*

16   Syracuse-Onondaga Planning Agency, "Onondaga County Trends 2007 Summary" (Syracuse, NY: Syracuse-Onondaga Planning Agency, 2007).

17   *Census Reporter*, "Census Profile: Syracuse, NY Urbanized Area," n.d., available at: *https://censusreporter.org/profiles/40000US86302-syracuse-ny-urbanized-area/*.

18   Paul Mackun, Steven Wilson, Thomas Fischetti, and Justyna Goworowska, "Population Distribution and Change: 2000 to 2010 2010 Census Briefs," 2011, available at: *https://www.census.gov/prod/cen2010/briefs/c2010br-01.pdf*.

19   US Bureau of the Census, "1950 Census of Population: Number of Inhabitants," 35-27 (Washington, DC: U.S. Census Bureau, 1950).

20   US Bureau of the Census, "U.S. Census Bureau QuickFacts," n.d., available at: *https://www.census.gov/quickfacts/fact/table/youngstowncityohio/INC110216*

21   Office of the New York State Comptroller, "Population Trends in New York State's Cities," n.d., available at: *https://www.osc.state.ny.us/localgov/pubs/research/pop_trends.pdf*

22   US Bureau of the Census, "U.S. Census Bureau QuickFacts," n.d., available at: *https://www.census.gov/quickfacts/fact/table/buffalocitynewyork/PST045216*

23   US Bureau of the Census, "1950 Census of Population: Number of Inhabitants" (Washington, DC: U.S. Census Bureau, 1952), 7.

24   US Bureau of the Census, "U.S. Census Bureau QuickFacts," n.d., available at: *https://www.census.gov/quickfacts/fact/table/detroitcitymichigan/PST045216*

25   US Bureau of the Census, "U.S. Census Bureau QuickFacts," n.d., available at: *https://www.census.gov/quickfacts/fact/table/neworleanscitylouisiana/PST045216*.

26   The Data Center, "Facts for Features: Katrina Impact," n.d., available at: *https://www.datacenterresearch.org/data-resources/katrina/facts-for-impact/#:~:text=The%20population%20of%20New%20Orleans*.

27   Philipp Oswalt, ed., *Shrinking Cities: Volume 1* (New York, NY: Distributed Art Publishers, 2005).

28   Much, much more about shrinking cities in ibid..

29   Ying Long and Kang Wu, ""Shrinking Cities in a Rapidly Urbanizing

China,"" *Environment and Planning A* 48, no. 2 (2016): 220–22.

30	Henry Petroski, *The Road Taken: The History and Future of America's Infrastructure* (New York, NY: Bloomsbury, 2016).

31	David A. Graham, "How Did the Oroville Dam Crisis Get so Dire?" *The Atlantic*, February 13, 2017, available at: *https://www.theatlantic.com/national/archive/2017/02/how-did-the-oroville-dam-get-so-bad/516429/*; Ralph Vartabedian, "Oroville Dam Repair Costs Soar Past $1 Billion," *Los Angeles Times*, September 6, 2018, available at: *https://www.latimes.com/local/california/la-me-oroville-cost-20180905-story.html?fbclid=IwAR1Pf7Z6SkXIZhMmTsIQqKHQz0w6UmhDPb-9tiTslJb_xtP04EJYxck15Dk.*

32	Solvejg Wastvedt. *Remembering The I-35W Bridge Collapse 10 Years Later* [Radio broadcast transcript], *Minnesota Public Radio*, August 1, 2017, available at: *https://www.npr.org/2017/08/01/540755188/remembering-the-i-35w-bridge-collapse-10-years-later.*

33	John Surico, "The History behind New York City's Crumbling Subway," *Vice*, June 30, 2017, available at: *https://www.vice.com/en_us/article/vbmmym/the-history-behind-new-york-citys-crumbling-subway.*

34	Robinson Meyer, "A Timeline of Hurricane Maria's Effects on Puerto Rico," *The Atlantic*, October 4, 2017, available at: *https://www.theatlantic.com/science/archive/2017/10/what-happened-in-puerto-rico-a-timeline-of-hurricane-maria/541956/.*

35	Theodore J. Kury, "Why Doesn't the U.S. Bury Its Power Lines?" *The Conversation*, n.d, available at: *https://theconversation.com/why-doesnt-the-u-s-bury-its-power-lines-104829.*

36	"Rural Electrification Administration (REA) (1935) –- Living New Deal," *Living New Deal*, 2016, available at: *https://livingnewdeal.org/glossary/rural-electrification-administration-rea-1935/.*

37	U.S. Census Bureau, Census History Staff, "1950 Fast Facts – History – U.S. Census Bureau," n.d., available at: *https://www.census.gov/history/www/through_the_decades/fast_facts/1950_fast_facts.html.*

38	Jason Gauthier, "2010 Fast Facts – History – U.S. Census Bureau," *Census. gov*, 2010, available at: *https://www.census.gov/history/www/through_the_decades/fast_facts/2010_fast_facts.html.*

39	Dale Kasler, "Final Verdict on Oroville Dam: 'Long-Term Systemic Failure," *The Sacramento Bee*, January 5, 2018.

40	Eric Holthaus, "The Dam Truth: Climate Change Means More Lake Orovilles," *Grist*, February 16, 2017, *https://grist.org/climate-energy/the-dam-truth-climate-change-means-more-lake-orovilles/.*

41	Susan Dieterlen. *Immigrant Pastoral: Midwestern Landscapes and Mexican-American Neighborhoods.* Research in Landscape and Environment Design. Hardcover ed. (London, UK: Routledge, 2015).

42	Business Insider, "You Are Paying 300 Times More for Bottled Water than Tap Water," *Slate Magazine*, July 12, 2013, available at: *https://slate.com/business/2013/07/cost-of-bottled-water-vs-tap-water-the-difference-will-shock-you.html.*

43	Ibid.

44   Ron Fonger, "State Spending on Bottled Water in Flint Averaging $22,000 a Day," *Mlive*, March 12, 2018, available at: *https://www.mlive.com/news/flint/2018/03/states_average_monthly_bottled.html*.

45   Howard Perlman, "Per Capita Water Use. Water Questions and Answers; USGS Water Science School," U.S. Geological Survey, 2016, available at: *https://water.usgs.gov/edu/qa-home-percapita.html*.

46   "Ron Fonger, "State Spending on Bottled Water in Flint Averaging $22,000 a Day," *Mlive*, March 12, 2018, available at: *https://www.mlive.com/news/flint/2018/03/states_average_monthly_bottled.html*.

47   Economic Development Research Group, "Failure to Act: Closing the Infrastructure Investment Gap for America's Economic Future" (Reston, VA: American Society of Civil Engineers, 2016).

48   Richard Campbell, "CRS Report for Congress Weather-Related Power Outages and Electric System Resiliency," 2012, available at: *https://fas.org/sgp/crs/misc/R42696.pdf*.

49   For a fascinating look at how moisture demolishes vacant buildings, see Alan Weisman, *The World without Us* (New York, NY: Picador, 2007).

50   James Hinton, "Self-Help and Socialism the Squatters' Movement of 1946," *History Workshop* 25 (1988): 100–26.

51   Student work: Ely Margolis, "Grow Heathrow: Property Outlaws and the Implications of a Movements' Actions Amidst the Greater Context of British Land Rights Activism and Housing Policy," paper for City Wild Seminar, Spring 2013.

52   Student work: Nathan LaPierre, "Viable Freeganism?" project for City Wild Seminar, Spring 2014.

53   Steve Neavling, "Decades-Long Devil's Night Ended This Year with a Handful of Fires in Detroit—Motor City Muckraker," *Motor City Muckraker*, November 1, 2018, available at: *http://motorcitymuckraker.com/2018/11/01/decades-long-devils-night-ended-year-handful-fires-detroit/*.

54   Here's a really entertaining account of one example of this: Mark Binelli, "City of Strays: Detroit's Epidemic of 50,000 Abandoned Dogs," *Rolling Stone*, March 20, 2012 available at: *http://www.rollingstone.com/culture/news/city-of-strays-detroits-epidemic-of-50-000-wild-dogs-20120320*

55   Richard Florida, "How Vacancy Traumatizes Cities," *CityLab*, July 30, 2018, available at: *https://www.citylab.com/equity/2018/07/vacancy-americas-other-housing-crisis/565901/*.

56   Frank S. Alexander, "Land Banks and Land Banking" (Flint, MI: Center for Community Progress, 2015).

57   John Gallagher, "Detroit Blight Removal Campaign Ramps Up, Long Way to Go," *Detroit Free Press*, December 14, 2014, available at: *https://www.freep.com/story/money/business/michigan/2014/12/14/detroit-blight-duggan/20360959/*.

58   "The 2018 Annual Homeless Assessment Report (AHAR) to Congress," 2018, available at: *https://www.hudexchange.info/resources/documents/2018-AHAR-Part-1.pdf*.

59   Hillary Hoffower, "A Minimum-Wage Worker Needs 2.5 Full-Time Jobs to Afford a One-Bedroom Apartment in Most of the US," *Business Insider*, June 14, 2018, available at: *https://www.businessinsider.com/minimum-wage-worker-cant-afford-one-bedroom-rent-us-2018-6.*

60   Susan Dieterlen, *Neighborhood Microgrids: Replicability and Revitalization* (Syracuse, NY: Syracuse University Center of Excellence for Energy and Environmental Systems, 2016), 1–24.]

61   Galen D. Newman, Ann O'M. Bowman, Ryun Jung Lee, and Boah Kim, "A Current Inventory of Vacant Urban Land in America," *Journal of Urban Design* 21, no. 3 (2016): 302–19, available at: *https://www.tandfonline.com/doi/abs/10.1080/13574809.2016.1167589.*

62   Douglas S. Massey and Nancy A. Denton, *American Apartheid: Segregation and the Making of the Underclass*, Cambridge, MA: Harvard University Press, 1993. A great source to learn more about this history, although it is not just a historical phenomenon, but an ongoing one.

63   John L. Crompton, "The Impact of Parks on Property Values: A Review of the Empirical Evidence," *Journal of Leisure Research* 33, no. 1 (2001): 1–31.

64   Andrew Boslett, "Hedonic Analyses of Urban Green Spaces and Urban Tree Cover in Syracuse, NY," Master's thesis. State University of New York College of Environmental Science and Forestry, December 2011.

65   Terry Hartig, Richard Mitchell, Sjerp de Vries, and Howard Frumkin, "Nature and Health," *Annual Review of Public Health* 35 (2014): 207–28.

66   Two good lists can be found in: Rodney Matsuoka and William C. Sullivan, "Urban Nature: Human Psychological and Community Health," in *The Routledge Handbook of Urban Ecology*, edited by Ian Douglas, David Goode, Mike Houck and Rusong Wang (London, UK: Routledge, 2011), 408–23; Howard Frumkin, Gregory N. Bratman, Sara Jo Breslow, Bobby Cochran, Peter H. Jr. Kahn, Joshua Lawler, Phillip Levin, et al. "Nature Contact and Human Health: A Research Agenda," *Environmental Health Perspectives* 125, no. 7 (July 2017): 075001-1–075001-18.

67   Rachel Kaplan and Stephen Kaplan, *The Experience of Nature: A Psychological Perspective*. Second ed. (Ann Arbor, MI: Ulrich's Bookstore, 1995; Cambridge University Press, 1989).

68   Roger S. Ulrich, Robert F. Simons, Barbara D. Losito, Evelyn Fiorito, Mark A. Miles, and Michael Zelson, "Stress Recovery During Exposure to Natural and Urban Environments," *Journal of Environmental Psychology* 11 (1991): 201–30.

69   ""Howard Frumkin, Gregory N. Bratman, Sara Jo Breslow, Bobby Cochran, Peter H. Jr. Kahn, Joshua Lawler, Phillip Levin, et al. "Nature Contact and Human Health: A Research Agenda," *Environmental Health Perspectives* 125, no. 7 (July 2017): 075001-1–075001-18.

70   Hugh D. Clout, Blake Ehrlich, and Michael John Hebbert, "London - Evolution of the Modern City," *Encyclopedia Britannica*, last revised Nov 22, 2019; originally posted online July 20, 1998, available at: *https://www.britannica.com/place/London/Tudor-London*

71   Susan Toby Evans, "How Many People Lived in Tenochtitlan?" in *An-*

cient Mexico and Central America: Archaeology and Culture History (New York, NY; London, UK: Thames & Hudson, 2013, available at: *https://anth.la.psu.edu/documents/ evans_2013_tenochtitlan.*

72   For example: Meghan Hazer, Margaret K. Formica, Susan Dieterlen, and Christopher P. Morley, "The Relationship between Self-Reported Exposure to Greenspace and Human Stress in Baltimore, Md," in *Landscape and Urban Planning* 169 (2017): 47–56; Geoffrey H. Donovan, David T. Butry, Yvonne L. Michael, Jeffrey P. Prestemon, Andrew M. Liebhold, Demetrios Gatziolis, and Megan Y. Mao, "The Relationship between Trees and Human Health: Evidence from the Spread of the Emerald Ash Borer," *American Journal of Preventative Medicine* 44, no. 2 (2013): 139-45; Chun-Yen Chang, William E. Hammitt, Ping-Kun Chen, Lisa Machnik, and Wei-Chia Su, "Psychophysiological Responses and Restorative Values of Natural Environments in Taiwan," *Landscape and Urban Planning* 85 (2008): 79–84.

73   Roger S. Ulrich, "View through a Window May Influence Recovery from Surgery," *Science* 224 (1984): 420–21.

74   For one example, see Meghan Holtan, Susan Dieterlen, and William C. Sullivan, "Social Life under Cover: Tree Canopy and Social Capital in Baltimore, Maryland," *Environment and Behavior* 47, no. 5 (June 2015): 502–25.

75   For example: Charles C. Branas, Rose A Cheney, John M MacDonald, Vicky W Tam, Tara D Jackson, and Thomas R Ten Have, "A Difference-in-Differences Analysis of Health, Safety, and Greening Vacant Urban Space," *American Journal of Epidemiology* 174, no. 11 (November 2011): 1296–306; Geoffrey H. Donovan and Jeffrey P. Prestemon, "The Effect of Trees on Crime in Portland, Oregon," *Environment and Behavior* 44, no. 1 (2012): 3–30; and the older but frequently cited Frances E. Kuo and William C. Sullivan. "Environment and Crime in the Inner City: Does Vegetation Reduce Crime?" *Environment and Behavior* 33, no. 3 (May 2001): 343–67.

76   For example: Jolanda Maas, Marijke Van Winsum-Westra, Robert A. Verheij, Sjerp De Vries, and Peter P. Groenewegen; "Is Green Space in the Living Environment Associated with People's Feelings of Social Safety?" *Environment and Planning A* 41, no. 7 (January 2009): 1763–77.

77   Howard Frumkin, Gregory N. Bratman, Sara Jo Breslow, Bobby Cochran, Peter H. Jr. Kahn, Joshua Lawler, Phillip Levin, et al. "Nature Contact and Human Health: A Research Agenda." *Environmental Health Perspectives* 125, no. 7 (July 2017): 075001-1–075001-18.

78   Joan Iverson Nassauer, "Messy Ecosystems, Orderly Frames," *Landscape Journal* 4, no. 2 (1995): 161–70.

79   To learn more about the Broken Windows hypothesis and its use in policing, this book presents a very positive view: George L. Kelling and Catherine M. Coles, *Fixing Broken Windows: Restoring Order and Reducing Crime in Our Communities*, Touchstone ed. (New York, NY: Simon and Schuster, 1997).

80   For more about current criticisms of Broken Windows, see Sarah Childress, "The Problem with 'Broken Windows' Policing," *Frontline*, June 28, 2016, available at: *https://www.pbs.org/wgbh/frontline/article/the-problem-with-broken-windows-policing/.*

81   Karen A. Franck and Quentin Stevens, *Loose Space: Possibility and Diversity in Urban Life* (London, UK: Routledge, 2006).

82   Centers for Disease Control and Prevention, "Childhood Obesity Preven-tion," Centers for Disease Control and Prevention, 2019, available at: *https://www.cdc.gov/healthyschools/obesity/index.htm.*

83   American Heart Association News, "Limit Screen Time among Kids, Ex-perts Caution." American Heart Association. August 6, 2018, available at: *https://www.heart.org/en/news/2018/08/06/limit-screen-time-among-kids-experts-caution.*

84   Centers for Disease Control and Prevention, "Preventing Bullying," 2019, available at: *https://www.cdc.gov/violenceprevention/youthviolence/bullyingresearch/fast-fact.html.*

85   Richard Louv, *Last Child in the Woods: Saving Our Children from Nature-Deficit Disorder* (Chapel Hill, NC: Algonquin Books of Chapel Hill, 2006); Richard Louv, *Vitamin N: The Essential Guide to a Nature-Rich Life* (Chapel Hill, NC: Algon-quin Books of Chapel Hill, 2016).

86   Student work: Stephanie Nick, "Wildness and Urban Playspaces," paper for City Wild Seminar, Spring 2015.

87   Catherine Ward Thompson, "Places to Be Wild in Nature," in *Wildscapes,* edited by Anna Jorgensen and Richard Keenan (London, UK: Routledge, 2012), 49–64.

88   City of Berkeley, California, "Adventure Playground – City of Berkeley, CA," 2019, available at: *https://www.cityofberkeley.info/adventureplayground/.*

89   Hanna Rosin, "The Overprotected Kid," *The Atlantic,* April 2014, available at: *https://www.theatlantic.com/magazine/archive/2014/04/hey-parents-leave-those-kids-alone/358631/.*

90   Woodland Play Centre, "Woodland Adventures | Woodland Play Centre" n.d., available at: *https://www.woodlandplaycentre.co.uk/.*

91   For more about wilder play spaces and their issues, see Hanna Rosin, "The Overprotected Kid," *The Atlantic,* April 2014, available at: *https://www.theatlantic.com/magazine/archive/2014/04/hey-parents-leave-those-kids-alone/358631/.*

92   Julie Pincus and Nichole Christian, *Canvas Detroit* (Detroit, MI: Wayne State University Press, 2014).

93   "The Heidelberg Project," n.d., available at: *https://www.heidelberg.org/.*

94   Susan Dieterlen, "Pieces of 81," design project brief created for Studio: Next, LSA 470/670, SUNY ESF, Spring 2014.

95   "Urban Relic Design," n.d., available at: *https://urbanrelicdesign.myshopify.com/*

96   Avery Hartmans, "The 21 US Cities with the Highest Startup Growth," *Business Insider,* n.d., available at: *http://www.businessinsider.com/us-cities-startup-growth-ranked-2017-10#1-washington-washington-arlington-alexandria-21.*

97   Daniel Sanchez, "Ohio Dominates Top 10 Midwest Cities for Startups: Rankings Reports," *Techli,* August 24, 2017, available at: *https://techli.com/2017/08/midwest-cities-startups/.*

98   "Green Garage Detroit—Coworking Space for Triple Bottom Line Busi-nesses in the Heart of Midtown Detroit," n.d. Green Garage Detroit, available at: *http://www.greengaragedetroit.com/site/*; "NextEnergy," n.d., available at: *https://nextenergy.*

org/; "TechTown Detroit | Where Detroit Businesses Launch and Grow," TechTown Detroit, n.d. available at: *https://techtowndetroit.org/*; and a lot more about the atmosphere in Ben Austen, "The Post-Post-Apocalyptic Detroit," *The New York Times*, July 11, 2014, available at: *https://www.nytimes.com/2014/07/13/magazine/the-post-post-apocalyptic-detroit.html*.

99   Jane Jacobs. *The Death and Life of Great American Cities* (New York, NY: The Modern Library, 1961, 1993).

100   C. Ray Jeffery, *Crime Prevention through Environmental Design* (Beverly Hills, CA: SAGE Publications, 1971).

101   Initially Oscar Newman, *Defensible Space: Crime Prevention through Urban Design* (New York, NY: Macmillan, 1972), then substantially revised in Oscar Newman, *Creating Defensible Space* (Washington, DC: U.S. Department of Housing and Urban Development Office of Policy Development and Research, 1996).

102   Much more about CPTED at "International CPTED Association Home Page," 2019, available at: *http://www.cpted.net/*.

103   Unpublished study as reported in Frances E. Kuo and William C. Sullivan, "Environment and Crime in the Inner City: Does Vegetation Reduce Crime?" *Environment and Behavior* 33, no. 3 (May 2001): 343–67.

104   To learn more, see Rachel Kaplan, Stephen Kaplan, and Robert Ryan, *With People in Mind: Design and Management of Everyday Nature* (Washington, DC: Island Press, 1998); Oscar Newman, *Creating Defensible Space* (Washington, DC: U.S. Department of Housing and Urban Development Office of Policy Development and Research, 1996); Jane Jacobs, *The Death and Life of Great American Cities* (New York, NY: The Modern Library, 1961, 1993).

105   For example: Austin Troy, J. Morgan Grove, and Jarlath O'Neil-Dunne, "The Relationship between Tree Canopy and Crime Rates across an Urban-Rural Gradient in the Greater Baltimore Regio," *Landscape and Urban Planning* 106 (2012): 262–70; Geoffrey H. Donovan and Jeffrey P. Prestemon, "The Effect of Trees on Crime in Portland, Oregon," *Environment and Behavior* 44, no. 1 (2012): 3–30.

106   Austin Troy, J. Morgan Grove, and Jarlath O'Neil-Dunne, "The Relationship between Tree Canopy and Crime Rates across an Urban-Rural Gradient in the Greater Baltimore Region," *Landscape and Urban Planning* 106 (2012): 262–70.

107   David Templeton, "Climate Change Is Making Poison Ivy Grow Bigger and Badder," *Pittsburgh Post-Gazette*, July 22, 2013, available at: *https://www.post-gazette.com/news/health/2013/07/22/Climate-change-is-making-poison-ivy-grow-bigger-and-badder/stories/201307220149*.

108   Michelle Nijhuis. "How Climate Change Is Helping Invasive Species Take Over," *Smithsonian Magazine*, December 2013, available at: *https://www.smithsonianmag.com/science-nature/how-climate-change-is-helping-invasive-species-take-over-180947630/*.

109   More information about green infrastructure at "What Is Green Infrastructure?" American Rivers, 2016, available at: *https://www.americanrivers.org/threats-solutions/clean-water/green-infrastructure/what-is-green-infrastructure/*.

110   This kind of centrally located older factories and their landscape legacy is

depicted in the Established Communities landscape type in my book: Susan Dieterlen, *Immigrant Pastoral: Midwestern Landscapes and Mexican-American Neighborhoods*. Research in Landscape and Environment Design, Hardcover ed. (London, UK: Routledge, 2015).

111   Darryl Fears, "Here's Why There Are So Many Coyotes and Why They Are Spreading So Fast," *The Washington Post*, May 22, 2018, available at: *https://www.washingtonpost.com/news/animalia/wp/2018/05/22/heres-why-there-are-so-many-coyotes-and-why-they-are-spreading-so-fast/?utm_term=.6fbd93185a2c*.

112   Tons more information about your city neighbor, the coyote, at "Urban Coyotes," Urban Coyote Initiative, December 12, 2017, available at: *https://urbancoyoteinitiative.com/*.

113   Colin Barras, "The Chernobyl Exclusion Zone Is Arguably a Nature Reserve," *BBC*, April 21, 2016, available at: *http://www.bbc.com/earth/story/20160421-the-chernobyl-exclusion-zone-is-arguably-a-nature-reserve*.

114   David J. Nowak and Eric J. Greenfield, "Tree and Impervious Cover Change in U.S. Cities," *Urban Forestry and Urban Greening* 11 (2012): 21–30.

115   H. Brian Underwood, ""Urban Greening and Impact on Wildlife Habitat," guest lecture for Susan Dieterlen's City Wild Seminar: Abandonment, Invasives, and Losing Control course, March 20, 2015, Syracuse, New York, State University of New York College of Environmental Science and Forestry, 2015.

116   Mark Binelli, "City of Strays: Detroit's Epidemic of 50,000 Abandoned Dogs," *Rolling Stone*, March 20, 2012, available at *http://www.rollingstone.com/culture/news/city-of-strays-detroits-epidemic-of-50-000-wild-dogs-20120320*.

117   Amanda Kolson Hurley, "We're Here. We're Deer. Get Used to It," *CityLab*, August 7, 2017, available at: *https://www.citylab.com/environment/2017/08/the-deer-in-your-yard-are-here-to-stay/535938/*.

118   Rachel E. Gross, "The Moral Cost of Cats," *Smithsonian*, 2016, available at: *https://www.smithsonianmag.com/science-nature/moral-cost-of-cats-180960505/*.

119   Geoffrey H. Donovan, David T. Butry, Yvonne L. Michael, Jeffrey P. Prestemon, Andrew M. Liebhold, Demetrios Gatziolis, and Megan Y. Mao, "The Relationship between Trees and Human Health: Evidence from the Spread of the Emerald Ash Borer," *American Journal of Preventative Medicine* 44, no. 2 (2013): 139–45. For more information about Emerald Ash Borer, its impacts, and control measures, see: "Emerald Ash Borer," available at: *http://www.emeraldashborer.info/index.php*.

120   For more information about control methods for different invasive species, see "*Invasive.org*," available at: *https://www.invasive.org/index.cfm*.

121   Peter Del Tredici, "The Flora of the Future," in *Projective Ecologies*, edited by C. Reed and N.M. Lister (New York, NY: Actar Press and Harvard Graduate School of Design, 2014), 198–217.

122   A staggering wealth of information about ecosystem services can be found here: "Millennium Ecosystem Assessment," 2019, available at: *https://www.millenniumassessment.org/en/index.html*.

123   Howard Frumkin, Gregory N. Bratman, Sara Jo Breslow, Bobby Cochran, Peter H. Jr. Kahn, Joshua Lawler, Phillip Levin et al., "Nature Contact and Human

Health: A Research Agenda," *Environmental Health Perspectives* 125, no. 7 (July 2017): 075001-1-075001-18.

124   "About Extreme Heat," Centers for Disease Control and Prevention, 2019, available at: *https://www.cdc.gov/disasters/extremeheat/heat_guide.html.*

125   This idea, of cities arriving in a hot future before the rest of the world does, is unpacked in Brian Stone Jr., *The City and the Coming Climate: Climate Change in the Places We Live* (Cambridge, UK: Cambridge University Press, 2012).

126   Kirsten Schwarz, Michail Fragkias, Christopher G. Boone, Weiqi Zhou, Melissa McHale, J. Morgan Grove, Jarlath O'Neil-Dunne et al., "Trees Grow on Money: Urban Tree Canopy and Environmental Justice," *PLoS ONE* 10, no. 4 (April 2015), doi:10.1371/journal.pone.0122051.

127   "U.S. Water Supply and Distribution Factsheet," Center for Sustainable Systems, University of Michigan, 2018, available at: *http://css.umich.edu/factsheets/us-water-supply-and-distribution-factsheet.*

128   Northern Institute of Applied Climate Science, "Carbon Sequestration – Forests Absorb Carbon Dioxide – Northern Institute of Applied Climate Science (NI-ACS) – Northern Research Station – USDA Forest Service," US Forest Service, 2010, available at: *https://www.nrs.fs.fed.us/niacs/forests/carbonsequestration/.*

129   "Resources for Writers | Gateway to Health Communication," Centers for Disease Control and Prevention, August 5, 2020, available at: *https://www.cdc.gov/ healthcommunication/ToolsTemplates/EntertainmentEd/Tips/Allergies.html.*

130   "Time to Rethink the Inner-City Asthma Epidemic? – 01/20/2015," Johns Hopkins Medicine, n.d., available at: *https://www.hopkinsmedicine.org/news/media/ releases/time_to_rethink_the_inner_city_asthma_epidemic.*

131   Diane E. Pataki, Margaret M. Carreiro, Jennifer Cherrier, Nancy E. Grulke, Viniece Jennings, Stephanie Pincetl, Richard V. Pouyat, Thomas H. Whitlow, and Wayne C. Zipperer, "Coupling Biogeochemical Cycles in Urban Environments: Ecosystem Services, Green Solutions and Misconceptions," *Frontiers in Ecology and the Environment* 9, no. 1 (2011): 27–36.

132   Union of Concerned Scientists, "Climate Change and Your Health: Rising Temperatures, Worsening Air Pollution," (Cambridge, MA: Union of Concerned Scientists, 2011).

133   Ibid.

134   Brian Stone, Jr., *The City and the Coming Climate: Climate Change in the Places We Live* (Cambridge, UK: Cambridge University Press, 2012).

135   David J. Nowak, "The Effects of Urban Trees on Air Quality," U.S. Forest Service, 2002, available at: *https://www.nrs.fs.fed.us/units/urban/local-resources/downloads/Tree_Air_Qual.pdf.*

136   Gerardo Ceballos, Paul R. Ehrlich, and Rodolfo Dirzo, "Biological Annihilation Via the Ongoing Sixth Mass Extinction Signaled by Vertebrate Population Losses and Declines," *Proceedings of the National Academy of Sciences* 114 (2017-07-25 00:00:00 2017): E6089–E96.

137   Damian Carrington, "Earth's Sixth Mass Extinction Event under Way, Scientists Warn," *The Guardian*, February 14, 2018, available at: *https://www.theguardian.*

com/environment/2017/jul/10/earths-sixth-mass-extinction-event-already-underway-scientists-warn.

138   Viviane Richter, "The Big Five Extinctions," *Cosmos Magazine*, July 6, 2015, available at: *https://cosmosmagazine.com/palaeontology/big-five-extinctions*.

139   Lena H. Sun, "Diseases Spread by Ticks, Mosquitoes and Fleas More than Tripled in the U.S. Since 2004," *The Washington Post*, May 1, 2018, available at: *https://www.washingtonpost.com/news/to-your-health/wp/2018/05/01/diseases-spread-by-ticks-mosquitoes-and-fleas-more-than-tripled-in-the-u-s/?utm_term=.4cdcb63d712e*.

140   "Climate Change Could Push Tropical Diseases to Alaska, according to a New Study," *Grist*. March 28, 2019, available at: *https://grist.org/article/climate-change-could-push-tropical-diseases-to-alaska-according-to-a-new-study/*.

141   Mark J. Statham, Benjamin N. Sacks, Keith B. Aubry, John D. Perrine, and Samantha M. Wisely, "The Origin of Recently Established Red Fox Populations in the United States: Translocations or Natural Range Expansions?" *Journal of Mammalogy* 93, no. 1 (2012): 52–65, available at: *https://www.fs.usda.gov/treesearch/pubs/40806*.

142   Mary Anna Evans, "The Sewage Crisis in America," *The Atlantic*, September 17, 2015, available at: *https://www.theatlantic.com/technology/archive/2015/09/americas-sewage-crisis-public-health/405541/*.

143   "Save the Rain," n.d., available at: *http://savetherain.us/*.

144   St. Michael's Hospital, "Inner-City Neighborhood May Affect Risk of Developing of Heart Disease, Research Finds," *ScienceDaily*, August 31, 2015, available at: *https://www.sciencedaily.com/releases/2015/08/150831101510.htm*.

145   There's a wealth, so to speak, of information available on this topic, but this is a concise place to start, if this idea is new to you: Rakesh Kochhar and Anthony Cilluffo, "Key Findings on the Rise in Income Inequality within America's Racial and Ethnic Groups," Pew Research Center, July 12, 2018, available at: *https://www.pewresearch.org/fact-tank/2018/07/12/key-findings-on-the-rise-in-income-inequality-within-americas-racial-and-ethnic-groups/*.

146   Susan Dieterlen, *Immigrant Pastoral: Midwestern Landscapes and Mexican-American Neighborhoods*. Research in Landscape and Environment Design, Hardcover ed. (London, UK: Routledge, 2015).

147   Mark Weiner, "Miner: Syracuse Water Main Breaks Decline 18 Percent," *Syracuse Post Standard*, March 17, 2017, available at: *https://www.syracuse.com/politics/2017/03/miner_syracuse_water_main_breaks_down_18_percent_but_city_needs_federal_aid.html*.

148   Margery Austin Turner, Robert Santos, Diane K. Levy, Douglas A. Wissoker, Claudia Aranda, and Rob Pitingolo, "Housing Discrimination against Racial and Ethnic Minorities 2012: Full Report," Urban Institute, June 4, 2016, available at: *https://www.urban.org/research/publication/housing-discrimination-against-racial-and-ethnic-minorities-2012-full-report*; Keeanga-Yamahtta Taylor, "Housing Market Racism Persists despite 'Fair Housing' Laws," *The Guardian*, January 24, 2019, available at: *https://www.theguardian.com/commentisfree/2019/jan/24/housing-market-racism-persists-despite-fair-housing-laws*.

149   All GHG emission numbers from "U.S. Emissions | Center for Climate and

Energy Solutions," Center for Climate and Energy Solutions, October 31, 2017, available at: *https://www.c2es.org/content/u-s-emissions/*.

150   "NOAA: 2017 Was 3rd Warmest Year on Record for the Globe," National Oceanic and Atmospheric Administration, January 18, 2018, available at: *http://www.noaa.gov/news/noaa-2017-was-3rd-warmest-year-on-record-for-globe*.

151   "Global Surface Temperature," Climate Change: Vital Signs of the Planet. National Aeronautics and Space Administration, February 19, 2019, available at: *https://climate.nasa.gov/vital-signs/global-temperature/*.

152   Adam Smith, "Billion-Dollar Weather and Climate Disasters," Billion-Dollar Weather and Climate Disasters: Time Series, National Centers for Environmental Information (NCEI), National Oceanic and Atmospheric Administration, 2020, available at: *https://www.ncdc.noaa.gov/billions/time-series*.

153   US Environmental Protection Agency OA (henceforth US EPA, OA), "Climate Change Impacts by Region," US Environmental Protection Agency, n.d., available at: https://19january2017snapshot.epa.gov/climate-impacts/climate-change-impacts-region_.html.

154   "National Climate Assessment," 2000, available at: *https://nca2014.globalchange.gov/report*.

155   US EPA, OA, "Climate Impacts in the Midwest," US Environmental Protection Agency, 2000, available at: https://19january2017snapshot.epa.gov/climate-impacts/climate-impacts-midwest_.html.]

156   Ibid.

157   US EPA, OA, "Climate Impacts in the Southeast," US Environmental Protection Agency, n.d., available at: https://19january2017snapshot.epa.gov/climate-impacts/climate-impacts-southeast_.html.

158   US EPA, OA, "Climate Impacts in the Great Plains," US Environmental Protection Agency, 2000, available at: https://19january2017snapshot.epa.gov/climate-impacts/climate-impacts-great-plains_.html.

159   US EPA, OA, "Climate Impacts in the Southwest," US Environmental Protection Agency, 2013, available at: https://19january2017snapshot.epa.gov/climate-impacts/climate-impacts-southwest_.html.

160   US EPA, OA, "Climate Impacts in the Northwest," US Environmental Protection Agency, 2015, available at: https://19january2017snapshot.epa.gov/climate-impacts/climate-impacts-northwest_.html.

161   US EPA, OA, "Climate Impacts in the U.S. Islands," US Environmental Protection Agency, n.d., Available at: https://19january2017snapshot.epa.gov/climate-impacts/climate-impacts-us-islands_.html.

162   US EPA, OA, "Climate Impacts on Coastal Areas," US Environmental Protection Agency, 2000, available at: https://19january2017snapshot.epa.gov/climate-impacts/climate-impacts-coastal-areas_.html.

163   "National Climate Assessment," 2014, available at: *https://nca2014.globalchange.gov/highlights/regions/coasts*.

164   2017 data from "U.S. Emissions," Center for Climate and Energy Solutions,

October 31, 2017, available at: *https://www.c2es.org/content/u-s-emissions/*.

165   Ibid.

166   E. Grizard, "The Dangers of Combustion-Based Power," *Better Elections: The Bloom Energy Blog*, 2019 available at: *https://www.bloomenergy.com/blog/dangers-combustion-based-power* 2021.

167   David Nowak, Jack Stevens, Susan Sisinni, and Christopher Luley, "Effects of Urban Tree Management and Species Selection on Atmospheric Carbon Dioxide," *Journal of Arboriculture* 28, no. 3 (2002), available at: *https://www.nrs.fs.fed.us/pubs/jrnl/2002/ne_2002_nowak_004.pdf*.

168   List drawn primarily from: H. Safford, E. Larry, E.G. McPherson, David J Nowak, and L.M. Westphal, "Urban Forests and Climate Change," US Department of Agriculture, Forest Service, 2013; Brian Stone Jr., *The City and the Coming Climate: Climate Change in the Places We Live* (Cambridge, UK: Cambridge University Press, 2012).

169   "CDC – Climate Change and Public Health – Health Effects – Temperature Extremes," Centers for Disease Control and Prevention, 2019, available at: *https://www.cdc.gov/climateandhealth/effects/temperature_extremes.htm*.

170   Emma Foehringer Merchant, "Puerto Rico Energy Commission Lays out Rules for a Future Microgrid Landscape," Green Tech Media, January 8, 2018,, available at: *https://www.greentechmedia.com/articles/read/puerto-rico-energy-commission-island-microgrid#gs.IDTbz6w*.

171   Larry Dzierzak and Louis Greenemeier, "As Electricity Returns to Puerto Rico, Its People Want More Power," *Scientific American*, July 10, 2018,, available at: *https://www.scientificamerican.com/article/as-electricity-returns-to-puerto-rico-its-people-want-more-power/*.

172   Emma Foehringer Merchant, "Department of Energy Issues Recommendations for Post-Maria Puerto Rico," Green Tech Media, June 20, 2018, a vailable at: *https://www.greentechmedia.com/articles/read/department-of-energy-issues-recommendations-for-post-maria-puerto-rico#gs.G5AUoKo*.

173   Ibid.

174   Larry Dzierzak and Louis Greenemeier, "As Electricity Returns to Puerto Rico, Its People Want More Power," *Scientific American*, July 10, 2018, available at: *https://www.scientificamerican.com/article/as-electricity-returns-to-puerto-rico-its-people-want-more-power/*.

175   Emma Foehringer Merchant, "Department of Energy Issues Recommendations for Post-Maria Puerto Rico," Green Tech Media, June 20, 2018, available at: *https://www.greentechmedia.com/articles/read/department-of-energy-issues-recommendations-for-post-maria-puerto-rico#gs.G5AUoKo*."

176   Larry Dzierzak and Louis Greenemeier, "As Electricity Returns to Puerto Rico, Its People Want More Power," *Scientific American*, July 10, 2018, available at: *https://www.scientificamerican.com/article/as-electricity-returns-to-puerto-rico-its-people-want-more-power/*.

177   US EPA, OA, "Sources of Greenhouse Gas Emissions," US Environmental Protection Agency, n.d., available at: https://*19january2017snapshot.epa.gov/ghgemis-*

sions/sources-greenhouse-gas-emissions_.html#commercial-and-residential.

178   Cventure LLC, Cathy Pasion, Christianah Oyenuga, and Kate Gouin, "City of New York Inventory of New York City's Greenhouse Gas Emissions in 2015," Mayor's Office of Sustainability, New York, April 2017, available at: *https://www1. nyc.gov/assets/dcas/downloads/pdf/energy/reportsandpublication/NYC_GHG_Inventory_2015_FINAL.pdf.*

179   US EPA, OA, "Sources of Greenhouse Gas Emissions," US Environmental Protection Agency, n.d., available at: https://19january2017snapshot.epa.gov/ghgemissions/sources-greenhouse-gas-emissions_.html#commercial-and-residential.

180   Obama Administration, "FACT SHEET: U.S. Reports Its 2025 Emissions Target to the UNFCCC," *Whitehouse.gov*, March 31, 2015, available at: *https:// obamawhitehouse.archives.gov/the-press-office/2015/03/31/fact-sheet-us-reports-its-2025-emissions-target-unfccc*

181   "Weatherize," *Energy.gov.*, n.d., available at: *https://www.energy.gov/public-services/homes/home-weatherization.*

182   Gerald T. Gardner and Paul C. Stern, "The Short List: The Most Effective Actions U.S. Households Can Take to Curb Climate Change," *Environment: Science and Policy for Sustainable Development*, September/October 2008, available at: *http://www. teachgreenpsych.com/wp-content/uploads/2018/01/Gardner-Stern-2008-The-short-list-The-most-effective-actions-U.S.-households-can-take-to-curb-climate-change.pdf.*

183   Lily Rothman, "How American Inequality in the Gilded Age Compares to Today," *Time*, February 5, 2018, available at: *http://time.com/5122375/american-inequality-gilded-age/.*

184   Drew DeSilver, "U.S. Income Inequality, on Rise for Decades, Is Now Highest since 1928," Pew Research Center, December 5, 2013, available at: *https://www.pewresearch.org/fact-tank/2013/12/05/u-s-income-inequality-on-rise-for-decades-is-now-highest-since-1928/.*

185   Rakesh Kochhar and Anthony Cilluffo, "Key Findings on the Rise in Income Inequality within America's Racial and Ethnic Groups," Pew Research Center, July 12, 2018, available at: https://www.pewresearch.org/fact-tank/2018/07/12/key-findings-on-the-rise-in-income-inequality-within-americas-racial-and-ethnic-groups/.

186   Gillian B. White, "Black-White Wealth Gap in Cities," The Atlantic, November 26, 2016, available at: https://www.theatlantic.com/business/archive/2016/11/racial-wealth-gap-dc/508631/.

187   Rakesh Kochhar and Anthony Cilluffo, "Key Findings on the Rise in Income Inequality within America's Racial and Ethnic Groups," Pew Research Center, July 12, 2018, available at: https://www.pewresearch.org/fact-tank/2018/07/12/key-findings-on-the-rise-in-income-inequality-within-americas-racial-and-ethnic-groups/.

188   Robert Reich and Heather McCulloch, "Op-Ed: Wealth, Not Just Wages, Is the Way to Measure Women's Equality," Los Angeles Times, August 25, 2017, available at: https://www.latimes.com/opinion/op-ed/la-oe-reich-mcculloch-womens-wealth-gap-20170825-story.html.

189   Ta Nehisi Coates's "Case for Reparations" lays out this argument better than I can, about the continuing financial cost of slavery and sharecropping to black

families. Ta-Nehisi Coates, "The Case for Reparations," *The Atlantic*, June 2014, *https://www.theatlantic.com/magazine/archive/2014/06/the-case-for-reparations/361631/.*

190 Much more about redlining and its impact on our cities in Douglas S. Massey and Nancy A. Denton, *American Apartheid: Segregation and the Making of the Underclass* (Cambridge, MA: Harvard University Press, 1993).

191 Alexis C. Madrigal, "The Racist Housing Policy That Made Your Neighborhood," *The Atlantic*, May 22, 2014, available at: *https://www.theatlantic.com/business/archive/2014/05/the-racist-housing-policy-that-made-your-neighborhood/371439/.*

192 Howard Frumkin, Gregory N. Bratman, Sara Jo Breslow, Bobby Cochran, Peter H. Jr. Kahn, Joshua Lawler, Phillip Levin et al., "Nature Contact and Human Health: A Research Agenda," *Environmental Health Perspectives* 125, no. 7 (July 2017): 075001-1–075001-18.

193 Kirsten Schwarz, Michail Fragkias, Christopher G. Boone, Weiqi Zhou, Melissa McHale, J. Morgan Grove, Jarlath O'Neil-Dunne et al., "Trees Grow on Money: Urban Tree Canopy and Environmental Justice," *PLoS ONE* 10, no. 4 (April 2015), doi:10.1371/journal.pone.0122051.

194 Douglas S. Massey and Nancy A. Denton, *American Apartheid: Segregation and the Making of the Underclass* (Cambridge, MA: Harvard University Press, 1993); Joseph P. Williams, "Segregation's Legacy," *US News & World Report*, April 20, 2018, available at: *https://www.usnews.com/news/the-report/articles/2018-04-20/us-is-still-segregated-even-after-fair-housing-act*; Aaron Williams and Armand Emamdjomeh, "Analysis | America Is More Diverse than Ever — but Still Segregated," *The Washington Post*, May 10, 2018, available at: *https://www.washingtonpost.com/graphics/2018/national/segregation-us-cities/?utm_term=.11907d3365ed.*

195 National Fair Housing Alliance, *The Case for Fair Housing: 2017 Fair Housing Trends Report* (Washington, DC, NFHA. 2017), available at: *https://nationalfairhousing.org/wp-content/uploads/2017/04/EXECUTIVE-SUMMARY-ONLY.pdf.*

196 US Bureau of the Census, "Figure 1: Real Median Household Income by Race and Hispanic Origin" (Washington, DC: US Bureau of the Census. 2018), available at: *https://www.census.gov/content/dam/Census/library/visualizations/2018/demo/p60-263/figure1.pdf.*

197 Susan Dieterlen, *Immigrant Pastoral: Midwestern Landscapes and Mexican-American Neighborhoods.* Research in Landscape and Environment Design, Hardcover ed. (London, UK: Routledge, 2015).

198 Ibid.

199 Ibid.

200 For more about the history of parks and other public spaces as arenas for social control and struggle, see Dorceta E. Taylor, *The Environment and the People in American Cities, 1600s-1900s: Disorder, Inequality, and Social Change* (Durham N.C.: Duke University Press, 2009); Don Mitchell, *The Right to the City: Social Justice and the Fight for Public Space* (New York, NY: Guilford Press, 2003).

201 More about FLO here: Olmsted Parks Administrator, "Frederick Law Olmsted Sr. - National Association for Olmsted Parks," *Olmsted.org*, 2016, available at: *http://www.olmsted.org/the-olmsted-legacy/frederick-law-olmsted-sr.*

202   More about Olmsted's park system for Buffalo: "Buffalo Olmsted Park System Map | 6 Parks, 7 Parkways, 8 Circle,." Buffalo Olmsted Parks, n.d., Available at: *https://www.bfloparks.org/mapandguide/*. More about Olmsted's park system for Louisville: "Our Parks," Olmsted Parks Conservancy, n.d., available at: *https://www.olmstedparks.org/our-parks/*. More about Kessler's parks and boulevards in Indy: "George Edward Kessler and the Park System--Indianapolis: A Discover Our Shared Heritage Travel Itinerary," National Park Service. n.d., available at: *https://www.nps.gov/nr/travel/indianapolis/kessleressay.htm*.

203   One take on this, from a legal point of view: Ann Eisenberg, "Rural Blight," Rochester, New York, July 30, 2018, available at: *https://papers.ssrn.com/sol3/papers.cfm?abstract_id=3222719*.

204   Meghan Holtan, Susan Dieterlen, and William C. Sullivan, "Social Life under Cover: Tree Canopy and Social Capital in Baltimore, Maryland," *Environment and Behavior* 47, no. 5 (June 2015): 502–25; Meghan Hazer, Margaret K. Formica, Susan Dieterlen, and Christopher P. Morley, "The Relationship between Self-Reported Exposure to Greenspace and Human Stress in Baltimore, Md," *Landscape and Urban Planning* 169 (2017): 47–56.

205   If you missed this phenomenon or want a refresher: Richard Florida, *The Rise of the Creative Class* (New York, NY: Basic Books, Inc., 2002).

206   "The Deadliest Types of Weather in 2017," The Weather Channel, n.d., available at: *https://weather.com/news/news/2018-05-02-noaa-weather-deaths-united-states-2017#:~:text=Extreme%20heat%20was%20responsible%20for*.

207   Alissa Walker, "Our Cities Are Getting Hotter—and It's Killing People," *Curbed*, July 6, 2018, available at: *https://www.curbed.com/2018/7/6/17539904/heat-wave-extreme-heat-cities-deadly*.

208   "Venomous Snakes," Centers for Disease Control and Prevention, February 21, 2020, available at: *https://www.cdc.gov/niosh/topics/snakes/default.html*.

209   US National Weather Service, "How Dangerous Is Lightning?" *Weather.gov*, 2018, available at: *https://www.weather.gov/safety/lightning-odds*.

210   "FastStats - Leading Causes of Death," Centers for Disease Control and Prevention, 2019, available at: *https://www.cdc.gov/nchs/fastats/leading-causes-of-death.htm*.

211   "Heart Disease Facts & Statistics," Centers for Disease Control and Prevention, September 8, 2020, available at: *https://www.cdc.gov/heartdisease/facts.htm*.

212   "Lead in Residential Soils: Sources, Testing, and Reducing Exposure," Penn State Extension, August 25, 2019, available at: *https://extension.psu.edu/lead-in-residential-soils-sources-testing-and-reducing-exposure*.

213   David Markowitz and Gerald Rosner, "Why It Took Decades of Blaming Parents before We Banned Lead Paint," *The Atlantic*, April 22, 2013, available at: *https://www.theatlantic.com/health/archive/2013/04/why-it-took-decades-of-blaming-parents-before-we-banned-lead-paint/275169/*.

214   American College of Allergy, Asthma and Immunology (ACAAI), "Mouse Infestations Cause More Asthma Symptoms Than Cockroach Exposure," *ScienceDaily*, November 7, 2014, available at: *https://www.sciencedaily.com/releas-*

es/2014/11/141107091226.htm.

215   John O. Whitaker, *National Audubon Society Field Guide to North American Mammals*, second ed.(New York, NY: Alfred A. Knopf, 1996).

216   Eugenia C South, Michelle C Kondo, Rose A Cheney, and Charles C Branas, "Neighborhood Blight, Stress, and Health: A Walking Trial of Urban Greening and Ambulatory Heart Rate," *American Journal of Public Health* 105, no. 5 (May 2015): 909–13.

217   "Regional Gun Violence Research Consortium," Rockefeller Institute of Government, n.d., available at: *http://rockinst.org/gun-violence/*.

218   An excellent example is here: Camiella Williams, "Communities Traumatized by Gun Violence Need Mental Health Care, Not More Cops," *NBC News*, February 9, 2018, available at: *https://www.nbcnews.com/think/opinion/communities-traumatized-gun-violence-need-mental-health-care-not-more-ncna846081.*

219   Such as Marc Gelkopf, Ilanit Hasson-Ohayon, Menashe Bikman, and Shlomo Kravetz, "Nature Adventure Rehabilitation for Combat-Related Posttraumatic Chronic Stress Disorder: A Randomized Control Trial," *Psychiatry Research* 209, no. 3 (October 30, 2013): 485–93.

220   Margaret K. Formica, Personal telephone interview, S. Dieterlen, June 8, 2018.

221   Anne Gunderson, "Breaking the Cycle of Inner City Violence with PTSD Care," *Chicago Policy Review* (June 2, 2017).

222   Sandra D. Lane, Robert A. Rubinstein, Dessa Bergen-Cico, Timothy Jennings-Bey, Linda Stone Fish, David A. Larsen, Mindy Thompson Fullilove et al., "Neighborhood Trauma Due to Violence: A Multilevel Analysis," *Journal of Health Care for the Poor and Underserved* 28, no. 1 (February 2017): 446–62.

223   Ibid.

224   Margaret K. Formica, Personal telephone interview, S. Dieterlen, June 8, 2018.

225   For more information on this, take a look at "Climate Change," American Public Health Association, 2018, available at: *https://www.apha.org/topics-and-issues/climate-change.*

226   Much more information about land banks is available from the Center for Community Progress, a national organization for land banks: "Center for Community Progress: Vacant Spaces into Vibrant Places," Center for Community Progress," n.d., available at: *http://www.communityprogress.net.*

227   One approach to evaluating parcel suitability for redevelopment via land bank or otherwise: Cleveland Land Lab at the Cleveland Urban Design Collaborative at Kent State University, *Re-Imagining a More Sustainable Cleveland: Citywide Strategies for Reuse of Vacant Land*, Cleveland, OH: Cleveland Planning Commission, December 19, 2008, available at: *http://www.clevelandnp.org/reimagining-cleveland/*.

228   Ian L. McHarg, *Design with Nature* (Garden City, NY: Natural History Press, 1969).

229   More information about McHarg and his legacy at "Ian L. McHarg," The

McHarg Center, October 9, 2017, available at: *https://mcharg.upenn.edu/ian-l-mcharg*.

230   Dolores Hayden, *The Power of Place: Urban Landscapes as Public History* (Cambridge, MA: Massachusetts Institute of Technology Press, 1995).

231   Kate Lachowycz and Andy P. Jones, "Does Walking Explain Associations between Access to Greenspace And lower Mortality?" *Social Science & Medicine* 107 (April 1, 2014): 9–17.

Jolanda Maas, Robert A. Verheij, Peter P. Groenewegen, Sjerp de Vries, and Peter Spre-euwenberg, "Green Space, Urbanity, and Health: How Strong Is the Relation?" *Journal of Epidemiology and Community Health* 60, no. 7 (2006): 587.

232   This section inspired by: Student work: Elysa Smigielski, "Shrinking Cities as the Next Healthy Cities: Utilizing Vacancy to Create a Walkable City," paper for City Wild Seminar, Spring 2014.

233   A wealth of information about walkability and why it's a good thing at "AmericaWalks | 20 Years of Making America a Great Place to Walk," *Americawalks. org.*, n.d., available at: *https://americawalks.org/*.

234   Such as Cleveland Land Lab at the Cleveland Urban Design Collaborative at Kent State University, *Re-Imagining a More Sustainable Cleveland: Citywide Strategies for Reuse of Vacant Land,* Cleveland, OH: Cleveland Planning Commission, December 19, 2008, available at: *http://www.clevelandnp.org/reimagining-cleveland/*.

INDEX

A

Abandoned buildings 15, 45, 47, 48, 49, 54, 82, 89, 106, 112, 126, 127, 159, 161, 164, 172, 185, 211, 227, 230, 243, 244, 245, 251, 262
African-American neighborhoods 31
African Americans 73, 86, 94, 187, 196, 200, 209, 210
Air conditioning 34, 46, 63, 138, 186, 191, 241, 272
Air quality 58, 67, 114, 136, 142, 143, 144, 145, 150, 165, 184, 225, 271
Allergies 143, 150, 187, 250, 251
American Society of Civil Engineers 25, 292
ASCE. *See* American Society of Civil Engineers
Anxiety 65, 66, 69
Architecture 12, 17, 188, 197, 198
Art 82, 83, 86, 87, 88, 89, 91
Asbestos 46, 183
Attention Restoration Theory 61

B

Benefit by neglect 159
Berlin 23
Britain 23, 47, 221, 232, 248
Broken Windows 73, 74, 99, 154, 156, 294
Brownfields 45, 120, 121, 125, 208, 263
Buffalo 20, 21, 222, 304
Built environment i, 9, 16, 26, 27, 50, 54, 98, 197, 198, 203, 269

C

Canvas Detroit 82, 295
Carbon 135, 142, 172, 182, 183, 184, 185, 191, 225, 237, 251, 272
Central Park 52, 221, 222
China 23, 132, 291
Christian, Nichole 82
Shrinking cities 3, 12, 18, 19, 22, 23, 25, 45, 48, 55, 88, 112, 134, 221, 230, 261, 263, 281, 282, 286, 290
Cleveland 48, 90, 305, 306
Climate iii, 2, 3, 28, 29, 34, 35, 36, 37, 38, 46, 63, 112, 114, 135, 137, 142, 144, 146, 147, 149, 157, 165, 166, 169, 172, 173, 175, 176, 177, 178, 179, 180, 181, 182, 183, 184, 185, 186, 187, 188, 190, 191, 193, 225, 230, 231, 237, 257, 258, 259, 271, 272, 286, 291, 296, 299, 300, 302, 305
Climate change iii, 2, 28, 29, 34, 35, 36, 37, 38, 112, 114, 142, 146, 147, 149,